UNBIASED
Editing in a Diverse Society

UNBIASED
Editing in a Diverse Society

Elizabeth Wissner-Gross

Iowa State University Press/Ames

Elizabeth Wissner-Gross, whose journalism career spans
more than 20 years, has edited and written as a staffer for *Newsday,*
the Associated Press and the *Daily News* (Los Angeles). Her articles have
also appeared in *The New York Times, The Los Angeles Times,*
The Washington Post and more than 30 domestic and foreign
newspapers and magazines. She has taught journalism at Hofstra University,
Fairleigh Dickinson University and Iona College and has
guest-lectured at New York University, Barnard College,
and the New School University. Having spent many years studying
bias in journalism, she has led workshops and participated in panel
discussions on media bias for college groups, civic clubs,
religious organizations and public schools. Wissner-Gross is a
graduate of the Columbia University Graduate School of Journalism after majoring
in political science at Barnard College.

© 1999 Iowa State University Press   All rights reserved

Iowa State University Press
2121 South State Avenue, Ames, Iowa 50014

Orders: 1-800-862-6657   Office: 1-515-292-0140

Fax: 1-515-292-3348   Web site: www.isupress.edu

Authorization to photocopy items for internal or personal use, or the
internal or personal use of specific clients, is granted by Iowa State University
Press, provided that the base fee of $.10 per copy is paid directly to the
Copyright Clearance Center, 222 Rosewood Drive, Danvers, MA 01923. For
those organizations that have been granted a photocopy license by CCC, a
separate system of payments has been arranged. The fee code for users of the
Transactional Reporting Service is 0-8138-2396-X/99 $.10.

♾ Printed on acid-free paper in the United States of America

First edition, 1999

Library of Congress Cataloging-in-Publication Data

Wissner-Gross, Elizabeth
Unbiased: editing in a diverse society / Elizabeth Wissner-Gross.—1st ed.
p.   cm.
Includes bibliographical references and index.
ISBN 0-8138-2396-X (alk. paper)
1. Journalism—Editing—Social aspects. 2. Pluralism (Social sciences). 3. Bias-free language.
I. Title.
PN4778.W57   1999
070.4′1—dc21   99-37053

The last digit is the print number: 9 8 7 6 5 4 3 2 1

—

To my father, Irwin Wissner,

who loved words and hated
prejudice. He was a most
demanding editor and a great
inspiration.

Contents

Preface

Editing in a diverse society is more than a matter of mere "political correctness." For journalists to be credible, they must vigilantly strive to remain unbiased and objective. Careful word selection, elimination of stereotyping and objective usage play key roles in fairness. As a result, a thorough understanding of nuance and subtle bias is essential to the editor. Detecting prejudice and "masked" terminology becomes an ongoing struggle as society and the English language continue to evolve and new challenges emerge.

Although journalism stylebooks generally touch on the subject for a paragraph or page or even a chapter, most professional stylebooks leave many bias-related questions unanswered. What is most lacking and needed is an overall policy to help journalists analyze words and word combinations as new expressions emerge.

This book, a reference guide for professional communicators and students, examines bias style policies of America's major print and broadcast news outlets, as well as style recommendations by a variety of advocacy organizations, in an attempt to define an unbiased American style of editing. The aim is to familiarize communicators with the issues in bias elimination, rather than to demand uniformity of all American publications. As a complement to other journalism stylebooks and reference books, this guide is vital for professional editors and writers, school newspaper editors and journalism students.

Acknowledgments

This book is the culmination of many years of editing copy and studying the intricacies of bias in journalism. I would like to thank the following organizations and institutions for contributing significant information toward this endeavor over the years:

American-Arab Anti-Discrimination Committee

American Civil Liberties Union

American Foundation for the Blind

American Moslem Foundation

American Society of Newspaper Editors

Anti-Defamation League

Barnard College

B'nai B'rith

Columbia University Graduate School of Journalism

International Romani Union

Little People of America

Mount Holyoke College

National Association for the Advancement of Colored People

National Association of the Deaf

National Organization for Women

Native American Journalists Association

The Newseum

News Watch Project

Oberlin College

St. John's University in New York, Public Relations

United States Hispanic Chamber of Commerce

University of Illinois, Public Relations

Numerous religious institutions and organizations

I also want to thank my sons, Alexander and Zachary, my husband, Sigmund, and my mother, Aileen Wissner, for their thoughtful insights and encouragement.

Introduction

Toward the beginning of each semester, when I am addressing the subject of "diversity and editing," I ask my journalism students if they have biases or prejudices.

"Raise your hand if you are prejudiced," I tell them.

Typically, no hands go up, and a few students squirm visibly. Others seem to look away or at their computer terminals, avoiding eye contact with me.

"*Nobody* is prejudiced?" I challenge. Again, the students look uncomfortable. There is a silence, but no hands go up.

"Do you know anybody who is prejudiced?" might get a greater response and sparks a more comfortable, third-person discussion. Sometimes people are more willing to discuss their own views by attributing those perspectives to a friend or some other third person.

In a few cases, I have had students who timidly confess to secretly harboring prejudices against people with differing taste: fellow students who wear baggy jeans or those who don't wear baggy jeans or people who are overweight or who dye their hair unnatural colors. Then usually a clever or diplomatic student pipes up, "It depends on how you define prejudice."

I follow up this awkward beginning with a Bias Quiz. I give students a long list of sentences, most of which contain examples of common bias, and ask the students to point out the bias in each. If they are unable to find bias, I explain that bias may be eluding them and they may be incorporating such hidden bias into their own writing or editing unwittingly.

I do not collect these quizzes. Instead, we analyze the sentences together in class, discussing our findings. The students grade their own papers, and no one else gets to see their shortcomings. The aim is to have the students determine their own biases and to then address them by "correcting" them. The premise is that in order to eliminate bias from other people's work, an editor first needs to be able to recognize bias, even subtle bias, when it appears on paper. Throughout this discussion, bias and prejudice are used interchangeably. However, prejudice is merely one form of bias, usually a bias against someone or something. Bias can also mean favoring someone or something over others.

In teaching college and graduate students for years, I have found that most students say they consider prejudice to be bad. Most journalism students I have worked with also genuinely seem to feel that they are free of prejudice. Some feel that they have petty prejudices, but nothing that would interfere with their ability to maintain complete objectivity in editing or writing.

I rarely find journalists or journalism students who intentionally discriminate or knowingly reveal personal biases. Instead, I find that most of the bias that appears in print or on student papers is subtle and a result of ignorance. Many journalists and journalism students are unaware of their biases, and therefore their biases occasionally "slip" into print seemingly unnoticed.

Probably the most common bias errors occur as a result of ignorance of a person's ways or a people's ways, without any ill intentions. On paper, this ignorance translates into or is perceived as prejudice. If a report were to quote a political candidate, for example, as stating, "All Americans should attend the church of their choice regularly," this may sound like an unbiased statement to many journalists at first glance. But a sharp editor, familiar with many religions' customs, would point out that the sentence incorrectly assumes that all religions gather in *churches*. Religious groups that gather in temples, mosques, synagogues or meeting houses would call the sentence biased, in that they would not consider *church* to be a generic term for *place of worship*. Obviously, American atheists would also have a problem with such a statement, because supposedly they do not have a church of choice.

The following list contains a sampling of sentences that have been known to appear on my bias quizzes. Professional journalists are invited to quiz themselves or discuss the samples. Journalism professors might want to offer the quiz to their students as a starting point for a discussion on editing in a diverse society.

When students look at the list initially, they ask if every sentence contains some form of bias. To increase the challenge, I usually include one or two sentences that do not, and I ask the students to find that sentence or those sentences as they work their way through the quiz. Some of the sentences suggest potential bias without containing any actual bias. They remind the reader, for example, that many people assume that robbers and kidnappers are always male, whereas nurses and secretaries are presumed to be female. Mixed in with these sentences are obvious examples of bias that most students recognize immediately.

■ Bias Quiz

What is wrong with the following statements? Circle any word or words that reveal bias. Note that some of the sentences may contain more than one example of bias, and one or two sentences may contain no real bias.

1. This is the season when everyone is hoping for a good tan.

2. The college coed was from Gainesville, Florida.

3. He complained that he got gypped at the store where they sold him an egg for $15.

4. The suspect was described as black and weighing about 150 pounds.

5. The 21-year-old girl was featured on the magazine cover about woman pilots.

6. The political party was searching for the best man for the job.

7. The 10-man team helped to evacuate the passengers from the burning train.

8. The breadwinner in the average household tends to earn twice as much as his wife.

9. The girls in the office threw a party for their boss.

10. Jane Anderson, an attractive blond, is married to Michael Anderson, a plumber.

11. The white militant and the black activist met together on racial issues.

12. When you wake up, there's nothing like shaving with coconut oil on your face.

13. The average American shopper prefers to buy her clothes at outlet stores.

14. The Afro-American man was a biology professor.

15. She taught philosophy even though she spoke with an accent.

16. "Miss Saigon" is about a petite Oriental girl's relationship with an American soldier.

17. Soldiers always make bad fathers because their children always have to travel.

18. She dressed like a JAP, called herself a CAP, but wasn't so Jappy after all.

19. She was a tomboy and played volleyball like a boy.

20. The proprietress rented rooms to a poetess, a waitress, an actress and an effeminate waiter.

21. For a female candidate, she certainly did not know how to dress.

22. The peace agreement is valid, the senator said with an Irish twinkle.

23. She was the American delegate, but she looked Chinese.

24. Although she was a fundamentalist, she was nonviolent.

25. The elderly woman had just celebrated her 50th birthday with her grandchildren.

26. The 30-year-old murderer, who had been an adopted child, was sent to prison.

27. Ask any doctor which aspirin he recommends most.

28. Melissa cradled her doll, while her brother was playing with his action figures.

29. Firefighters rescued the boy's adoptive mother as his real mother watched in horror.

30. Although he had retired, he was still agile enough to play tennis every day.

31. Although she was old, she was still fashionable and feminine.

32. The 13-year-old adopted girl had a reunion with her natural parents.

33. The suspect, who had dark eyes and olive skin, looked very Mediterranean.

34. The man admitted his part in the murder, but insisted that the other accused men, who were both members of a Harlem mosque, were not accomplices.

35. She was a pretty girl—blond hair, blue eyes—and smarter than you would expect a typical blonde to be.

36. In federal court today, the plaintiff wore an orange plaid ski sweater, gold earrings and matching slacks, and her hair was pulled back neatly in braids.

37. In Austria, Gypsies are being victimized by some of the worst racial violence in 50 years.

38. The Gypsies are targeted by neo-Nazis who want to rid the country of foreigners.

39. Our mailman said she had just started working for the U.S. Post Office.

40. He was chairman of the budget committee, and his wife was co-chairperson.

41. The birth certificate listed the boy's father's last name and his mother's maiden name.

42. The girls on the team argued about who would play first baseman.

43. Diamonds are a girl's best friend, and it's every girl's dream to marry rich; dogs are a man's best friend.

44. He behaved like a real boy—wild, careless and assertive. She was bossy—wild, careless and assertive.

45. He was a very nurturing, caring father. When his children were sick, he would offer to stay home from work for the day to take care of them. She, in contrast, was a very unreliable employee. When her children were sick, she would make excuses to stay home from work for the day to take care of them.

46. The two women were having a catfight. They could not agree on anything, and their claws were starting to show. At the same time, their husbands were having an intellectual dispute. They too could not agree on anything, and were heard making loud barbs at each other.

47. She always toted a purse, and he carried a wallet.

48. The doctor was recommending that the nurse take his wife to the same resort where the doctor and her husband had just been.

49. If a strange man offers you candy and tells you he will only give it to you if you get in his car, don't listen.

50. The robber was last seen wearing high heels and a white dress.

51. After the *Titanic* went down, she was the subject of many investigations.

52. Hurricane Gloria was a feisty storm; she knocked down many trees.

53. The room was decorated with feminine pastel colors and lace curtains.

54. Her husband baby-sat their kids while she went out shopping and then helped out in the kitchen before the company arrived.

55. She spoke Jewish and English with a Jewish accent.

56. Although her parents came from Syria, she could pass for a typical American.

57. A reporter must be a thorough researcher if he wants to be fair to all sides.

58. While she was off at work, her kids were tearing up the neighborhood.

59. Despite her Irish heritage, she did not drink.

60. The tour offered something for everyone: While the men met with religious leaders, special shopping trips were scheduled for their wives.

61. In order to be fair to all students, the school board allocated equal

amounts of money to the boys' football team and the girls' cheer-leading team.

62. Although Justin was taking ballet lessons, he still found time for football.

63. She told all her girlfriends; but he rarely spoke openly with his boyfriends.

64. Although he was on welfare, he seemed to show some intelligence.

After students have completed the quiz, the class discussion is usually animated. I ask them, "How many students were able to detect all of the bias contained in all of the sentences?"

No hands go up.

"No perfect scores?" I challenge.

Most students smile or look directly at me; they appear to be relieved. In class discussion, they say that they realize that although they may have been unaware of some of their own biases, they see that they are not alone. Everyone else in the class—regardless of age, sex, ethnic background, nationality, disabilities, etc.—discovers unrecognized (and unaddressed) bias as well. This is somehow reassuring.

I explain to the students that we all are guilty of bias, even those of us with the best intentions. A lot depends on our environment and exposure. Meeting and reading about different kinds of people helps to sensitize us to differing perspectives and helps us to recognize our biases. Elimination of bias is an ongoing but essential struggle. It is not a sudden process or a mission exclusive to liberals or conservatives. Objectivity is the backbone of American journalism. (A biased journalist is not a journalist, but a propagandist.) Fairness and objectivity require elimination of bias. So writers who want to be objective need to first recognize their own biases in order to eliminate them. Many otherwise kind-hearted, thoughtful and dedicated writers are unable to admit that they have bias. This quiz provides a first step.

I warn my students that as journalists, they will be faced with many more biased statements in the future. No book can expose all bias because language is constantly changing. New expressions of bias emerge as language evolves. This is only the beginning. I explain that the task of recognizing and removing this bias from journalism may at times be painstaking and at other times seem like nit-picking. But it is probably the most important responsibility that editors have. I advise them that the task is not as simple as it may appear at first. It takes a very perceptive and committed journalist to be able to detect and "catch" all of the bias before it appears in print. And sometimes, before eliminating bias, an editor is required to justify the edit to a supervising editor or a defensive writer who is not as sensitized, perceptive or aware of what constitutes bias. As a result, the job may occasionally seem thankless or unappreciated.

I want my students to know, however, that editing is one of the noblest endeavors. This mission of vigilantly preserving objectivity is the ultimate weapon against corruption as well as the most powerful defense of democracy, fairness and American journalism.

UNBIASED
Editing in a Diverse Society

Overview

In a business that strives to maintain objectivity and fairness, inclusion of bias—whether intentional or inadvertent—is not to be tolerated. Thus, a major part of the copy editor's job is to seek out bias and to eliminate it from copy.

Yet, some media critics contend that bias is appearing increasingly in the journalism media. They claim that elimination of bias from journalism is a naïve goal and that because journalists are human, a certain amount of subjectivity is to be expected and even tolerated. In publications that are written and edited by a single individual or interest group, this indeed is often the case. At larger, general interest publications, however, where staff diversity is valued, elimination of bias becomes more realistic, in that more eyes (with more diverse perspectives) monitor usage, focus and assignment of articles. Such publications are more likely to have ongoing dialogues and sharing of ideas, particularly if dialogue is encouraged.

Journalism students often inquire about bias at major journalism publications. Some novices even fallaciously assume that journalists are required to write with a slant toward a particular political position, and that if they do not share what is supposedly a common political perspective, they may be unable to work as journalists. They hear arguments from critics who contend that many major publications have "a strong liberal bias," for example, and who commonly categorize journalism as "the liberal media." They hear other media critics contending that some publications have reactionary or conservative leanings, or even that major publications have singled out specific ethnic or religious groups to oppose or belittle.

When students presume that all newspapers have political leanings and special biases, I encourage them to visit a newsroom, preferably the newsroom of a major urban daily newspaper. I tell them that they should expect to encounter a diverse population at work: Newsrooms generally include men and women ranging from age 18 to mid-80s, who are of differing races, religions, national origins, ethnic backgrounds and physical conditions. Many of these journalists are not affiliated with any political party, as a reinforcement of their objectivity and fairness in covering political stories.

Could there be bias in such a setting? Unfortunately, the answer is yes. But the more diverse and educated representation there is within a news publication, particularly on the copy desk, the better the chances are that biased writing will be caught and eliminated.

Not all newsrooms or all parts of all newsrooms are diverse, however. A West Coast journalist spoke of a major urban daily in the Northeast, where a Native American intern believed that the publication's editing revealed a strong bias against American Indians. The news editors seemed open-minded, but would not acknowledge any such bias. Perhaps they thought that the intern was overly sensitive. After all, the newspaper editors believed that their publication had a proud reputation for providing objective, unbiased and even sensitive news coverage. The young intern argued that many of the sports headlines in particular belittled Native Americans. But the sports editors were at a loss to find anything offensive about a headline like "Indians Scalp Rivals." After all, the name of the team was the Indians, and most sports sections permitted plays on words and puns in sports headlines. Eventually, the intern left the publication, disillusioned about the integrity of America's major journalism institutions.

What the young intern did not know was that removing bias from any major publication is an ongoing struggle. It is the copy editor's duty to point out bias and to continue to explain why certain usage is biased, persisting until the other editors understand. Different writers have different biases, and most journalists admit to having none. It is helpful in this struggle to have diversity on the copy desk. This is a helpful resource to reporters who are sometimes asked to cover stories on segments of the population about whom they have no prior knowledge. It is also useful to have editors on hand who are familiar with the language of a particular population, to make sure that the news of this group is written objectively, sensitively and accurately.

At large publications, this need for diversity should not be a license for tokenism or minimal representation of diversity, since it is better to have more than one person representing each different ethnicity, religion, nationality, age, race and physical condition. Otherwise, the lone representative may not find a sympathetic ear. Devoted editors use their stylebooks as defense when elimination of bias is contested. But when the stylebook makes no mention of how to handle a particular perceived bias, allies can be vital within a news organization. It is difficult and wearing to defend the same cause all day every day. When there is a second voice at a major publication, the task becomes easier.

Not all publications are able to provide a "second voice," however, or even a lone voice representing each ethnicity, religion, nationality, age, race and physical condition. Smaller publications with very limited budgets, for example, often cannot support large diverse staffs. In such situations, the copy editor's sensitivity and awareness of bias become even more crucial to the fairness and objectivity of the publication. At such publications, the copy editor has a larger responsibility to become familiar with the many forms and manifestations of bias.

Well-run journalistic institutions encourage copy editors to speak up to defend their publications against all forms of bias and biased writing, since such vigilance is in the best interest of journalism.

1

Political Bias

■ Political Bias Examples

The following are examples of different kinds of political bias that commonly appear in publications. Examine the sentences, and then determine how they should best be rewritten to eliminate political bias.

The senator called for economic restraint and tightening of the belt, despite his self-proclaimed liberal leanings.

The pro-abortion activists demonstrated peacefully across the street from sign-wielding anti-abortion militants.

Along the mountainous border, ultra-rightist guerrillas destroyed villages, where women and children were innocently tending their homes.

The candidate, who has been known to cross party lines, turned her back on her party to oppose the mandatory curfew.

The new regime was worse than the primitive leadership it replaced, the moderates contended, running the country like a banana republic.

■ Simplistic Labels

Political bias is most commonly unleashed through labeling. Careless journalists borrow the usage of heavily biased politicians, political publicists and lobbyists and categorize people according to some of their political views or according to public image. As a general rule, journalists should refrain from labeling people based on a mere sampling of their political views.

Unsophisticated politicians are sometimes the first to identify themselves with a political label, believing that such a categorization may appeal to their constituents. Savvy politicians have been labeling themselves as well, particularly in regions where a certain leaning or *buzzword* is believed to be popular. This is not license, however, for a journalist to use that same label when referring to the politician.

Many newspapers, magazines and news broadcasts are quick to label people as *liberals, conservatives, moderates, leftists, rightists, radicals, reactionaries, activists, militants* and even *card-holders,* based on the way the reporter would characterize people's philosophies. Such labels appear frequently in headlines, as a means of summarizing who (or what type of person) is involved in a particular story in abbreviated form. What do these terms mean in modern society?

Objective journalists need to recognize not only the inadequacy of such simplistic labeling, but also the harm of categorizing people under these headings.

If a person is affiliated with a political party, such as the Conservative Party or the Liberal Party, that person correctly can be called a Conservative or Liberal, using an uppercase *C* or *L*. When describing a political philosophy using these terms, lowercase letters are generally used, but much more caution is needed.

If the writer does not mean to imply any affiliation with a party, editors should be wary of references to individuals as *conservatives* or *liberals.* As a general rule, thinking individuals with independent philosophies and perspectives cannot and should not be classified into such categories. To label them is to deliberately oversimplify and stereotype the individual, even if the interview subject prefers to be characterized in a simplistic way.

A radio talk show recently asked callers to state their political leanings before posing their questions or commenting on the issue discussed. Callers had to declare themselves *liberals* or *conservatives,* and many clearly felt uncomfortable with this categorization. A typical response: "I identified myself as a *liberal,* but I didn't mean to." Then the caller awkwardly explained that he went along with the categorization in order to "get on the air." Editors should remind themselves that not every issue has a *liberal* or *conservative* side. And those that do often have other sides as well. Not every person feels comfortable or should feel comfortable wearing a political label. Not every person who takes a *liberal* stance on one issue, takes the same stance on every other issue.

If, in the course of journalism, the writer must characterize the views of a person, only the relevant views should be characterized if the writer is to maintain objectivity. Each view on each issue must be characterized separately. Do not attempt to characterize all of an individual's opinions with a single label. Views may be described as conservative, liberal or reactionary. People should not be, however. In the vast majority of articles, attempting to characterize an entire person is inappropriate, unsophisticated and even demeaning. Simplistic labels imply that the individual is incapable of evaluating each issue separately, and thus prefers to wear a label.

In the rare instance that a particular article requires characterization of an entire person, the journalist should not presume that any thinking person can be characterized with a single political label. To say that one is a conservative, no matter what the issue, displays either a lack of sophistication on the part of the labeling journalist or a lack of independent thought on the part of the article subject.

Thinking people are generally *conservative* on some issues, while being *liberal* on others and *activist* on still others. For example, a person who is against permitting the sale of alcohol to children might be considered *conservative* on that issue. The same person might have *liberal* views when it comes to demanding an investigation of water quality. When it comes to donating money toward cancer research, the same person might have *activist* or *radical* ideas on new fund-raising methods. Such a conglomerate is not unusual, yet it would be wrong to label this person *conservative, liberal* or *radical*.

Activists and Militants

When writers use the word *militant* incorrectly, this usage may reveal the writers' otherwise hidden political bias. An *activist* is perceived as a "good person," who is dedicated to a cause and is determined to improve society. At the very worst, *activists* are perceived as naïve people, who fight windmills and fight the good fight, although their odds of triumphing are minimal. More typically, however, an *activist* is perceived as one who protests or promotes a cause by handing out leaflets, demonstrating, picketing, organizing marches, raising money, participating in strikes, assisting in phone-a-thons or petition drives, picketing or protesting in some other nonviolent fashion. *Activists* are more popularly associated with so-called *liberal* causes, although news publications also mention *activists* in pieces about *conservative* and *traditional* causes. In general, *activists* are perceived as committed people, sometimes overly obsessed with a particular cause at the expense of other aspects of life. They may be pushy and intimidating at times, but they are not really feared and certainly are not criminal. They are perceived as good citizens who use legal channels. The range of causes with which *activists* are commonly associated includes anti-abortion, pro-abortion, lowering taxes, raising taxes, improving education, busing, anti-busing, ecology, civil rights, women's rights, pro-democracy, increasing literacy, animal rights, pro-war, anti-war, among others.

The word *militant,* however, implies some *military* connection and violence. A *militant* is a "bad person." A *militant* is someone who blows up a federal building in Oklahoma City or sets off a bomb in the World Trade Center. A *militant* may also be devoted to a political or religious cause, but the *militant*'s tactics differ. Instead of peacefully demonstrating or handing out leaflets, the *militant* uses weapons and violence or threats of violence to terrorize people or try to force them to cooperate.

When labeling someone a *militant,* the writer needs to understand whether or not that person actually performed a violent act, intended to, or threatened violence. When editing a piece that mentions a *militant,* the editor should ask the following questions:

1. Was the person carrying a weapon?

2. Did the person pose a danger?

3. Did the person intend to pose a danger?

4. Did the person threaten violence or to terrorize?

5. Was anybody physically harmed or endangered?

6. Did the person destroy someone else's property?

7. Did the person intend to destroy property?

Obviously, the reporter may not be able to determine the intentions of the so-called *militant.* Nevertheless, if the answer to any of these questions is *yes,* the reporter is probably justified in referring to the person as a *militant.* If the answer to all of the questions is *no,* the reporter should not use the word *militant,* and should use *activist* instead.

Even if the reporter does not trust the protester or secretly despises the cause, even if the cause seems unjust, trivial, unpopular or a threat to rational society, if no violence is committed or intended, the article subject is most objectively described as an *activist.*

Some writers sloppily use *militant* in the lead as a means of avoiding repetition of the word *activist.* They presume incorrectly that both words share approximately the same meaning.

Example: "A black *activist* met today in Washington with a white *militant* leader to discuss race issues."

This sentence is unbiased only if the white leader is indeed *militant,* having displayed weapons, threatened force or committed an act of violence. If that is not the case, then the white leader must be called an *activist* also. A better way to state the lead without repeating words would be to write:

"Black and white *activists* met today in Washington to discuss race issues."

Because *activist* is viewed as a relatively benign term and *militant* is viewed as violent and negative, many writers unwittingly find themselves referring to people or groups with whom they do not sympathize as *militants.* The ones they favor are referred to as *activists.* This subtle bias should be corrected by alert editors, in order to keep the coverage objective.

Conservative

In reference to people, *conservative* connotes those who prefer a combination of tradition and preservation of existing conditions. *Conservative* is sometimes used interchangeably with *moderate.* In all cases, editors should be wary of political labels that attempt to characterize people. Such labels are better applied to specific views and approaches that provide the reader with a more concrete understanding of the individual described.

For example, it is better to write, "The Senator held a *conservative* view on teen smoking and a *liberal* view on class size in public education," than to write, "The Senator was *conservative.*"

The *Broadcast News Writing Stylebook* advises caution when describing people as *conservative* (as well as *left, liberal, moderate* and *right*):

"Although we use these terms all the time, their meaning is, at best, subjective—and probably says more about the political views of the writer than the person labeled. Generally, it is best to avoid the terms unless someone so designated agrees with the label or you're quoting."

Evaders and Resisters

Although both words are used in similar contexts, the term *evaders* should be used for people who run away from or hide from forces or institutions that they oppose. A *resister* stays to protest and face the consequences. *Newsday's* stylebook cites the following example: "The young man who evaded the draft by fleeing to Canada...should be identified as a draft *evader,* while the man who went to jail for opposing it should be called a draft *resister.*"

Extremists

Be careful when editing articles that label people *extremists,* even when violence is committed. If a person resorts to violence, *militant* may be a more appropriate label. *Extremist* obviously implies that a person goes to *extremes.* What is an *extreme* in one reporter's eyes may not be an *extreme* in another person's eyes. When writing about one who is extremely dedicated to a cause—a vegetarian who refuses to wear leather shoes, a member of a religious group who believes in wearing a head covering at all times, a person who is opposed to blood transfusions or medication for religious reasons, a person who refuses to drink alcohol under any circumstances—the reporter and editor should not presume the right to label such people *extremists.* Use the words *dedicated* or *committed* instead, explaining clearly to what cause or belief this person is dedicated or committed. Without this added information, *dedicated* and *committed* sound like biased personality judgments.

Although *political extremist* is generally a term to be avoided, it is considered more acceptable and less judgmental than *religious extremist.* Be particularly wary when editing articles that label people as *religious extremists.* Many religions and religious groups do not allow for partial or supposedly moderate belief, with the philosophy that either you believe or you do not. This should not be interpreted to mean that all followers of such religions are *extremists,* even if they view themselves as extremely devout. (Refer to the Extremists listing in chapter 6, Religious Bias.)

Guerrillas, Rebels, Insurgents

The *Broadcast News Writing Stylebook* advises caution when using the word *guerrilla.* "*Guerrilla* fighters generally conduct their anti-government campaign by hit-and-run tactics. *Insurgents* or *rebels* fight against the government generally; these are usually more appropriate terms to use." *Rebel* is more of an accepted catch word. It is not necessarily violent and is sometimes used merely to connote individuality or nonconformity. The term can be applied to an opponent of any particular authority or custom, not necessarily one that is political or military. A person with a divergent view on popular clothing style, for example, can be referred to as a fashion *rebel.* An artist who violates the accepted conventions of music or painting may be referred to as an artistic *rebel.*

The *Associated Press Stylebook* is less particular in defining *guerrillas* as "unorthodox soldiers and their tactics." UPI's definition is "irregular soldiers or their tactics."

Note that *guerrilla* has two double letters: *rr* and *ll.* This is one of the most commonly misspelled words in newspapers and magazines.

Liberators

Be very careful about describing a person as a *liberator* or a faction as *liberators,* particularly when violence is involved in the so-called *liberation.* Such terms are very revealing of a writer's sympathies. An anti-government group that is viewed as liberating by some may be viewed as terrorizing by its opponents and supporters of the government.

Moderate

Moderate sounds like a positive title, a label of endorsement by the writer. When a person is labeled a *moderate,* the implication is that the individual's views are sensible and not too extreme. Unlike an *extremist,* a *moderate* sounds reasonable, rational, mainstream and trustworthy. At worst, a *moderate* may imply stodginess, indecisiveness, timidity or hesitation to act on an issue or issues that require immediacy.

Although few people would complain if they were called *moderates,* editors should be careful of the usage. What one person calls *moderate,* another may call *radical* or *reactionary. Moderate* is a comparative term and is generally used in contrast to one who is perceived to have *extreme* views. In other words, using *moderate* implies that opponents are *extremists* to some degree.

As a general rule, it is better to label approaches to specific issues as *moderate*—a *moderate* solution, a *moderate* plan, a *moderate* approach—using attribution, rather than attaching the adjective to a person.

Power Advocates

Not every black or white person who advocates black power or white power is a *militant.* Nor are the majority of people who advocate in favor of Northern Ireland, Israel and Zionism, a separate Palestine, or Kurds. When people say they are advocating power for a particular population or segment of the population, the writer needs to understand what they mean. The meaning varies according to the group and the political situation. The editor's understanding and unbiased explanation can influence the readers heavily. The editor needs to know answers to the following questions.

1. Does the group's call for power mean that the group demands to be officially recognized?

2. Are they asking that some other group be violently opposed?

3. Are they seeking to take over a government?

4. Are they advocating that their group deserves equal treatment and equal rights?

5. Are they arguing that they are superior to other groups and need to be accorded privileges that others should not get?

6. Are they contending that they have been disadvantaged over the course of history and need to be compensated specially to make up for their group's handicap?

When the public is not told what is meant by a call for power, individual interpretations influence views, prejudicing many of the readers and possibly inciting others to behave irresponsibly. When journalists mention that a group is advocating power, the journalists have a professional responsibility to elaborate on what is meant by these advocates.

Radicals and Reactionaries

Both *radicals* and *reactionaries* are labels that are commonly used to describe people who advocate extreme political change at each end of the political spectrum. Like other labels, these two are more accurate and informative when applied to specific views and approaches rather than being used in an attempt to characterize people.

It is better to write, for example, "The Senator held a *radical* view on cleaning up nuclear waste and a *reactionary* view on capital punishment" than to write, "The Senator was *radical*" or "The Senator was perceived as *reactionary.*"

As labels, both terms suggest unwillingness to compromise and imply unreasonable behavior. Both terms appear occasionally in political speeches to undermine others whose views may be perceived as divergent, challenging or threatening. If a political speaker labels other people as *radicals* or *reactionaries,* reporters may quote both terms. Editors should make sure, however, that the labels are clearly attributed and that the context is explained.

Rightist and Leftist

The Associated Press advises editors to avoid the terms *rightist, ultra-rightist, leftist* and *ultra-leftist* and instead to use "more precise descriptions of an individual's political philosophy." Although many editors find these words useful in headline writing, which requires concise or even abbreviated usage, such terms can mislead the readers.

Most commonly, the terms *rightist* and *leftist* appear in stories that originate overseas. The terms are used as a simplified means of summarizing to the American public the politics abroad. Such oversimplification, however, is often confusing to the reader. Who is the *rightist* for example in the former Yugoslavia? In the former U.S.S.R.? In the Middle East? What makes these so-called *rightists* further *right* in their politics than *leftists* in the eyes of the American reader? And weren't some of these so-called *rightists* referred to as *leftists* a decade ago in the same American publications? How did their labels change without their politics changing?

AP suggests that "*rightist* often applies to someone who is *conservative* or *opposed to socialism.* It also often indicates an individual who supports an authoritarian government that is militantly anti-communist or anti-socialist." Again, an editor reading a piece about the former U.S.S.R. should ask, in this context, what a *rightist* could possibly be.

AP defines an *ultra-rightist* as "an individual who subscribes to rigid interpretations of a conservative doctrine or to forms of fascism that stress authoritarian, often militaristic, views." Editors handling hard news stories should be wary of flippant use of these words. In most cases, more specific terms should be used instead. The same person who is labeled *ultra-rightist* by some editors, may be considered *ultra-leftist* by others, with equal validity.

According to the Associated Press, "*leftist* often applies to someone who is merely liberal or believes in a form of democratic socialism." Who are the *leftists* in the Middle East, according to this definition? Editors should be careful about references to political philosophies as *leftist* if they are unsure about what makes the particular philosophy more *left* than any other philosophy. Editors should also realize that even if they are clear about what makes a philosophy *leftist* abroad, the reader will not necessarily be as informed or clear unless the designation is clearly explained within the piece. This means that if the story develops and follow-up pieces are published each day, the designation should be explained anew each day. Editors should not assume that readers are following the developments of a particular story on a daily basis, or remember the details from day to day. If *left* and *right* are to be used, the readers need to be brought up to date regularly on who is being labeled *left* and who is being called *right* and why. *Ultra-leftist,* meanwhile, is defined as "an individual who subscribes to a communist view or one holding that liberal or socialist change cannot come within the present form of government."

The *Broadcast News Writing Stylebook* advises caution with the words *leftist, rightist,* and *radical.* "Different people use and hear these terms differently. Use clearer, more precise political descriptions." The book specifies that "A *radical* wants the upheaval of the existing governmental system—so be particularly careful here."

SAMPLE POLITICAL ISSUES.   In articles about violent confrontations abroad, writers and editors are sometimes too fast to label any two opposing factions as *rightist* and *leftist* as a shorthand for describing the two positions or as a way to refer to the sides after initially describing their positions. In many situations, the labels are embarrassingly inappropriate.

Consider the following sample American conflicts. Assume that one group is in favor of the change, and the other is opposed. Would it be correct to label one side *leftist* and the other *rightist*?

1. Should major American cities have public pay toilets available to tourists?

2. Should the local public high school offer courses in Japanese as one of the foreign language options?

3. Should day-care centers be permitted to admit infants less than 3 months old?

4. Should local street signs be black and white or blue and white?

Obviously, *leftist* and *rightist* do not apply to these situations. Yet some writers will use the terms anyway, particularly when writing about the same issues abroad: pay toilets in London or day care in France, for example. Editors should watch for this lazy usage and correct it. Often the labels encourage readers to take sides based on which leaning (*right* or *left*) the readers generally prefer or usually identify with, while inhibiting the readers' understanding of the specific issues.

Wings Are for Birds

People do not have wings, left or right. Nor would most people consider themselves *wingers,* left or right, even if they acknowledge that they have strong views. Editors should be very cautious with copy that labels people as *right-wing* John Doe or *left-winger* Jane Doe. While some writers contend that such labels clarify the copy by abbreviating the explanation of the factions of a particular issue, in most cases such labels add little to a reader's understanding of either side of a complex situation.

In cases where the editor deems the terms *right wing* and *left wing* appropriate, *The Associated Press Stylebook* dictates that as nouns, *right wing* and *left wing* each be written as two separate words, no hyphen. As adjectives, the words are hyphenated: *right-wing* faction and *left-wing* faction, as are the nouns *right-winger* and *left-winger*. Many publications' styles dictate that *right-winger* and *left-winger* are inappropriate terms in all instances.

■ Crossing Party Lines

Occasionally reporters portray a politician who *crosses party lines* as a traitor or confused individual. Obviously, depending upon the party and the circumstance, *crossing party lines* can be a very courageous act by a devoted leader who is attempting to follow his or her conscience. Writers need to be very careful about characterizing such people as turncoats or fools, as such labeling often reveals the writer's own biases concerning a political issue.

■ Geographical Designations

The way in which a location is described can reveal a writer's geographical and political bias. (See the section on Geographical Designations in chapter 4, Nationality Bias.)

■ Pro-Life, Pro-Choice

As a shorthand in covering potentially complex stories on the topic, writers sometimes resort to fast labels summarizing people who feel strongly about the very political issue of abortion. Whether describing people who favor abortion, those who oppose it, or those who have mixed feelings, writers often categorize people with a one-word oversimplified label, instead of recognizing that the issue has complexities. Many people may support some aspects of a political position but not others. The United Press International Stylebook advises writers to "shun labels like anti-abortion, anti-choice, pro-abortion, pro-life" in reference to people, arguing that "such labels overgeneralize" and may be "objectionable."

■ Regime

A *regime* is a political system, not a government. Many writers use the term incorrectly to connote government. Some use the term to reveal bias against a government of which the writers do not approve. Editors should be alert to both incorrect uses of *regime*. It is incorrect to write: "The Serbian *regime* announced today ..." or "India's ruling *regime* declared that ...".

Regime is not a biased term in itself, although constant incorrect usage has given it a negative connotation. Writers rarely refer to a "democratic *regime*," and more commonly refer to an "authoritarian *regime*" or a "communist *regime*," as if *regime* were synonymous with "backward system," "corrupt government," "threatening system" or "primitive government." Nevertheless, the term is still considered usable and unbiased when applied correctly.

Editors should observe how the writer uses the term. If it is only applied to political systems that the writer views as unstable, primitive or negative, other words should be substituted that do not reveal the writer's bias.

2

Racial Bias

■ **Racial Bias Examples**

The following are examples of different kinds of racial bias that commonly appear in publications. Examine the sentences, and then determine how they should best be rewritten to eliminate racial bias.

The suspect was described as Afro-American, weighing about 170 pounds and wearing jeans and a T-shirt.

Austrian authorities reported some of the worst racial violence against Gypsies in years.

The Latino players rarely socialized with the more mainstream team members.

Orientals tend to be better students than typical American children, because their families value education more.

The Jewish community has tended to vote for more liberals than the Hispanic race.

■ **Background and Overview**

Racial bias means simply prejudice against a race. Although this definition seems obvious, racial bias is perhaps the most commonly confused and misunderstood form of bias, largely because to understand what constitutes racial bias, it is necessary to first agree on a common definition of race. Such a definition, however, has eluded biologists, anthropologists and social scientists for hundreds of years.

First, it should be emphasized that for centuries scientists have recognized that all human beings are members of the same species, *Homo sapiens.* This classification was determined and announced by Swedish naturalist Carolus Linnaeus (1707–1778). With that given, Linnaeus proceeded to divide humans into four "varieties," according to the *Encyclopedia of Multiculturalism.* The categories were *Homo Europaeus, Homo Asiaticus, Homo After* and *Homo Americanus*, corresponding "to the perceived skin colors of white, yellow, black and red/brown."

This categorization is not necessarily uniformly accepted, however. Many anthropologists and biologists argue that there are only three major races: Negroid, Mongoloid and Caucasoid. "Some investigators designated other major races, such as the Amerind and the Oceanian," according to the *Social Science Encyclopedia.* The book also states that "within the major races, several dozen minor races (or simply, races) were recognized, the number identified varying, with the investigator."

Those who contend that there are three races generally classify Asians and American Indians together as Mongoloid.

On what characteristics are these racial groups based? Not genetic research—which has not found any significant genetic differences among people of different races. Not biological research, either. Biologists tend to argue that there is no real racial difference, that all humans belong to one race. Yet society has insisted on categorization. The classification of racial groupings is based largely on physical appearance, observation and geographical origins. As a result, there are many exceptions, many combinations, and many people who do not fit the overall boundaries of any given race.

Defining Races

The *Encyclopedia of Multiculturalism,* admitting that the racial characteristics are "overgeneralized," and the boundaries are fuzzy, describes *Caucasians* as a race that originated in Europe, northern Africa and western Asia. It says Caucasians are characterized by a lighter (whitish, pinkish or reddish) skin complexion, blond or brown hair that is wavy or straight, with a tendency toward balding. Caucasians typically have blue or green eyes, and noses that are straight, hooked or pug. They have "conspicuous jaws" and "relatively long torsos."

Mongoloids, according to the same book, originated in northern and eastern Asia. Their skin color is described as ranging from yellow to brown with hair that is black and straight. Their facial structure includes wide cheekbones, low nose bridges, and almond-shaped or slanted eyes.

Negroids, meanwhile, trace their roots to Africa, according to the book. Their skin color ranges from light tan to dark brown. Their hair is brown or black and is described as kinky, curly or woolly. They have high foreheads and thick lips and noses.

With these three races described, the encyclopedia asserts that "modern scientists cannot agree on the exact number of races...or even an acceptable definition of race." It contends that Polynesians and Australian aborigines "defy simple categorization." It also adds, "While some people of presumed Caucasoid stock, such as Asian Indians with dark skins, were physically more like Negroid peoples, others classified as Negroid, such as the Kalahari Bushmen, were light-skinned. This confusion has led many to attempt to develop more precise classification systems, which resulted in the identification of as few as four and as many as two thousand racial groups."

Editors need to realize that racial categorization is an extremely inexact social classification system. Racial boundaries are not based on precise, scientific lines, but rather on fuzzy perceptions and images. Racial labels are therefore sensitive, and editors should be careful about writing that attempts to categorize people. In most cases, racial descriptions do not pertain to news and feature pieces and should not be included in such articles. Racial classification, like other categorizations and generalizations about people, should only be mentioned in a piece if it pertains to the story.

■ Some Overall Principles of Eliminating Bias from Copy

1. Avoid categorizing people by race.

2. Only mention a person's race if you have determined that race is necessary to the story.

3. When describing people, avoid buzzwords and limited descriptions that only enhance bias. Demand *defining descriptions* instead.

4. Do not describe people as *pure-blooded* or *purebred.*

5. Do not assume that individuals mentioned in stories trace their roots to a single race, or that tracing roots to a single race is somehow better than having a multiracial background.

6. Do not let any one race dominate a description of a person with a multiracial background. (It is incorrect to describe a person who is half black and half white as black, for example.)

7. Do not write that any one skin color is *mainstream* or *typical,* implying that others are not.

8. Eliminate derogatory terms and words that promote racial bias.

Race Categorization

Writers and editors should avoid categorizing people as belonging to races, particularly when referring to groupings that are not universally accepted as independent races. It is better to be more specific in categorizing people by nationality, ethnic identification, religion or political affiliation if such categorization is necessary to the story.

Race classification played a major role in Nazi Germany during World War II. Dictator Adolf Hitler claimed to make a "science" of classifying people in his rise to power. His aim was to advance the so-called Aryan race. In addition to recognizing the African race and Asian race, Hitler referred to the Nordic people as a separate, superior race from non-Nordic Europeans. He considered Jews a distinct race, and classified Gypsies as a separate race. Nazi publications promulgated these supposed racial differences and used this information to promote division and hatred, pitting racial groups against each other. Historians have documented the contention that Hitler aimed to ultimately promote the so-called Nordic or Aryan race, by annihilating other races that he considered "undesirable."

"VISIBLE" MINORITIES.   One of the problems with categorizing people by race is that many people trace their roots to more than one race and therefore defy categorization. Writers sometimes label people "visible" minorities, which becomes a euphemism for saying that their skin color is darker than "white," but lighter than "black." To avoid bias, editors should eliminate racial categorization, rather than create new terminology to define every racial combination.

When Race Is Pertinent

The major stylebooks specify that articles should not name the race of each person mentioned, unless race is pertinent to the story.

How does a reporter determine whether or not race is pertinent? In pieces that focus on issues or conflicts of race, the race of each person quoted may bear some relevance to the story and should probably be mentioned.

The Associated Press Stylebook and *United Press International*'s *Stylebook* both specify (with identical wording) that race is also pertinent "in biographical and announcement stories, particularly when they involve a feat or appointment that has not routinely been associated with members of a particular race." Any article on the breaking of barriers or historical firsts for a particular race makes race pertinent.

In addition, UPI specifies that race should be mentioned when describing someone sought by police. Many publications prohibit mention of race, however, if that is all the description that is available to the reporter. The argument is that such a limited description only promotes bias without providing enough information to be useful in the search. Race may be mentioned at such publications, however, if there is enough additional information available on a sought individual's features to provide a *defining description*.

Defining Descriptions

As a general principle, when a writer describes a suspect, criminal or missing person, the writer should strive to provide a *defining description*.

Many crime reports describe a suspect on the loose in terms of sex, race and either height or weight or both. These four features combined provide an inadequate description. The writer's rationale may be that these four features were the only descriptive details available from the police. By failing to provide enough of a *defining description*, however, the report carelessly and subtly promotes prejudice without offering useful clues.

For example, if a suspect is only described as "a white male weighing about 170 pounds," this profile fits millions of Americans and cannot help police or the public find a criminal. Obviously, the same holds true if other skin colors are used in place of white. While such descriptions may seem harmless at first, many editors feel these vague descriptions only promote fear or hatred without giving the reader any useful information.

Some editors argue that writers should use every bit of descriptive information available, without attempting to predict the potential impact if information is scant. They say that, as a general rule, objective description is important for the "flavor" of a news story.

The response to this argument is that such minimal information, such as height, weight, or skin color, does not contribute to the "flavor" of an article unless there is something unusual about the person's height, weight or color. If a person has green-painted skin, for example, that information could be very useful to both the police and the public in trying to identify the suspect, while adding to the "flavor" of a story. Likewise, if the suspect's skin were bright yellow as a result perhaps of liver cancer, skin color could be very pertinent. When there is nothing unusual about the person's color, however, there is no reason to specify skin color. White, tan, dark brown, light brown, olive, reddish brown, beige and peach skin colors are not considered unusual colors, and do not enhance "flavor."

Some writers disguise their lack of an adequate description by adding to it a description of the suspect's clothing. Again, the editor should be very cautious about including this enhanced but still inadequate description. To say that the suspect was described by police as "a white male weighing about 170 pounds and wearing a white T-shirt with jeans and white jogging shoes" does not contribute to either the so-called flavor of a story or to the ability of the public to locate this person. Such clothing is worn by millions of Americans each day, and suspects who know they have been spotted are likely to change their clothes quickly. What service is the news medium providing in describing a suspect as wearing jeans if the suspect has already changed to jogging pants?

NOTEWORTHY FEATURES. A defining description is one that helps the public and police locate a missing person. Some obvious examples of features that might contribute to a defining description are:

1. An unusual but obvious tattoo on someone's hand or face

2. An unusual but obvious mole, scar, bruise or freckle on someone's hand or face

3. A pierced nose or noticeable facial punctures

4. Hair that is dyed purple or some other unusual color

5. An obvious handicap or broken bone

6. An unusual way of standing, walking or moving

7. An unusual speech impediment or rare accent

8. An unusual skin coloration or birthmark

9. A physical disfiguration

10. Baldness or distinguishing facial hair

11. Obesity

12. Extreme thinness

13. An unusual nervous twitch

14. A glass eye, or very thick glasses

WHEN A LIMITED DESCRIPTION MAY BE USED. Editors should note that a suspect's height, weight and skin color do not necessarily need to be eliminated from a news story. If there is additional descriptive material that when combined with this information helps to "define" the person more fully, then this limited description can become more useful and may be included. The more information that is known and provided, the more helpful each element of the description becomes.

Before eliminating any such description, the editor should decide whether or not the description plays a vital role in the story. If the story is about a racial incident, for example, the skin color or racial identification could become essential to the story, even if there is little further description of the people involved.

Assuming that the focus of a story is unrelated to issues of race, height, sex or weight, and the writer only provides an inadequate description, the copy editor should do more digging. Contact the reporter to find out if there is any additional descriptive information available. In many cases, the police are able to provide more information as the story develops. Without a defining description, however, the editor should seriously consider eliminating any description.

As a rule, if there is no potential benefit to providing a very limited description and there is only potential harm, it is better to eliminate the description entirely.

Pure-Blooded

People of different racial backgrounds should not be presumed to have blood types exclusive to or dependent upon their race. Blood types cross all cultural, ethnic and racial lines. To refer to a person as *pure-blooded* or a *pure-blooded* patriot, implies that other people or patriots have tainted, inferior or impure blood as a result of cultural mixing. Obviously, this is a false notion. Although the expression is meant to be figurative, and is often used to flatter rather than insult, the term *pure-blooded* implies bias and should be avoided in most instances. (See the section titled Pure-Blooded in chapter 4, Nationality Bias.)

Purebred

People of different backgrounds are not of different *breeds*. *Breed* is not an accepted synonym for race, nationality, ethnicity or religion.

Animals are classified into *breeds*. In articles that refer to pets and animal breeding, it is more accurate to say *pure-breed* or *purebred,* rather than *pure-blooded.*

Race Inquiries

Writers should not assume that all people, or even most, are of a single race. Nor should articles imply that it is somehow better to be of a single race. Many individuals are biracial or multiracial, as are many families.

Many application forms include an "optional" section to inquire about each applicant's racial or ethnic background. Such a section typically contains a disclaimer that specifies: "This information is used for statistical reporting purposes. Providing the information is voluntary. The fact that an applicant chooses not to respond to the question does not play a role in our admission decisions." Many application forms dictate that the applicant may only check one category. Typical categories include: African American or Black, Puerto Rican, Mexican American or Chicano, Latin American or other Hispanic, Native Hawaiian, American Indian, Eskimo or Aleut, Asian, Asian American or Pacific Islander, and White or Caucasian American.

While the aim of the question might be to help companies or universities eliminate bias, the applicants are asked to classify themselves. Sometimes this task requires the applicant to weigh others' biases or to promote their own biases. Does an applicant whose mother is black and whose father is Chinese American check the box in front of African American or Asian American? Does a person whose father is African American and whose mother is Swedish American check the box for Black or White? Should the applicant check both? Should an Israeli American or Turkish American check the Asian American box, since Israel and parts of Turkey are located in Asia?

Some applications have provided resolutions of these kinds of questions with the addition of an "Other (please explain)" category. Increasingly, applications are adding the category "Mixed (please specify)."

■ Community

Community should be used to mean neighborhood. It should not be used, however, as a euphemism for race, ethnicity, nationality, sexual grouping, political grouping, religious grouping or age grouping, or as a means of classifying people of similar backgrounds together as a single unit with a single view.

Incorrect usage:

The black *community* supports affirmative action.
The gay *community* opposes the law.
The Estonian *community* votes conservatively.
The conservative *community* uses pesticides on their lawns.
The senior citizen *community* opposes early retirement.
The Hispanic *community* supports bilingual education.
The Catholic *community* is against cigarette smoking.

Instead of the word *community,* insert the word or name of the organization or grouping that is meant. An editor should consult the writer if the meaning is unclear or if the specific organization is not known.

Correct usage:

Many black organizations support affirmative action.
The university's gay rights organization opposes the law.
Estonian-American political organizations traditionally support conservative candidates.
The Conservative Party in the county was opposed to banning pesticides.
Many older Americans oppose forced retirement.
Many Hispanic educators support bilingual education.
Many Catholic youth groups do not endorse cigarette smoking.

It is correct to refer to a *religious community,* when describing a group of people who attend the same religious institution, know each other and act as a *community* together. Just being affiliated with the same religion, does not constitute being part of the same religious *community.* (See the heading Religious Community in chapter 6, Religious Bias.)

■ Caucasian Portrayal

Anglo

Some writers, when specifying racial background, use the word *Anglo* instead of *Caucasian,* as if *Anglo* were a more polite way to indicate *white. Anglo* means English. To use it as a synonym for *Caucasian* is incorrect.

Armenians, Middle East Christians, Eastern Europeans, Greeks, Jews, Italians and people of many other ethnic backgrounds who might consider themselves *Caucasian* would not consider themselves *Anglo.*

"Dear White Reader"

Editors of general-interest publications should not assume that all of their readers are white by permitting writers to address a white audience only. The same applies to assumptions of other skin colors. (The exception is when writing for a publication that is targeted for either an ethnic audience that shares a common skin color or when writing for a publication targeted toward a specific skin color. Two examples: a magazine targeted for black business executives, and a magazine on cosmetology published in Swedish for Swedish Americans.)

One of the most common examples of this kind of bias in general-audience publications appears each spring in articles focusing on tanning lotions or sun block. Writers, eager to impart the latest medical wisdom on avoiding skin cancer, suddenly assume that their readers are all white, or that "everyone" is white. Such bias is discrimination by exclusion, implying that those readers to whom this information does not apply are not important or, even worse, do not exist.

Consider the following sentences:

This is the season when everyone is hoping for a good tan.
Doctors recommend that all people—regardless of age—use tanning lotion with sunblock before going outdoors in summer.

Parents should all encourage their children to use a protective sun-tanning lotion.

All teenagers like to lie in the sun for a good tan.

While the writers' intentions may be good and protective, all of these sentences assume that all of the readers are white or pale-skinned. All of these statements are therefore inappropriate for general audience publications. As a rule, unless the publication is tailored specifically for a white audience, a dermatology journal on pale skin disorders, for example, the editor should eliminate the assumption that all readers have pale skin.

Consider the following changes:

This is the season when many people seek suntans.

Doctors recommend that light-skinned people—regardless of age—use tanning lotion with sunblock before going outdoors in summer.

Parents whose children have fair skin should encourage use of protective sun-tanning lotion.

Many pale-skinned teenagers like to tan themselves in the sun.

PERFECT TAN.   Writers have been known to discuss pursuit of suntans in terms of the *perfect tan.* Editors should note that even in feature stories, there is no such thing as a *perfect tan.* The usage implies that some skin shades are better than others, more imperfect or perfect, or universally more attractive or less attractive. These are obviously biased notions.

Typical American Skin Color

There is no *typical American* skin color. Many publications inadvertently present white people as *normal* and people of color as an aberration or the exception to the rule. They do this by excluding any mention of skin color when referring to light-skinned people, while specifying a skin color for people with darker skin tones, even when skin color is completely irrelevant to the story. Some writers have the tendency to refer to all people as either *whites* or *nonwhites,* implying that *white* is some kind of standard.

Obviously, there are many American skin colors. Among so-called white people, skin tones vary. Asian people and Native Americans should not be presumed to have yellow skin or red skin. Middle

Eastern people, Jews, Greeks and southern Italians should not be presumed to have so-called olive-colored skin. Writers should not presume that all Irish people have red hair or freckles.

As a rule, a publication should not describe skin color for every nonwhite mentioned in articles, unless the publication describes skin tone for white people as well. If it bears no relevance to the story, description of skin color should be eliminated from the article.

When to Use White

When referring to person's skin color in an article where skin color is relevant, *white* is preferred over *European American, Caucasian* or *Anglo*. Not all white people trace their roots to Europe. *Anglo* means English, and many white people do not trace their ancestry to England or consider themselves *Anglo*. Caucasian is generally used in an anthropological discussion, and should be avoided in reference to a person's skin color or ethnic background.

■ Portrayal of People of Color

Nonwhites are sometimes referred to as *people of color,* although the usage is confusing. The implication is that so-called white people do not have color or pigmentation. The term is applied to Africans, Native Americans, Latinos and many Asians, including those who may have lighter skin than the whites who are not considered *people of color.*

Many publications do not use the phrase *people of color,* because it sounds like a flowery euphemism for *nonwhite,* and they prefer to avoid euphemisms. Other publications consider *people of color* a positive label and prefer it to a negative (or negating) one like *nonwhite.* If race is not pertinent to the story, remove all references to *whites, nonwhites* and *people of color.* If race is vital to the story, the writer should try to specify which racial (or ethnic) groups are involved rather than generalizing about coalitions of *people of color.*

Some writers substitute the word *minorities* instead of *people of color,* but editors should be cautious about this usage. If all Americans are technically from somewhere, all are *minorities.* The *minority* designation cannot be the exclusive domain of *nonwhites.* In many American towns, cities and neighborhoods, whites are the minority.

Never substitute *colored people* for *people of color.* The terms are not interchangeable. Both have very different connotations.

Colored

At one time, *colored* was considered a polite way to say *black*. It no longer is. Editors should eliminate references to *colored people* in copy. An exception is in the name of an organization like NAACP, the National Association for the Advancement of Colored People.

A second exception is when the word appears in an old quotation. If the quotation is pertinent to the piece, the writer should keep the word in quotation marks, attribute the quotation, and explain the context. If a direct quotation is not essential to the context, writers may prefer to paraphrase the quotation outside of quotation marks, using *black* instead of *colored.*

The *United Press International Stylebook* notes that "in some African countries, *colored* denotes those of mixed racial ancestry. If *colored* is used, place it in quotation marks and explain its meaning." Even when writing about such populations, however, it is generally better to write "of mixed racial ancestry" (and to specify this ancestry if relevant to the story) than to describe people as *colored,* which many view as offensive.

Minorities and People of Color

Do not use *minorities* and *people of color* interchangeably. While the euphemism, *people of color,* generally includes only nonwhites, the term, *minorities,* is used more broadly, and its meaning may vary depending upon the context. While readers typically equate the two words, the term *minorities* may also include white Latinos, for example, as well as every other white ethnic group that considers itself a minority in America: Armenians, Jews, Syrians, Turks, Kurds, Pennsylvania Dutch, Estonians, Latvians, etc.

In some contexts, *minorities* is not exclusively an ethnic reference. For example, people with differing social situations sometimes count themselves among America's *minorities*: gay people, dwarfs, blind people, deaf people, wheelchair users, women (although they are in the majority), welfare recipients, etc.

The term *minority* becomes especially inappropriate when the so-called *minorities* referred to in any particular article actually make up a majority in that article. For example editors should eliminate references to "women and other minorities" that imply that women constitute a minority of the general population. Likewise, in neighborhoods, cities or states where any nonwhite racial groups make up a majority of the population, it is inappropriate to label members of this population "minorities." Such labeling presumes incorrectly that white people are uniformly the majority when, in fact, white people would be the minority in this context.

■ Portrayal of Africans and African Americans

African American or Afro-American?

African American is the correct usage. In general, *Afro* is used as a noun in reference to a hairstyle, rather than to a continent or culture. If a reporter argues that *African American* sounds too unwieldy, the editor can explain that *African* contains fewer syllables than *American,* and that if anything should get cut in the name of smoothness, *American* would be the likely candidate. Obviously *Amer-African* does not work, and alters the meaning.

In general, an American should only be described as *African American* if the person's heritage bears some relevance to the story. Theoretically, specification of a person being *African American* should be no more common in a publication than specification of a person being European American or Asian American. Some writers inadvertently make a special point of singling out *African Americans* as opposed to other Americans for no justifiable reason, implying that *African Americans* are an oddity, or exceptions to the rule.

African American or Caribbean American?

Editors should note that not all black Americans consider themselves *African Americans,* and that the two descriptions are not necessarily interchangeable. Some black Americans identify more with Caribbean nations, tracing their roots back for many generations. These Americans might consider themselves *Jamaican Americans* or *Cuban Americans,* for example, or *Caribbean Americans.* At the same time, many *Caribbean Americans* identify themselves as *African Americans,* tracing ancestry back to Africa. Some *Caribbean Americans* have light skin and trace their roots to Europe, India or other locations. Some *Caribbean Americans* trace their roots back to a combination of continents, Africa and Europe, for example.

Assuming ethnicity or ancestry is important to a particular story, a good reporter should inquire about the subject's ancestry, without being presumptuous based on skin color. ("To where do you trace your ancestry?" would be a reasonable question. If the answer is "Jamaica," for example, the reporter might then ask, "Would you consider yourself a *Jamaican American?* Would you consider yourself an *African American?"*)

Reporters should try to be as specific as possible. An interview subject who merely volunteers that he or she can trace ancestry to the Caribbean should be asked to specify which nation or nations. If ethnic background is important to the story, it is better to be more specific and write *Cuban American* or *Jamaican American* than to merely indicate *Caribbean American,* which encompasses a broad range of national and ethnic heritages. If a person has roots in more than one Caribbean nation, multiple nations can be specified within the story, although the lead would probably be more comprehensible if it only identified the person as Caribbean American.

The same principles apply to people who claim African ancestry. When ethnicity is important to an article, the editor should make sure that if the writer calls the person *African American,* the subject of the article traces his or her roots to Africa. In Africa as in the Caribbean, the specific country of ancestry should be mentioned when known, recognizing that Africa is not a single country, but a continent of many countries and many varied cultures and ethnic groups. Just as writers would describe an American who traces roots back to Italy as an *Italian American* instead of a *European American* in most contexts, writers should identify someone whose roots go back to Nigeria as a *Nigerian American* rather than an *African American,* if the national roots are known.

If ethnicity and nationality are not important to the article, the editor might question why *African American* or *Caribbean American* are even mentioned in the copy. If the writer is mentioning ethnicity as a euphemism for skin color, the editor should eliminate this usage.

Black or African American?

Some editors believe that it is more polite to describe someone as *African American* in all instances rather than *black American.* There is no basis for this, particularly in a story about color or color-related issues. When a writer uses *African American* consistently as a euphemism for *black,* it becomes obvious that the writer is uncomfortable with the word *black,* revealing some personal bias. Both *African American* and *black* may be used in journalism, depending upon the context. Editors should evaluate the usage in each instance, to check the context and to be sensitive to any biases on the part of the writer.

Maintain parallelism. In a sentence that mentions *"white Americans and African Americans,"* for example, one of the references should be changed to maintain parallelism. The correct sentence would either refer to *"white and black Americans"* or *"European and African Americans."*

WHEN TO USE BLACK.   When referring to a person's skin color in an article where skin color is relevant, *black* and *white* are the preferred terms. *African American* and *European American* are inappropriate.

In articles about race or racism, *black* and *white* are generally accepted adjectives. Brown may also be acceptable in many cases. Yellow, red and other colors, however, are generally to be avoided. Do not write, for example, that a racial conflict erupted "between black people and yellow people," or "between white people and red people." Such color designations are not acceptable shorthand for the ethnic or national groupings that they supposedly represent.

In articles about skin coloring (a fashion story on selecting flattering makeup, for example), *black* and *white* are preferred adjectives. In such articles, however, a writer will probably need to be more specific about skin tones and colors, since *black* and *white* include a wide range of colors.

WHEN TO USE AFRICAN AMERICAN.   In an article about ethnic heritage, *African American* may be the preferred usage if and only if the person or event described traces roots to Africa. (A Jamaican-American parade, for example, is not an *African-American* event.) *African-American* is preferred in articles about African-American celebrations, arts, heritage, politics, travel and customs. If a specific African nation is tied to the event or news item, however, writers should specify that nation, rather than merely labeling the event or news item *African American*. For example, if there is an Egyptian-American arts festival, the writer should specify that the event is *Egyptian American,* rather than merely labeling it generically as an *African-American* arts festival. Likewise, if the writer is reviewing a restaurant that is *Moroccan American,* or covering an ethnic dance performance by a *Nigerian-American* troupe, specifying these national affiliations provides more information and is therefore preferred over generic references to an *African-American* restaurant or dance troupe.

Writers should be cautioned, however, not to specify ethnicity or national heritage in articles in which heritage does not pertain. If the mayor of a particular American city happens to be *Tunisian American,* for example, the writer covering city hall should not gratuitously point out this ethnic heritage in every article about the mayor. If the mayor announces a new annual *Tunisian-American* parade in the city, the mayor's ethnicity becomes relevant to the story, and *Tunisian American* should be mentioned in reference to the mayor. If the writer is covering a speech by the mayor on local transportation or budget or housing, the mayor's ethnicity is not relevant to the speech and should not be included in the article.

The Black Perspective

There is no such thing as the "black perspective," just as there is no singular "white perspective" or "Asian perspective" on any issue. (Refer to the section Women's Perspective, chapter 5, Gender Bias, for a discussion on assigning a single perspective to a wide-ranging group of millions of thinking people.) A reporter seeking to incorporate a fair mixture of perspectives in a story about race may indeed quote a variety of black leaders and white leaders. However, it should not be presumed anywhere within the piece that any one single black individual or even leader represents the views of all black people (or that any single white or Asian individual or leader represents the views of all white or Asian people). Leaders only represent the particular groups that elected them to lead. Even when the reporter has gathered a group of prominent leaders, it should not be presumed that the reporter can then summarize an official *black perspective* from the group.

A reporter who interviews only one black person to gain the *black perspective* in an article is guilty of tokenism, a form of racism, even if the expression *black perspective* is never used. A diligent reporter should find leaders to interview, and the article should state whom those leaders represent (which organizations and the size of the membership). In this way, the readers are able to understand clearly how influential these leaders' views are (and to understand that these views are not the entire *black perspective,* but only one group's or a few groups' perspectives). Even if a leader presides over a large organization, it should not be presumed that this singular view represents the universal *black perspective.*

An exception may be in a local story, where the numbers of people involved are smaller and an individual (a civic leader, elected to officially represent a neighborhood, for example) may, in fact, represent the majority of ethnic voters in that neighborhood. But this only applies if the elected official has a specific mandate restricted to leadership of a limited ethnic group. (The president of a Haitian-American settlement and cultural committee, for example, could speak authoritatively about the "local Haitian-American perspective" on housing integration, if this organization's membership includes a majority of the local Haitian Americans in a largely Jamaican-American neighborhood.)

This exception does not apply to officials elected to represent diverse populations. A reporter should be cautioned, therefore, not to assume that because the mayor of a large city is black that he or she is representing the *black perspective,* rather than the diverse city's best interests, although these two causes may have the same interests on many issues. In the same way, a mayor who is Asian American should not be presumed to be representing only the "Asian-American perspective" instead of all of his or her constituents' interests. If a politician who is elected to serve a diverse population only represents his or her minority group, the politician would be considered negligent.

Black and White, "Opposite Races"

Black and white may be opposite colors, but black and white are not "opposite races." There are no opposites when it comes to race. There are *different* races, but no opposites. It is correct to refer to "the opposite sex," because there are only two, but "opposite race" is not acceptable.

In calling black and white "opposite races," the implication is that *black* and *white* are at opposite ends of a social/racial spectrum, with every other race somewhere in the middle, and lighter-skinned people nearing the *white* side of the racial and social spectrum. According to this obviously fallacious racial "scale," Indians and Pakistanis are somehow more Caucasian than Nigerians, and Koreans are generally more Caucasian than Indians.

As a general rule, editors should be careful about handling articles about race, in which *black* and *white* are compared, without mentioning other races, as if only two skin colors apply to race stories or as if every other race falls somewhere in the middle.

The following sentence may sound innocent enough or even positive, but it contrasts only *black* and *white* people, failing to mention other skin colors or racial groupings, thereby implying and reinforcing the notion that *black* and *white* people are generally opposites.

"In black neighborhoods, just as in white neighborhoods, parents want their children to get the best possible education."

Although the writer's intention may be to break down stereotypes, the sentence reinforces stereotypes.

Busing

The word *busing* should not be used as a euphemism for *integration*. Editors need to be vigilant about eliminating this biased usage. Although many opponents of school integration programs feel more comfortable discussing *busing* inconveniences, the term may not be used interchangeably with *integration* in objective journalism.

If the writer is covering an integration story and is interviewing people who claim to be opposed to busing, the reporter needs to ask specifically what aspect of busing the interviewees oppose. Unfortunately, this discussion tends to become a cat-and-mouse game, in that the interviewees then feel obligated to defend their stance and elaborate on the hassles and hazards of school buses, when it is usually integration that they really oppose. A clever reporter might ask, "Would you favor integration if there were a way to integrate without busing?" At that point the interview subject might admit that he or she is opposed to integration in general, or the particular method proposed. If the interview subject insists that the argument is a matter of busing, the reporter could follow up by asking, "May I quote you as saying you would favor integration as long as it would occur without busing?"

Ultimately the aim is not to corner an interview subject, but rather to get to the heart of the issue. Is it integration that is opposed or the particular method of integration that is opposed? Is there a better method that the interview subject can suggest, perhaps that would benefit more people? Does the interview subject believe that integration in general has been shown not to work? Does the person believe that the form of integration proposed has been proven not to work? What is it, really, about the particular method of integration that disturbs the interviewee?

If a writer turns in a story about busing hassles, a copy editor should begin asking questions. Good editing does not permit "codes" and "euphemisms" that help cloud an uncomfortable story rather than shedding light on an issue.

Black Is Bad, White Is Good

Editors should watch vigilantly for writing that equates black with evil and white with good. This usage goes beyond skin color discussions to descriptions of material objects, ambiance, and actions. In old movies, for example, the villain always wore black, and heroes and heroines wore lighter colors; most newer films have moved away from that cliché.

COMMON EXPRESSIONS THAT SAY BLACK IS BAD.   The following types of expressions may reinforce a stereotype:

He did not want his name/reputation blackened.
She dealt on the black market.
His name appeared on the blacklist.
The woman believed in the black art of black magic.
In every class, there is always one black sheep.
She was so distraught, that she blacked out her memory.
The plague was referred to as Black Death.
The employment record contained a black mark.
The unemployed worker was accused of blacklegging.
They were accused of blackmail.
The dirty child's hands were black with mud.
The comedian resorted to a little black humor.
The stepmother was portrayed as blackhearted.
A black cat crossed my path.
That is a black lie!
The plant was killed by black rot.
The angry boss responded blackly.
The criminals belonged to the Black Hand society.
The stock market crashed on Black Friday.
The bride wore black and had a black outlook.

COMMON EXPRESSIONS THAT SAY WHITE IS GOOD.   Likewise, these statements also reinforce an image:

> The young bride wore white.
> In a bid for peace, they displayed the white flag.
> The floor was clean and white.
> Tom Sawyer whitewashed the fence.
> To make him happy, she told a little white lie.
> Snow White's skin was as pure and white as snow.
> The tourist visited the "Great White Way."
> The law firm was strictly white shoe.
> As a doctor, he was considered a white hope.
> The military white alert meant that all was clear.
> I'm dreaming of a white Christmas.
> That was very white of you to be so honest.
> You were considerate to perform some white magic.
> She was a white-collar worker.
> She was white-hot with enthusiasm.

Dark Is Bad, Light Is Good

Editors should be careful about references that equate darkness with evil and lightness with good. Such caution should extend beyond discussions of skin color to general descriptions and metaphors selected by the writers. At the same time, not all metaphors that refer to darkness as negative or lightness as positive need to be stricken from an article. Each reference should be considered separately and in context. But the editor needs to be sensitive to the issue, particularly if metaphors about darkness and lightness constantly appear in different forms in the writing.

COMMON METAPHORS THAT SUGGEST THAT DARK IS BAD. The following types of expressions should be approached with caution, particularly if overused.

> He lived on the dark side.
> The candidate was in the dark about the issues.
> The professor's lecture seemed rather dim.
> She was called dim-witted.
> His chances were dim, and so were his views.

He had suffered a dark past.
He held onto a dark secret.
The candidate was considered a dark horse.
They studied the Dark Ages.
The sign was interpreted as a dark cloud.

COMMON METAPHORS THAT SUGGEST THAT LIGHT IS GOOD.
Editors should note that there is often a subtle difference between
words that say "lightness" is good and words that suggest that "light"
is good. If light is equated with visibility or clarity, there may be nothing wrong with referring to light. If lightness is equated with beauty or
superiority, however, the usage should be questioned. The following
expressions are common, but not necessarily negative.

Look to the bright side.
There's a light at the end of the tunnel.
Let there be light... and it was good.
The book may shed light on the issue.
The room was light and airy.
The actor stole the spotlight.
The politician was in the limelight.
He saw the light of day.
The student was enlightened.
The dark cloud had a silver lining.

African-American Celebrations

Writers covering an African-American celebration should make sure
that the event is exclusive to African Americans before labeling the celebration an African-American holiday. If the celebration honors Civil
Rights or a celebrity who happens to be of African-American heritage,
for example, that does not make the holiday an African-American holiday.

JUNETEENTH.   Juneteenth is considered an African-American his-
toric celebration and the nation's oldest African-American holiday.
The June 19th holiday commemorates the June 19, 1865 arrival of
Gen. Gordon Granger in Galveston, Texas, where he was sent to force
slave owners to release their slaves in the aftermath of the
Emancipation Proclamation.

KWANZAA.   Kwanzaa is a cultural holiday observed by African Americans of all faiths from December 26th through January 1st. Although the dates coincide with Christmas celebrations, Kwanzaa is not correctly described as the *black Christmas, African Christmas,* or *African-American Christmas.* It is also incorrect to describe it as an African religious holiday. According to the book *Holiday Symbols* by Dr. Maulana Karenga, a UCLA professor from Nigeria, the seven-day celebration was established as a means of reconnecting African Americans with African roots and harvest traditions.

MARTIN LUTHER KING DAY.   Writers have been known to refer to Martin Luther King Day as "a major African-American celebration." To describe it that way is just as biased as calling George Washington's birthday a major white-American holiday or Anglo-American holiday. Both birthdays are correctly considered American federal holidays or national holidays; each celebrates an American hero. Neither should be singled out as an ethnic or racial celebration.

Likewise, in a general-interest publication, Dr. Martin Luther King Jr. should not be described on first reference as "black American hero Dr. Martin Luther King Jr." or as "African-American hero Dr. Martin Luther King Jr." Both indicate bias in implying that he is only a hero to a segment of the American population, rather than embracing him as an American hero. This does not mean that his racial background should be omitted or ignored. After establishing the fact that King was an American hero, it is appropriate to follow up by discussing his heritage, talents and contributions.

Dr. Martin Luther King Jr.'s birthday, celebrated in the United States on the third Monday of January, became an official national holiday in 1983. His actual birthday was January 15, 1929.

■ Portrayal of Asians and Asian Americans

Asians and Asian Americans are sometimes portrayed in the media as being quiet, conformist, unemotional, introverted, insensitive, hard-working, secretive, fragile-looking and power-hungry. Editors should eliminate usage that reinforces these stereotypes, particularly when groups of people are characterized in copy. (See chapter 4, Nationality Bias, for a discussion of the portrayal of China and Chinese people.)

Oriental, Asian or Asiatic?

When referring to Asian people or Asian Americans, use *Asian* or *Asian American* instead of *Oriental,* if and only if the person's national or ethnic heritage is pertinent to the story. Otherwise, an *Asian American* should be referred to as an *American. Oriental* is an adjective and the correct term to use when discussing rugs, as in *"Oriental* rug," vases as in *"Oriental* vases," or, occasionally, in cooking as in *"Oriental* cuisine." (In food stories, it is generally better to specify the national or regional origin instead of using the generic label of *Oriental* cuisine. *Japanese* cuisine and *Cantonese* cuisine are preferred over the less specific *Oriental* cuisine. This is not always possible, however, since some restaurants do not specify the ethnic or national origins of their own cooking, preferring to label all of their dishes *Oriental.*)

Because Asia is such a large continent, *Asian American* is very vague. The label includes people whose roots are linked to India, China, Vietnam and those who trace their heritage to every other Asian country. As a rule, it is better to be specific about national origin when ethnicity or national origin pertain to the article. Specifying *Japanese American* or *Korean American,* is far more informative than merely referring to someone as *Asian American.*

Assuming ethnicity and ancestry are important to a particular story, a good reporter should inquire about the subject's ancestry, without being presumptuous based on the way the person appears to the reporter. ("To where do you trace your ancestry?" would be a reasonable question, if ancestry or ethnicity pertain to the article topic.) If a person has roots in more than one Asian nation, multiple nations can be specified within the body of the story, although the lead of the article would probably be more comprehensible if it only indicated that the person is *Asian American.*

If ethnicity is not relevant to the article, the editor should question why *Asian American* or any national heritage reference is even mentioned in the copy. If the writer is mentioning ethnicity as a way of distancing the reader from the article subject, or prejudicing the reader, the editor should eliminate this usage.

Oriental is not used as a noun. Asian Americans are not *Orientals,* they are *Americans* or *Asian Americans,* depending upon the context.

The term *Asiatic* should be eliminated by editors or replaced with either *Asian* or *Asian American,* depending upon the context. *Asiatic* "implies enemy race," according to the *News Watch Project Style Guide.*

Confucian Work Ethic

Editors should eliminate references to a Confucian work ethic, even if the term sounds flattering or affirmative of hard work. According to the *News Watch Project Style Guide, Confucian work ethic* has appeared in descriptions of Asians as a "stereotypical term used to describe the tendency of some Asians to work hard and keep quiet. Many Asian Americans cringe when the generalization is made, because it evokes images of Asians as mindless hordes unable to think or act creatively."

Confucius Say

Editors should eliminate the expression *Confucius say* from copy. The usage implies that Asians do not use correct grammar in quoting Confucius. (Correct usage would be: "Confucius said.") But more importantly, the expression is a "stereotypical saying that pokes fun at Asian Americans as always speaking in proverbs and not having original thoughts or actions," according to *News Watch Project Style Guide.*

Dragon Lady and Madame Butterfly

Editors should watch for usage that characterizes every Asian woman as either a sinister dragon lady or a fragile Madame Butterfly (a reference to Puccini's opera).

Model Minority

Asian people should not be referred to as the *model minority* in copy. Although the designation might seem flattering or positive (see chapter 13, Appeals to "Positive Bias"), the expression is considered offensive and revealing of bias. The *News Watch Project Style Guide* specifies that the term reinforces "the misleading belief that they [Asian Americans] have [all] achieved success in the United States. Such references ignore the large groups of Asians and Asian Americans who have failed to achieve success, or who suffer from poverty, unemployment, language barriers, drug abuse and other problems."

Petite Oriental

A newspaper review of "Miss Saigon" said the Broadway show was about a "petite Oriental." Not only is the use of the word *Oriental* incorrect, but the attachment of the word *petite* is considered offensive. *Petite* connotes *trivial, cute* or even *insignificant*. Editors should assume that men and women do not want to be described as *petite,* and they should avoid stereotyping any ethnic group by size.

Portrayal of Other Races

Race versus Ethnicity

Calling an ethnic group a separate *race* can be construed as a form of either racism or ethnic discrimination or both. One cannot correctly write that a riot was racially motivated, for example, if there is no racial difference between the parties involved in the incident. To say that the incident is racially motivated, means that the reporter acknowledges a racial difference.

(Not all publications' styles agree on this issue. At some publications, if the instigator of trouble views the conflict as a *racial* difference, the publication is correct in calling the conflict a *racial incident,* even if no *racial* difference has been objectively established.)

Gypsy Race

German dictator Adolf Hitler declared the Gypsies to be a separate race and attempted to have them annihilated during World War II. Although in recent years the Austrian press has perhaps unwittingly promoted this distinction by describing violence against Gypsies in Austria as *racial* violence, Gypsies are an ethnicity and a culture, not a race. (See chapter 3 on Ethnic Bias for a discussion on portrayal of Gypsies and Roma.)

The American news media have been picking up Austria's usage. American editors should examine their usage carefully. If a speaker refers to the *"Gypsy race,"* the writer may rephrase the quotation outside of quotation marks, to change the reference to *"Gypsy people,"* or *"Gypsy culture."* If the writer describes the violence as *racial* conflict, the editor should change that usage to *ethnic* conflict. If the quotation is vital to the story and needs to be maintained, the writer should attribute the quotation and explain to the reader that *Gypsy* is not commonly accepted as a distinct race.

In some older reference books, Gypsies have been described as a separate "dark Caucasian race," originating in India and living primarily in Europe and the United States. Journalists should be wary about classifying people into races.

Indians

The people classified as Native Americans vary in population, depending upon who does the categorization. The U.S. Census Bureau classifies American Indians and "Alaska Natives" as Native Americans. Native Hawaiians and people from Guam are classified as Pacific Islanders. Editors should note that many common definitions of *race* would not distinguish Native Americans as a separate race. (See chapter 3 on Ethnic Bias for a discussion of portrayal of Native Americans.)

Indians from India and Pakistan

People from India and Pakistan are not considered a separate race by most common definitions. People from India should be referred to as either *"people from India"* or *"Indian American"* (if they are American citizens), according to *News Watch Project Style Guide*. People from Pakistan are Pakistani or Pakistani Americans. If ethnicity and national origin do not pertain to the piece, do not describe article subjects as *people from India, Indian Americans, people from Pakistan,* or *Pakistani Americans. Pakis* is derogatory and should not be used in reference to *Pakistanis.*

Jewish Race

During World War II, German dictator Adolf Hitler declared that the Jews were a separate race. According to the Anti-Defamation League, Jews are not a race, and the word *race* should not be used with Jews. Alan Schwartz, Research Director for ADL, explains that Nazi racial theories sought to portray Jews as a separate race, promoting "pseudo-science notions about size of skull and other features...[using] a gloss of scientific vocabulary." This classification served Nazi political purposes, "but was simply a reflection of hateful Nazi theories."

"Nowadays we should be aware that Jews are not a single race as an anthropological category," Schwartz says. "Race would apply to skin tone, and other recognizable physical characteristics. Jews are found in all parts of the world" and have different skin colors, hair color and physical features. "The Ethiopian Jews do not look like Jews of Canada, and many Jews in Israel from Arabic countries have darker skin than Jews who grew up in Poland."

According to the Anti-Defamation League, Jews fit various anthropological and racial categories. "What links them is their religious traditions and cultural traditions rather than anything one could call race."

Old references to the Jews as a race, are sometimes without ill intentions, Schwartz notes. Various Christian groups have referred to Jews as the *chosen race*. "If you go back 50 to 100 years, one can find sympathetic treatments of the Jewish people using the word *race*: *persecuted race* or *intellectual race*." He adds, "Today we would prefer to be called an *ethnic group*," which he calls a more accurate distinction.

SEMITES AND ANTI-SEMITES.   Although Semites technically include both Jews and Arabs, all descendants of Noah's son, Shem or Sem, *anti-Semitic* has meant anti-Jewish from the outset. Anti-Semitism cannot journalistically be considered a form of racism if the prejudiced party is of the same race as the Jewish people, even if the prejudiced party believes him- or herself to be of another race and claims the hatred is racially motivated. While legal systems may define racism differently, journalists should consider anti-Semitism a form of *ethnic* or *cultural* discrimination, hatred or violence.

If someone is charged legally with *racial* violence for committing an act of anti-Semitism, the writer should explain clearly that the charge was racial violence and the reason was anti-Semitism.

Can Arabs Be Anti-Semitic?   Because *anti-Semitic* has been used as a synonym for *anti-Jewish,* Arabs that are anti-Jewish may correctly be called anti-Semitic. Any people, including those of Jewish descent, who are anti-Jewish may be called anti-Semitic.

According to the research director of the Anti-Defamation League, the term *anti-Semitism* comes from late 19th century Germany, where a small-time politician named Wilhelm Marr coined the term as a euphemism for Jew hatred. Alan Schwartz of ADL says the term "has always essentially meant hatred of the Jews." He says those who claim that anti-Semitism means prejudice against both Arabs and Jews are in error. "Some have tried to advance a political agenda, by claiming that since Arabs are also Semites, anti-Semitism is also an anti-Arab term, but that is false."

Latino Race

If an article focuses on racism against Latino people, an editor should change the usage to *cultural bias* or *discrimination* against Latino People.

The category *Latinos* refers to Spanish-speaking people of a variety of ethnic backgrounds and physical characteristics. Latinos may belong to any race, although European Americans sometimes classify Latinos as a separate race based on generalizations about skin color. By most classification systems, however, skin color alone does not constitute a separate race, and there is no one Latino skin color. Editors should be wary, therefore, of references to the *Latino race* or *Hispanic race*. Latino people are part of a culture, not a distinct *race*. (See chapter 3 on Ethnic Bias for a discussion on portrayal of Latin People.)

Mixed Heritage

Many writers wrongly label a person who is half Asian and half Caucasian as "Asian." Likewise, it is not uncommon in the American press to see a person whose father is black and whose mother is white (or whose mother is black and whose father is white) described as *black* or even *a light-skinned black*. Yet this same person is never described as *a dark-skinned white*.

In editing, the general principle stands that no skin color or race should be gratuitously mentioned in a news or feature piece in which color and race are irrelevant. If color or race is relevant to a story and needs to be mentioned, editors should note that no race or color should be viewed as more dominant than any other. In other words, if the subject of the article is half Japanese and half Egyptian and this is relevant to the story, the person should be described as half Japanese and half Egyptian—not *Asian*, nor *Oriental*, nor *African*. If the person's background is relevant to the story but the writer is not sure to which specific countries the subject's ancestry can be traced, it would be correct to describe the person as *half Asian and half African*. It would be incorrect, however, to describe the person as only *Asian* or *African*.

Writers should not assume that people who come from mixed ancestry only trace their roots to two countries. Each grandparent, for example, may trace ancestry back to a different continent. If ancestry is not relevant to the story, the writer should not attempt to offer an in-depth discussion ironing out the article subject's racial or ethnic roots. If ancestry is vital to the story, the writer might want to state in the lead that the person's ancestry includes a multicultural mix that can be traced back to four continents. Later in the piece, the writer can spell out the details of which continents and, more specifically, which countries on each continent.

■ Racially Loaded Terms

Editors should eliminate derogatory terms and words that promote bias, as a general rule. There is no place in objective journalism for incorporation of abusive or bias-loaded terms.

The main exception, and one that confuses many journalists, is when a derogatory word appears as part of a quotation. Some publications allow writers to include epithets, for example, as part of quotations. Some ban use of all derogatory words. Most American publications handle such words on a case-by-case or article-by-article basis, evaluating what the quotation contributes to the story and how essential it is toward telling the story objectively.

One factor in the decision-making process at many publications is the severity of the word itself. Not all derogatory terms are considered equally offensive. Some publications ban specific derogatory words, but permit others.

At first, the idea of banning all derogatory words from a publication may sound appealing. An editor who is quick to ban all epithet words, however, should understand that quoting a limited amount of offensive language is not necessarily tantamount to endorsing or even promoting such usage. Sometimes by quoting the abusive language, the editor is allowing the reader to understand the severity of the abuse on the part of the speaker. By shielding the reader from hearing the abusive language, the editor is, in effect, protecting the abusive speaker from being seen as he or she really is. In extreme cases, this can be construed as a subjective endorsement of the speaker, particularly if a substantial portion of the speaker's language is consistently censored or "cleansed."

At many publications, the general philosophy is: When speakers are their own worst enemies, provide enough rope to let them hang themselves. In other words, quote people's abusive language, and the readers, who we presume are intelligent people, will see the abusiveness and will better understand the reason to oppose the speaker.

For this reason, sometimes it is deemed important to the meaning of the story to report what wording the speaker actually used, no matter how ugly it sounds, so that the reader gains a full and objective understanding of the speaker.

An editor needs to ask, "Who am I protecting by not including abusive or insulting language contained within a quotation?" In some cases, the answer legitimately may be children who might be reading the publication and whose parents may not want them exposed to harsh or ugly language or images. (Does the publication attempt to lure young readers, with special pages or articles targeted for children and teenagers, as well as an adult audience?) If the answer is "the adult reader," however, the editor should think twice about automatically eliminating unpleasant or inappropriate language.

Including sensitive words on a case-by-case basis should not give license, however, to constant repetition of derogatory words. Most newsmakers do not use epithets and other derogatory words in their speeches and statements to the media. Such words appear as the exception rather than the rule. A speaker who constantly resorts to such usage should not be automatically and slavishly quoted by the writer. Instead, a single quotation or sampling generally suffices to give the reader a taste of the speech. Parroting every nasty word only gives publicity and promotion to a nasty speaker. In the same way that censoring all unpleasant usage is not viewed as the aim of the objective journalist, drawing attention to all unpleasant usage is also not the aim. Responsible publications do not want to provide a propaganda vehicle for subjective speakers, particularly those who do not seem to have a mastery over their own speech.

Cotton-Picking Hands

In plantation days, cotton was picked by black slaves. The phrase *cotton-pickin' or cotton-picking hands* could be construed as the equivalent of *black hands* or, more offensively, *dirty black hands.* While the phrase is still heard in common speech, particularly in supposedly humorous monologues, its meaning is essentially derogatory.

Editors should eliminate this usage from copy, even though it generally only appears in quoted matter. People who say *cotton-picking hands* rarely mean to be offensive and tend to be ignorant of the expression's origins. If the phrase appears within a quotation that is essential to the story, rephrase the quotation and remove the quotation marks.

Merriam Webster's Dictionary lists *cotton-picking* as synonymous with *damned,* and explains that it is "used as a generalized expression of disapproval" or as an "intensive" ("out of his *cotton-picking* mind"). In either case, avoid it.

Cracker

The term *cracker* is used disparagingly in reference to poor Southern whites. The usage should be avoided, since it reveals both racial and economic bias. When it appears within a quotation, it may be used within quotation marks if the information is vital to the story. In that case, it should appear with attribution and an explanation of context.

(This should not be confused with another contemporary use of the term *cracker,* meaning a computer hacker who breaks into computer systems illegally.)

Gringo

Gringo is a derogatory term used among Hispanic Americans in reference to Caucasian Americans and Britons. UPI style dictates that writers should "avoid this contemptuous term." Not all journalism stylebooks concur. An American travel writer, visiting a depressed Caribbean nation, saw several examples of spray-painted graffiti that warned, "Gringo go home!" throughout the island. Because travel writers' and other journalists' first responsibility is to their readers, the travel writer wanted to let her readers know about this graffiti, rather than shielding them from it. (Novices often assume that the job of the travel writer is to sell a destination—to only write about the positive aspects, rather than informing readers of what to expect realistically when they travel.) The resulting question was whether to quote the word *gringo* in the travel story, or to just write that graffiti bearing anti-white epithets was seen along the roadside throughout the island nation.

Common journalistic practice is to use the word only if it is part of a direct quote that is deemed necessary for the story. In most styles, if such a derogatory word is ultimately used, it should appear within quotation marks with a lowercase *g,* if it is not the first word of the quotation. If the quotation is being rephrased, there is no reason to use the word *gringo.* When used, the term should be attributed and its context or apparent context should be explained clearly in the article.

In the case of the travel writer, the graffiti was quoted in the story, because merely saying "graffiti bearing epithets was seen," did not seem to provide readers with a clear enough sense of the tension on the particular island at the time and who was being blamed.

Honky

Honky is a derogatory term meaning *white* or *whitey,* sometimes used by nonwhites. In most cases, the word should not be used in a journalistic piece. If, however, the word appears in a direct quote that is deemed necessary for the story, it may be used, according to many stylebooks. When such a derogatory word is printed, it should appear within quotation marks and start with a lowercase *h,* if it is not the first word of the quotation. The quotation should then be attributed and carefully explained in context.

Mr. Charlie and Gook

Editors should monitor derogatory terms that emerge from war stories. In most cases, if racial slurs appear within material quoted from soldiers, the usage should be rephrased outside of quotation marks, eliminating the racist usage, if the statement is pertinent to the story.

Mr. Charlie is used as a war-related derogatory term for *white man, white soldier* or *white people* and comes from the proper name Charles. The usage should be eliminated from copy, unless it appears in a direct quote that is vital to the story. If it is used within a quotation, quotation marks should be used, and the remark should be attributed and explained in context.

The term *gook* is a derogatory term for Asian enemies, "widely used by American GIs during the Korean War and again during the Vietnam War," according to the *News Watch Project Style Guide.* The term should be eliminated from copy.

Negro and Negroid

Negro is no longer considered an accepted synonym for black. The preferred term is *black. Negro* may still be used, however, within the name of an organization, for example the United Negro College Fund, or within quotations, particularly quotations from decades ago when *Negro* was a more widely accepted term.

Contemporary quotations that use the word *Negro* should only appear as quotations in a story if vital to the story. When used, *Negro* should begin with an uppercase *N.* If the exact quotation is not necessary to the story, editors should paraphrase the quotation outside of quotation marks, using *black, African, African American,* or *Carib-*

bean American, depending upon the context and requirements of the article.

Negroid may only be used in reference to historic and scientific studies of race.

NEGRESS AND MAMMY.   *Negress* is considered a derogatory term for black women for two reasons. It combines the word Negro, which is no longer accepted as a synonym for *black,* with an *-ess* suffix, which is gradually being eliminated from English usage because of sexist connotations.

The preferred term is *black. Negress* may be used within a quotation only if the quotation is deemed essential for the story. In almost every case, paraphrasing outside of quotation marks is preferred. When used, *Negress* should begin with an uppercase *N.*

Editors should eliminate the term *mammy* in reference to a black woman who is a mother or child care provider. The term implies servitude and is demeaning.

The *N* Word

During the O.J. Simpson legal proceedings, the word *nigger* was heard in discussions. This created an issue for the various news organizations covering the trial. Policy decisions had to be made on how to handle this word, which was previously banned from use in most American publications and broadcasts. Should the print media quote the word directly, immediately attributing it to the speaker? Should they just say that some "epithets" were overheard in audiotapes, without specifying which epithets? Was the word itself an important element of the story?

At some news outlets, uncomfortable with the mere mention of the term, editors labeled *nigger* the *N word,* and continued to refer to it that way. In some radio broadcasts, every quote that mentioned the word *nigger* was edited out entirely or paraphrased. In other broadcasts only the word itself was bleeped from a sentence or sound bite that was used in the broadcast.

Most American news media have a policy against using the word, regardless of the context. They feel that the word is more extreme than other epithets and has no place in the media, or that the mere mention of the word encourages other people to use it. Even when the term is being quoted as an example of the extent of racism, most editors specify that *nigger* may not be used.

The Associated Press Stylebook treats the word like other derogatory terms. It specifies that within a quotation, the word should only be used "in direct quotes when essential to the story."

Niggardly

Although it sounds like it is related to "nigger," the term *niggardly* is unrelated to any racial or ethnic slur and is not a derivation of the word *Negro*. *Niggardly* means "stingy." Although the use is clearly judgmental, it is not considered an ethnically or racially biased term. Nevertheless writers, particularly broadcast writers, are cautioned against using this term because it sounds too similar to "nigger." Well-meaning readers and listeners are likely to be offended unnecessarily and to presume that the usage reflects prejudice.

Oreos, Bananas, Eggs and Twinkies

Editors should eliminate usage that insinuates that people can be one race on the outside and a different race on the inside, as if behavior is determined by race. The concept reveals strong racial bias. An *Oreo* refers to a black person who behaves like a white person, implying that there exists a *white behavior*. A *banana* refers to an Asian American who behaves like a white person, as a result of growing up in a white environment. An *egg,* according to the *News Watch Project Style Guide*, is "a pejorative term used by Asian Americans to describe whites who are enamored with Asians or Asian culture (white on the outside, yellow on the inside)." A *Twinkie* refers to Asian Americans who knowingly reject their Asian identity and identify more with whites, according to *News Watch*.

Redneck

The term *redneck* refers to "a white member of the Southern rural laboring class" and any person who shares similar behavior and opinions with this class, according to *Merriam Webster's Dictionary*. The usage is generally disparaging and should be avoided. It may be used in direct quotations if such a quotation is vital to the story and is accompanied by attribution and an explanation of the context.

Sambo

The Helen Bannerman children's story *Little Black Sambo* is considered by many to be racially biased. Regardless of the viewpoint of the individual editor, references to Sambo should be monitored carefully. Eliminate any comparison of a child or children to Sambo. Be wary of writing that endorses or refers endearingly to the original illustrations.

Spade and Superspade

In reference to black people, the terms *spade* and *superspade* should be eliminated. Both are racial slurs.

White Trash

White trash is synonymous with *poor white.* It is often used as a synonym for *redneck* as well. The usage is disparaging both racially and economically and should be avoided. In a quotation, the term may be used within quotation marks if it is vital to the story and is attributed and explained in context.

WHITEY.   Used as a disparaging label, *whitey* means *white man* or *white society.* The term should only be used within a quotation, if the quotation is vital to the story. In such a case, the entire sentence should appear within quotation marks, and the term should be attributed and explained in context.

ZEBRA AND MULATTO.   People of mixed heritage should not be compared with animals or inanimate objects in copy. The term *zebra,* as a casual reference to people of mixed races, should be eliminated. The term *mulatto,* referring to the offspring of one white parent and one black parent, should also be eliminated. The term comes from *mulatto mule,* an animal with medium brown coloring.

3

Ethnic Bias

■ Ethnic Bias Examples

The following are examples of different forms of ethnic bias that commonly appear in publications or on broadcasts. Examine the sentences, and then determine how they should best be rewritten to eliminate ethnic bias.

The Indians are making lots of wampum from their new casino.

He was gypped and reported his loss to the Better Business Bureau.

The Latin-looking suspect had a mañana attitude about confessing.

"Long time, no see," she yelled to her long lost friend.

Witnesses described the suspect as short, shifty-eyed and Mediterranean.

■ Overview of Ethnic Bias

Ethnic biases are sometimes revealed within journalism in the form of headlines that poke fun at ethnic traditions, generalizations about ethnic customs, stereotypical descriptions and illustrations that belittle ethnic groups and promote prejudice.

Editors need to be aware of ethnic subtleties and sensitivities in order to eliminate unintended ethnic bias. In referring to people of different ethnic backgrounds, the word *ethnic* should only be used as an adjective, not a noun. People are not *ethnics*.

■ Arabs

By some definitions, the term *Arab* refers to all people whose native language is Arabic, regardless of their religion or ethnic affiliation. Yet many Middle East Christians, who do not consider themselves Arabs, dispute this definition. Other definitions link the word *Arab* to all Semitic people inhabiting countries where Arabic is the primary language. But this definition cannot be applied to Sephardic Jews, who are also Semitic and, in many cases, born in countries where Arabic is the primary language.

Be careful about describing people as Arab. The term is not synonymous with *Muslim*. Editors also should be careful about writers who label all people from the Middle East Arabs.

As a rule, it is always better to be specific when discussing a person's national or ethnic heritage, rather than generalizing about all Arabs or Arab traditions. An Egyptian has a different cultural experience than an Iraqi, for example. In Kuwait, the experience is different than in the United Arab Emirates.

Iranians

Iranians are not considered Arabs, since Iran is not an Arab country. Most Iranian people are Persian. The language of Iran is Farsi.

Media Contacts

The American-Arab Anti-Discrimination Committee (ADC) is a civil rights organization committed to defending the rights of people of Arab descent and promoting their rich cultural heritage. ADC is non-sectarian, nonartisan and claims to be the largest Arab American grass-roots organization in the United States. It was founded in 1980 by former Senator James Abourezk and has chapters nationwide.

The organization's mission includes "combating defamation and negative stereotyping of Arab Americans in the media and wherever else it is practiced." The organization promotes events "correcting anti-Arab stereotypes and humanizing the image of the Arab people."

Contact the ADC at 4201 Connecticut Ave., NW; Suite 300, Washington, DC 20008, (202) 244-2990.

Stereotyping

People should not be described as *Arab-looking* in the media, as there is no single Arab look. While Arabs often have black hair, brown eyes and olive skin coloring, many Arabs are black, and many have light skin and blond hair. Arab is a cultural and ethnic designation, rather than a racial one. Eliminate *camel driver, sandsucker* and other ethnic slurs from copy, even in quoted material. If slurs occur within a quoted statement, either eliminate the quotation or rephrase the quotation to eliminate derogatory language, removing the quotation marks.

ARAB TERRORISTS, HOLY WARS AND JIHADS.   The term *Arab* should not be equated with or automatically linked with *terrorist* in copy. Arab people should not be presumed to be violent, sneaky, dangerous or irresponsible. The term *Arab* also should not be equated with *holy war* or *jihad*. Arab people should not be presumed to be supporters of violent causes.

SHIFTY-EYED.   Years ago, children's mystery book series commonly described suspects as being "shifty-eyed," particularly when the suspects were from the Middle East or Turkey. According to the stereotype, Arabs and Muslims were sneaky and as they whispered evil plans, their eyeballs moved rapidly from side-to-side, suspiciously checking to see that nobody overheard their secret.

Obviously, people from the Middle East have no more of a tendency toward shifty eyes than do people from other places. Yet even in cartoons and animated films, Arabs are often portrayed that way. Editors should watch for usage of *shifty-eyed* to make sure that the writer is not inserting the cliché gratuitously to promote some old stereotype.

■ Gypsies and Roma

Major international newspapers have covered Gypsy struggles within Austria in recent years. But many of the accounts reveal careless anti-Gypsy bias by the writer. Even use of the word *Gypsy* may be perceived as derogatory by some in reference to itinerant ethnic groups in Europe. *Roma* or *Romani* is generally preferred. Some editors may argue that readers recognize the *Gypsy* designation more readily and will not understand a reference to *Roma*. In that case, it is the task of the editors and writers to educate the readers on current usage. An editor could substitute the word *Roma* for each reference to *Gypsies,* inserting an explanation after the initial reference (*"Roma,* more commonly known in North America as *Gypsies"* or even *"Roma,* previously referred to as *Gypsies"*).

The *Dictionary of Bias-Free Usage* suggests that whenever possible, writers should "refer to specific Romani groups (Romanichal, Kalderash, Bashaldo)" rather than generalizing about all Romani people or traditions. The book notes that "For centuries the Roma have been severely oppressed and regarded as second-class citizens (and in some countries as no citizens at all)." The author, Rosalie Maggio, contends, "There is virtually no mention of the Roma in references to the Holocaust; although there is some debate about the actual figures, it is possible that up to 80 percent of the Romani population perished."

Roma

When referring to the *Romani* people, the plural form is *Roma. Romani* is the singular as well as an adjective.

Capitalizing the *G* in Gypsy

When *Gypsy* is used instead of *Romani,* the *G* is most commonly capitalized in reference to ethnic *Gypsies.* But when using *gypsy* to mean a generic itinerant or in any other sense (gypsy moth, gypsy cab, etc.) the *g* is lowercase. UPI style dictates that the *G* should be capitalized "in a direct reference to the tribes of itinerant dark-skinned people believed to have come from India in the 14th or 15th century." AP style concurs: "Capitalize references to the wandering Caucasoid people found throughout the world." *The New York Times* uses uppercase as well.

Gypsy Ethnicity versus Race

Newspaper reports from Austria frequently refer to violence against Gypsies as "racially motivated," but such usage implies that Gypsies and Austrians are of different races, a notion that the Nazis promulgated during World War II. The terminology used by publications in referring to Gypsies is very revealing. (Refer to the section Gypsy race in chapter 2, Racial Bias.)

Gypsies are generally considered an ethnicity, not a race. (Note that AP style considers Gypsies part of the Caucasian race, "wandering Caucasoid people.")

At a publication where Gypsies are considered an ethnicity, an American journalist would have to call violence against Gypsies an example of ethnic violence, rather than racial violence.

Some dictionaries define *Gypsy* as a separate "dark Caucasian race" originating in India and living primarily in Europe and the United States. Journalists should be wary about classifying people into races. If a publication has no set style on Gypsies, conflicts between Gypsies and other European people should be characterized as ethnic violence, if ethnicity or ethnic prejudice seems to be a factor in the issue. Gypsy conflicts should not, however, automatically be characterized as *ethnic,* unless specific ethnic issues pertain. Likewise, unless the conflict is specifically linked to some aspect of culture (i.e., preference for one form of music competing with another style of music for performance time at a local concert hall), the conflict should not be referred to as a *cultural conflict.*

Roma and Romani News Sources

Lazy journalists are sometimes guilty of printing only government-originating stories about Gypsies, contending that Gypsy sources are too difficult to locate.

The European Roma Rights Center (ERRC) bills itself as an international public-interest law organization that monitors the situation of Roma in Europe and provides legal defense in cases of human rights abuse. Contact them at their Web site: http://www.errc.com. The International Romani Union claims to be "an umbrella organization" coordinating regional and national groups in 30 countries. The aim of the organization "is to foster a sense of reunification among all Romani peoples through our language and culture, and to combat anti-Gypsy [discrimination]...in all its forms."

According to organization literature, "One means of achieving this is to provide educational materials about Gypsy peoples to non-Gypsy peoples, and to monitor media misrepresentation." Contact the International Romani Union at their Web site: http://www.unionromani.org.

Gypsy Blood

Gypsy blood is sometimes used as a synonym for wanderlust or a love of travel. While unsuspecting writers may find the usage colorful, bold or even romantic, the terms can also be perceived as offensive, literally reinforcing the false notion that Roma have a different kind of blood than other people and promoting age-old stereotypes. In fact, *Gypsy blood* also has been used pejoratively to connote a tendency toward wildness, violence, irresponsibility, lack of commitment or sloppiness. Figurative references to *Gypsy blood* should be eliminated in most cases.

Responsible editors, who otherwise judiciously eliminate disparaging references to other ethnic groups, are sometimes hesitant to remove references to *Gypsy blood.* The usage is perceived as an inoffensive example of supposedly positive bias, and therefore the reference remains in the copy. Editors should note, however, that there is no room for so-called positive bias in objective journalism.(Refer to chapter 13, Appeals to "Positive Bias.")

For editors who consider this edit to be overly cautious, try substituting the blood of other ethnic groups as a comparison test. Nordic blood, Jewish blood, Arab blood, English blood, African blood, Kurdish blood, Mexican blood: If any of these references seem offensive, *Gypsy blood* too should be edited out of copy.

Gyp

The words *gyp* or *gypped,* as in "The salesman *gypped* him by charging $15 for an apple," originated as an ethnic slur and should not be used in journalism. Most dictionaries indicate that *gyp* is slang. Some specify that *gyp* stems from the word *Gypsy.* The word *gyp* should be changed to *cheat. Gypped* becomes *cheated.* In quoted material, remove the quotation marks and paraphrase what was said, using the word *cheat* instead of *gyp.*

In place of the noun *gyp,* as in "The deal turned out to be a *gyp,*" use *fake, fraud* or *scam.*

■ Latin People

Chicano and Chicana

Chicano means *Mexican American* and is often considered derogatory. *Chicana* is the feminine form. Journalists should avoid using the terms unless they appear in quoted matter, in which case they should appear only within quotation marks, with attribution, and with the context explained. *Mexican American* is preferred usage in discussing the ethnic origins of Americans from Mexico. As a rule, do not mention a person's ethnicity in an article unless this information is pertinent to the piece.

The *United Press International Stylebook* specifies that "*Chicano* has been adopted by some social activists of Mexican descent, and may be used when activists use it to describe themselves."

Hispanic

Latino and *Hispanic* are generally considered synonymous. The word *Latino* is more commonly used on the West Coast of the United States, although it has been gradually gaining in usage in the rest of the United States as well. Some stylebooks prefer *Latino,* a broader term, since it more readily embraces Portuguese-speaking Americans in addition to Spanish-speaking Americans. *Hispanic* implies Spanish-speaking only. Like *Latino, Hispanic* can refer to a person of any race.

Reporters and editors with bias questions concerning representation of Hispanic Americans in the media can contact the United States Hispanic Chamber of Commerce at (800) USHCC-86.

Latin Americans

Latin American is not a synonym for *Latino, Latina* or *Hispanic. Latin American* refers specifically to a person who comes from Latin America. (Latin America consists of the countries south of the United States, where Romance languages, including French, are the national languages.)

Latin-Looking

Occasionally a police report or crime story describes a suspect as *Latin-looking.* Editors should be wary of this usage and ask the reporter to get a more definitive description of the suspect or omit this biased reference. If the reporter is trying to say that the suspect has tan skin, black hair and dark eyes, that is more definitive than a vague ethnic reference to "Latin-looking." Latin America includes all of the nations south of the United States. This includes a wide range of ethnic and racial populations, and makes the adjective "*Latin-looking*" meaningless.

Latinos

Latinos are Spanish-speaking Americans, most of whom come from southern North America or South America. The term is considered an ethnic and cultural designation. The largest percentage of Latinos traces ancestry to Mexico. Second largest percentage is from Puerto Rico; third largest, Cuba. Latinos stem from many other places as well, representing a wide array of cultural and historic diversity. Some books classify Portuguese-speaking Americans as Latinos, adding to the diversity. The designation *Latinos* does not refer to a separate race, and in fact includes members of the three or four major races.

Latino and *Latina* are the singular masculine and feminine forms. The plural is *Latinos*.

ARE LATINOS "PEOPLE OF COLOR"?   Whether or not Latinos are considered people of color depends a lot upon the Latino or Latina, and who is making the determination. There is no right answer, since Latino is an inclusive term that represents people of a variety of cultures, historic backgrounds, national origins, races and skin colors. According to the 1990 U.S. Census, about half of the Mexican-American population classified themselves as white.

In covering Latinos or Latino events, writers should not assume that the people about whom they are reporting want to be counted as people of color, Caucasians or members of an independent race.

LA RAZA.   Latino people are also referred to as *La Raza,* a Spanish word for *race.* Sometimes *Raza* is used to refer to Latino culture and heritage, according to the *News Watch Project Style Guide.* Although so-called insiders may use the term *La Raza,* writers for English-language publications (*outsiders* by definition) should use the terms *Latino* or *Hispanic* instead.

Spanish Words

As a rule, when words in an English-language publication are borrowed from another language, the editor should monitor the usage to make sure that the words are not being used to disparage an ethnic population (supposedly in their own terms) or to create negative images. Make sure the word selection includes a variety of words if the purpose of the usage is to add ethnic flavor to the piece. Eliminate the usage if all of the borrowed words are negative or demeaning.

BARRIO.   *Barrio* means *neighborhood* in Spanish. When the word is the only Spanish word (or one of very few Spanish words) to appear in an English-language publication, the implication is that the English word *neighborhood* is not equivalent and that a *barrio* is somehow different. *Barrio* may be acceptable usage among so-called insiders, people who live in a Latino neighborhood. But in an English-language publication (by definition, an *outsider*), *barrio* has a negative connotation. The *News Watch Project Style Guide* suggests avoiding the usage "because the term conjures up stereotypes about Latino neighborhoods." The guide recommends specifying the name of the neighborhood instead.

MAÑANA ATTITUDE.   *Mañana* means *tomorrow* in Spanish. To describe someone as having a *mañana attitude* means the person is lazy or slow and would rather put off some task until an indefinite tomorrow. Because the word is quoted in Spanish, it becomes a slur, as if to imply that writing *lazy* or *slow* in English is not enough to communicate the degree of laziness or slowness. The implication is that Hispanics or Spanish-speaking people are somehow lazier or slower or less caring about promptness.

The word most commonly appears in articles about Caribbean nations and South America, by political, business and travel writers. Editors should be very wary about the usage, since it promotes a common stereotype. At the very least, *mañana attitude* makes readers associate slowness with the Spanish language. This becomes particularly noticeable when *mañana* is the only example in the publication of a word borrowed from the Spanish language.

As a rule, writers should avoid the term in an English-language publication when writing about Caribbean nations or South America.

■ Mediterranean-Looking

Occasionally a police report or crime story describes a suspect as *Mediterranean-looking*. Editors should be wary of this usage and ask the reporter to get a more definitive description of the suspect or omit this biased reference. If the reporter is trying to say that the suspect has olive skin, dark hair and dark eyes, that is more definitive than a vague ethnic reference to "Mediterranean-looking."

Obviously the Mediterranean region encompasses a broad area and includes such varied locations as the French Riviera, the Greek Islands, the Egyptian desert, Morocco, Israel, Spain, Italy and Gibraltar, all of which have different ethnic populations. This makes *Mediterranean-looking* meaningless.

■ Native Americans

Contrary to popular portrayal in the media, Native Americans include more than 500 cultures, ethnic traditions and languages. There is no one singular Native American culture. Editors should question writing that implies that any one person represents the American Indian culture, or that any one ritual or tradition is representative of all Native American customs.

American Indians or Native Americans?

According to the Native American Journalists Association, the style on whether to call people *American Indians* or *Native Americans* is largely a matter of different publications' preferences and the context. Neither reference is considered offensive.

A representative for the organization said many publications currently favor *Native American* instead of *American Indians,* with the explanation that "We were never those Indians" that the Europeans thought they had found as they sailed for India.

The Associated Press style uses *American Indian* in reference to "those in the United States." But it advises that writers "be precise and use the name of the [nation] tribe" where possible. AP permits *Native American* in quotations and names of organizations. United Press International also does not use *Native American* in reference to *American Indians.* The stylebook poses the argument that "All people born in this country are *Native Americans.* Avoid as a reference to races that preceded the white man [person] to this continent."

News Watch Project Style Guide suggests using *native-born* instead of *native* in reference to people born in the United States who are not American Indians.

NATIVES.   Many publications shorten *Native Americans* to *natives,* and that usage seems to be gradually gaining acceptance. Most of the major stylebooks do not accept *native,* however, arguing that the term is still widely perceived as pejorative. Editors should probably avoid using *native* as a noun in reference to indigenous people. The usage appears most often in pieces about rights for indigenous people, archeology articles, and travel stories.

As an adjective, *native* becomes more acceptable. *Native* American, for example, is considered proper usage at many major publications, as is *native* Alaskan.

In reference to nonindigenous people, the noun forms may be acceptable. "He described himself as a *native* of New York," or "He was a Vermont *native,*" are both acceptable.

Should the N in Native Be Capitalized?   Styles vary on whether or not to capitalize the *n* in *native/Native American* or *native/Native Alaskan*. The argument against capitalization is that native is used as an adjective rather than the proper name of a specific ethnic group. When used with American, however, many styles would argue that *Native American* does refer to a specific ethnic group.

Native American Language

There is no single official Native American language. According to the Native American Journalists Association, there are 500 federally recognized nations, and an equal number of languages. There are also some nations that are not federally recognized. When referring to a native language, the writer should specify the language, and not presume that all Native Americans speak one language.

Tribes

The word *tribe* is to be avoided, according to the *News Watch Project Style Guide*. The guide suggests using *nation* or *ethnic group* instead. Within the United States, "Native Americans prefer *nation,* because their people have signed treaties" with the United States "that recognize them as nations." (The guide notes that in reference to Africa, as well, the different ethnic groups should not be described as *tribes.*")

When writing about Native American nations, the writer should specify which group or groups are discussed in the article. Because there are hundreds of ethnic groups, customs and traditions vary enormously. Editors should be suspicious of any generalizations about the practices of Native Americans, particularly if no specific nation is mentioned.

TRIBAL WARFARE.   Avoid describing any disagreement as *tribal warfare*. The expression is often used by writers with a Eurocentric bias to describe conflicts among non-European people. The usage is pejorative and implies *primitive*. The *News Watch Project Style Guide* says *tribal warfare* has been applied to conflicts "between Hutus and Tutsis in Rwanda," whereas "the civil war in the former Yugoslavia between Serbs, Croats, and Muslims" has been called *ethnic cleansing*. The guide suggests that both conflicts should be described as either *ethnic conflicts* or *civil wars*.

Indian Reservations

Some Indians prefer the term *nation* to *reservation*. The *News Watch Project Style Guide* cites as an example the *Navajo Nation*, instead of *Navajo Reservation*.

Writers should not assume that all Native Americans, or even most, live on reservations or in Indian nations. According to the 1990 Census, only half of all Native Americans lived on or near reservations. Most of the remaining Indians lived in major cities. American Indians are not *confined* to *reservations*. Using the word *confined* in reference to *reservations* is incorrect.

Expressions to Avoid

Many expressions used years ago in Hollywood depictions of Native Americans gradually have made their way into popular speech. Some of these expressions may seem harmless and innocuous, but have demeaning or biased overtones. Most of these expressions add nothing to the authentic flavor of a piece (generally detracting from an article's authenticity), and even less in the way of information. Editors should eliminate such expressions from writing.

"How!"   In old Hollywood movies, cartoons and television series, no matter what group of Native Americans were supposedly being depicted and no matter where these groups lived, the first word out of the chief's mouth was always "How!"

Contrary to Hollywood stereotypes, all Native Americans do not greet each other by saying "How!" and raising their right hand. Editors should eliminate this stereotype, even when used in a supposedly whimsical way in cartoons or feature stories. Nor should journalistic writing imply that Native Americans greet people with folded arms and frowns.

"LONG TIME, NO SEE!"   Although people who use this expression rarely mean to degrade Native Americans, the line is taken from a cliché Hollywood depiction of how Indians speak. Indians do not speak this way, and repeating the expression is promoting an insulting and outdated image.

While old westerns occasionally reverted to this single broken-English expression in trying to portray dialogue with and among Indians, many contemporary films are attempting to portray Indian dialogue in a more authentic way, as audiences become more sophisticated. Creating dialogues of broken English to belittle ethnic groups is generally considered tasteless—both in drama and comedy.

Nevertheless the expression lives on. In its newest incarnation, "Long time, no see" suddenly appears in sitcoms and comedies that have nothing to do with Native Americans or native heritage. It is used by old friends of all ethnic backgrounds as an icebreaker and a greeting. Because of the expression's origins, however, "Long time, no see" is derogatory. It is also hackneyed. Eliminate the expression from all copy. In quoted material, it adds nothing to a news or feature piece, except to point out the speaker's insensitivity toward Native Americans.

"Long time, no hear!" "Long time, no write!" and "Long time, no speak!" are all variations of the expression. They should not be used for the same reasons.

"ME BIG CHIEF, YOU PALEFACE".   Contrary to depictions in old Hollywood westerns, Native Americans do not call all non-Native Americans *paleface*. In the same way that "Long time, no see!" makes fun of broken English, so does "Me big chief, you paleface." Any reference *to paleface* should be eliminated.

CRIMSON-RED SKIN.   A populated town in New York State uses as its emblem the face of an Indian chief with crimson-colored skin. While the aim may not be to offend, the depiction serves to further a myth about Native Americans instead of paying tribute to a great chief. Contrary to pictures in old storybooks and at modern-day Web sites, Native Americans do not have crimson-red skin. As with many ethnic groups, Native Americans' skin colors can vary from pale white to peach to tan to reddish tan to reddish brown to dark brown. Traffic-light-red skin does not exist. Editors should be wary of references that exaggerate the skin color of American Indians.

REDSKINS.   The term *Redskins* is not an acceptable synonym for Native Americans or Indians. The term is considered particularly offensive, whether used in speech, journalism or in naming a team. Some historians say the term originally referred to a form of "currency" by European settlers, who traded animal furs and skins of dead Indians for other "products."

Editors should note that journalists never refer to other ethnic groups by their skin tone. Whiteskins, Blackskins, Brownskins, and Yellowskins, are obviously offensive and unacceptable. The same applies to Redskins.

LOTS OF WAMPUM.   As a rule, do not use the term *wampum* in stories in place of the word *money,* unless the article is about genuine wampum. Speakers and writers who feel uncomfortable discussing finances or fund-raising sometimes resort to euphemistic language. Popular euphemisms include big bucks, moolah, greenbacks, green, and dough. Good journalism has little use for such euphemisms, which only reveal the speaker's (or writer's) discomfort with money. If a speaker claims to be seeking *"lots of wampum"* for a project, the usage becomes offensive in addition to being euphemistic. The writer should take the expression out of quotation marks and rephrase by substituting *a significant amount of money,* or *serious funding.*

SMOKING PEACE PIPES.   As a rule, editors should eliminate *peace pipes* references from copy, when used as a euphemism for *negotiations.* In quoted material, it also should be eliminated or paraphrased outside of quotation marks. When two leaders are meeting to resolve a conflict, the writer should not write that they are smoking peace pipes. The reference to peace pipes, a cliché in articles about serious negotiations, is usually based on the writer's image of old Hollywood stereotypes rather than research into authentic Native American negotiations procedures. Discussion of peace pipes should be limited to articles about genuine peace pipes.

Occasionally, an editor inserts the usage into a headline, because it seems more concise (and takes up less headline space) than the words *Negotiations* or *Settlement Agreement*. Find a different word. There are many shorter, albeit "headlinese," words for peace agreements: *Accord, Pact, Talks, Truce, Deal,* etc.

POWWOW.   *Powwow* should not be used casually as a synonym for *meeting,* whether in reference to Native Americans or others. Only use the term when referring to a genuine Indian *powwow.*

INDIAN GIVER.   An *Indian giver* has come to mean a person who gives something and then takes it away again. It is not acceptable usage. The term probably stemmed from European settlers' confusion about some Indian traditions of sharing and property. The usage implies that Indians do not know how to give or cannot be trusted to give fully. Because the expression promotes false images and is insulting, this name-calling should be eliminated from copy. In quoted material, *Indian giver* should be eliminated as well. Editors should rephrase the quotation outside of quotation marks and attribute it.

FEATHER IN YOUR CAP.   When people perform good deeds or accomplish feats, others say, as a compliment "There's a feather in your cap," or "You've added another feather in your cap." In theory, this is meant as a compliment for an achievement. It is loosely based on a stereotyped notion of an American Indian reward system that supposedly dictates that each time an Indian achieves something, he or she is rewarded with another feather to wear in a headdress, eventually becoming chief after accumulating so many feathers.

While the expression is not necessarily meant to be derogatory, it is based on a cartoon image of Native American tradition rather than an understanding of culture. *Feather in your cap* is flippant and cliché and should be eliminated from copy that is not specifically about Indian traditions.

SMOKE SIGNALS.   *Smoke signals* should not be used as a metaphor to mean *implications, vague communications* or *hints*. Nor should a writer or cartoonist imply that Native Americans communicate by smoke signals.

CULTURAL TRIBUTES.   Editors should be cautious about coverage of cultural commemorations if the tributes are meant to honor groups that are not represented in the planning process, not participating in the event and not permitted to offer input. Editors should be particularly cautious if members of the group supposedly being celebrated claim to be offended by the commemoration.

Domineering cultural groups that design pageants, displays or ceremonies to honor other groups' cultural heritage, may in fact be doing the opposite if these other groups are excluded from the planning. (At the same time, a commemoration may be offered legitimately to stimulate thought or sensitize others about a segment of the population that is not available to participate.) Before providing coverage, editors should determine whether or not a good-faith effort has been made at authenticity and if participation was invited from the group being honored. Otherwise, such pageantry can provide misinformation, and editors may find themselves unwittingly acting as propaganda vehicles.

Among of the most common contemporary examples of nonauthentic tributes are many American Indian rites fabricated by non-Indian groups.

Teams with Indian Names

Many American sports teams have names that supposedly honor Native Americans. In some cases, Indians have contested the names, contending that such names are, in fact, disrespectful. According to the argument, the images are insulting, are belittling and promote disrespect or disregard for authentic native tradition. Many of the mascots and gestures associated with these team names are also said to encourage stereotypes.

Some of the names that have been used by national and local teams have included the Reds, Redskins, Indians, Chiefs, Seminoles, Chieftains, Tomahawks, Warriors and Braves. Not all of the team names are perceived to be equally offensive. In some cases, the gestures (particularly the Atlanta Braves' "tomahawk chop") and mascots may be viewed as more offensive than the team names.

CHIEF ILLINWEK.   Probably the most publicized example of controversy regarding a team mascot has been at the University of Illinois in Urbana-Champaign. Argument about the team name and mascot, based on an Indian theme, began in the 1980s, according to a university spokesman, who said very strong feelings persist on both sides. The name of the team is the Fighting Illini, supposedly honoring the Illini Indians, the indigenous people of Illinois who were "wiped out in the early 18th century." The mascot is a white student dressed as Chief Illiniwek, a fictitious character who wears war paint and performs an interpretation of ritual dances during halftime. The university claims that the chief mascot "represents the noble characteristics to which our team members aspire." However, opponents say that the mascot is a demeaning caricature of a Native American that abuses sacred lore in order to amuse and entertain sports fans. Many students claim that the image is offensive to them.

The university claims that students are split on the issue; the faculty is predominantly opposed to the pageant; and alumni are split, but predominantly in favor of it. The board of trustees voted in 1990 to retain the chief and has said it has no intention of addressing the issue again, unless new information is introduced, the university spokesman said.

The pageant began in 1926. Since then, the mascot has been appearing at halftime at football, volleyball, and men's and women's basketball games.

In the last decade, the controversy grew and the state government became involved. In 1996, both houses of the Illinois legislature overwhelmingly passed a measure stating that the chief must be the symbol of Illinois. The governor changed verb from *must be* to *may be*, according to the university. The controversy became the focus of a film by Jay Rosenstein, *In Whose Honor* about Charlene Teters, a Spokane Indian, who became a leader in opposing the merchandising of Native American sacred symbols. The film first aired on public television in 1997.

OTHER TEAMS.   Other teams with long-standing traditions of Indian names and symbols have changed their names to eliminate images that were construed as offensive. St. John's University in New York, for example, in 1994 changed the name of its men's athletic teams from the Redmen, symbolized by an Indian logo, to the current name, Red Storm, with a horse mascot and a lightning-bolt-in-a-cloud logo. A spokeswoman said the change was made because the original name was considered insulting.

Similarly, Miami University in Ohio changed its team names from the Redskins to the RedHawks during the academic year 1996–97.

Sometimes when a name is put into retirement after it is no longer deemed tasteful on the national level, smaller hometown teams, often children's teams, continue to use the name, allowing the negative stereotypes to proliferate.

THE EDITOR'S ROLE.   While a sports journalist cannot change the name of team or ignore a team because its name promotes bias, the editor should pay special attention to the use of team names and symbols in sports stories, both in print and broadcast journalism. Editors need to be aware that some team names are so offensive to Native Americans and other sympathetic citizens that every mention seems hurtful and insulting.

Writers, trying to write "bright" articles, occasionally resort to puns or what they perceive to be clever turns of phrase that inadvertently promote biases. Copy editors, trying to create spirited headlines, sometimes resort to the same bias promotion. Editors do not have license to make Indian jokes and puns in a headline just because the name of the team is Indian related.

Watch out for pejorative uses of totem poles and war paint in headlines, for example. Here are some other sample headlines that offend:

Indians Scalp Yankees
Indians Pay Wampum for Pitcher
Redskins in the Pink
Smoke Signals from the Braves Camp
Chiefs' Powwow with Mets
Seminoles Beat Their Tom-Toms
War Paint for Navajos
A New Feather in the Seminoles' Cap
Braves Get a New Chief
Indians Show 'Em "How"

OTHER WORDS TO AVOID.   *The Associated Press Stylebook* suggests avoiding the following words in reference to Native Americans: *warpath, teepee* (also *tepee* or *tipi*), *brave, buck,* and *squaw.* The stylebook notes that these terms "can be disparaging and offensive." And it warns writers who use the words to "Be careful and certain of their usage." In addition, eliminate references to going *Navajo style*, meaning "in a pickup truck." If the usage appears in a direct quotation, eliminate the quotation, and substitute *in a pickup truck,* if the mode of transportation is important to the story. (Refer to the Demeaning Illustrations and Demeaning Photographs sections in chapter 14, Editing Art for Bias.)

■ Eskimos, Aleuts, or Inuits?

Aleuts refers specifically to the native population of the Aleutian Islands off the coast of Alaska; the term is limited to those people and is not interchangeable with *Eskimos* or *Inuits.*

The term *Inuit* means simply "the people," and refers to a specific ethnic group. *Eskimo* is derived from an Indian word that means *eaters of meat,* and is considered derogatory by *Inuits.*

Eskimo is a valid term in reference to Inupiat or Yupik Eskimos, according to *News Watch Project Style Guide.*

■ The Most Offensive Ethnic Slurs

Some ethnic slurs are considered so abusive and offensive that most editors will not permit them to appear in the paper for any reason, even if contained in an otherwise vital quotation or on graffiti. Because they are slang words, the vocabulary tends to change quickly, and editors are responsible for keeping up-to-date with the current usage. Among the more well-known banned words are: *Jap* (Japanese), *Chink* (Chinese), *Kraut* (German), *Spic* (Hispanic or Spanish), *Kike* (Jewish), *Hymies* (Jewish), *Polack* (Polish), *Shanty Irish* and *Wop* (Italian). (See chapter 4 on Nationality Bias.)

4

Nationality Bias

■ Nationality Bias Examples

The following are examples of different forms of nationality bias that commonly appear in publications or on broadcasts. Examine the sentences, and then determine how they should best be rewritten to eliminate nationality bias.

The speaker was of Lithuanian persuasion, although she could have passed for a pure-blooded Estonian.

The delegate from Indiana looked Chinese, although she didn't speak with an accent.

The politician delivered the Polish joke with an Irish twinkle.

The real estate agent spoke about the immigrants, complaining that foreigners were taking over the community.

The Frenchman ordered Chinese, and the Chinaman ordered French food.

■ Overview of Nationality Bias

Nationality biases are commonly revealed within news stories as well as in the overall selection of stories and publication layout. These biases may appear in the form of mimicry of different accents and customs, value judgments determining what stories (from which destinations) merit up-front coverage and follow-up coverage, decisions about what places merit minimal coverage, descriptions of geographical locations, and oversimplification of national and international issues.

■ International Coverage

Readers often complain that American newspapers and magazines do not provide enough coverage of international news and that American journalism tends to be very isolationist, self-absorbed and biased against many of the smaller countries. Some of the decision making by editors entails a circular argument. Editors do not perceive significant interest in certain countries, so they do not devote as much space to those countries. Readers then are not exposed to news from those countries and assume that nothing of interest is happening there. Because they are told little about those countries, readers lose interest in the countries. If news is scant or irregular, readers find it difficult to follow ongoing situations in other countries and also lose interest.

Sometimes the lack of coverage is a matter of limited resources. A publication that can only fund 10 overseas reporters must make a value decision as to where the reporters would be most efficient, thus providing the most "useful" and abundant news. Certain locations obviously attract more coverage, particularly large countries that generate a lot of news, countries that directly impact the United States and centrally located countries where nearby news is guaranteed. As a result, a bias emerges against some of the smaller, more isolated countries.

Although good reporters are able to link events in remote corners of the world to their readers, such reporters often do not get to go to these remote locations. This does not mean that they are biased, but rather that they are limited by budgets. As a result, much of the international coverage at major newspapers is skewed and may appear biased, relying on wire service reports and stringers of varying quality.

Most of the major publications strive for balance in international coverage. But what ultimately is covered, and what stories are awarded up-front space, reveals a lot about the assigning editors' biases and their understanding of what the readers want.

International Politics

Smaller countries in remote areas tend to be ignored, and often the readers never hear about a country unless an international crisis erupts. Readers are unfamiliar with the form of government in most countries, know little about the geography, language and customs of smaller countries, and are not given enough regular information to follow the politics in most smaller nations. In some cases, readers may not even recognize the names of some of the smaller countries, as a result of lack of coverage.

Editors might ask themselves what they know of the political systems of some less-publicized countries. For example, try naming the leader of 10 of the following countries:

1. Togo

2. Uzbekistan

3. Tadzhikistan

4. Turkmenistan

5. Kirghizistan (Kyrgystan)

6. Burkina

7. Cape Verde

8. Gabon

9. Nauru

10. Sao Tome and Principe

11. Kiribati

12. Tuvalu

13. Vanuatu

14. Tonga

15. Cameroon

16. St. Lucia

17. Andorra

18. Lesotho

19. Surinam

20. Moldava

An editor's lack of knowledge could influence the editor's lack of interest in a country, and ultimately, a publication's lack of coverage, and readers' lack of interest. Editors may argue that such countries are not politically pivotal. With limited financial resources, editors find such countries among the ones where coverage is least crucial. Nevertheless, such news judgment and budgetary decisions are based on bias—popular bias within the country that the media operation is based.

Travel Destinations

The destinations that a travel editor selects reveals a lot about that editor's bias regarding national and international destinations. Travel editors use a variety of considerations in creating interesting sections that inform and appeal to readers. They seek pieces about unique experiences, new attractions, budget strategies, travel trends, changes in regulations, new modes of transportation, hotel amenities and exotic scenery. Travel sections tend to feature the most popular and accessible destinations more frequently than those that are remote or dangerous, partly because it is assumed that more readers will be interested in reading about places they can access comfortably. (Articles on accessible locations are also featured more often partly because they are in greater supply—more travel writers submit articles on these places.)

In selecting a mix of stories, however, many travel editors do not realize that they are revealing bias toward and against certain countries. There is an obvious bias toward domestic destinations, for example, but that bias is justifiable in that there is large reader demand for information about accessible, "affordable" domestic trips. Coverage of international destinations, which tends to be far more uneven, is more difficult to rationalize. Sometimes editors are at the mercy of freelance writers. If nobody submits an article from the African nation Togo, for example, an editor cannot publish an article about Togo. But sometimes the unevenness is a result of the editor's own interests and taste. Does the editor find safe destinations in Africa interesting? Is the editor captivated by new destinations in Asia? Has the editor ever traveled in South America? Does the editor speak any foreign languages, and is the editor more comfortable including articles about countries where English is the primary language?

Granted, some publications are influenced heavily by the advertising dollar, but this kind of promotional bias should not be a factor at a publication that offers quality journalism. Objective journalists should regularly monitor their coverage to ensure a fair variety of destinations and to guarantee that individual biases do not influence the coverage.

BANANA REPUBLICS. In descriptions of countries and governments, *banana republic* is often used disparagingly as a put-down of a tropical nation—often a Caribbean nation, but not restricted to the Caribbean—that bases much of its economy on growing and selling fruit. According to the *Merriam Webster's Dictionary, banana republic* means "a small dependent country usually of the tropics; especially one run despotically." The usage is also meant to imply "primitive," "backward," "inefficient," or "overly bureaucratic." Editors should eliminate this usage, particularly in political or international affairs stories. Instead of characterizing an entire country as a banana republic, a more specific description should be provided, as this is potentially more useful to the reader. If a country's political system seems inefficient, for example, and this inefficiency is relevant to the story, the reporter should specify how the operation is lacking, rather than resorting to a cliché label.

If used in a quotation that is deemed necessary to the story, the writer should attribute the usage and explain the context. The label should be avoided in travel articles, even when the intention is not pejorative, because the usage has become cliché.

■ Describing People from Other Nations

Accents

National biases are sometimes revealed in the way editors handle accents. Many writers don't realize that everyone has an accent. Americans who insist they are accent-free would be laughed at in England, for example. Some people boast that they speak "with a pure American accent" and without any regionalism. What such boasters do not understand is that there is no single pure American English, that even correct pronunciation varies. When writers, who falsely assume that they are masters of the pure American accent, poke fun at their subjects' speech, editors need to pay special attention. Emphasizing an accent is generally inappropriate and tasteless, unless the accent is relevant to the subject of the story.

Writers sometimes point out that a subject of their writing speaks with a particular accent as a means of put-down or as a means of subtly inserting an ethnic, national, regional or class reference, without realizing they are revealing personal biases. If the particular accent is not relevant, eliminate all mention of it. If the accent is relevant, make sure the writer has credited the correct accent or dialect. For example, is the accent that the writer calls "Irish" actually Scottish or Australian? Might it be from Liverpool or Wales? Did the writer confirm the source of the accent with the subject of the article, or did the writer rely on his or her own ear or presumption about the person's background?

People are commonly offended when their accent is pegged incorrectly. It is not unusual for an American writer to label all Irish, Australian, South African and even Danish accents as English accents or British accents. Within each country, accents vary as well, and to many Americans, Cockney may not sound different from so-called high-English accents.

If the writer inserts mention of an accent as a way of telling the reader that the subject is a foreigner or of some distinct ethnicity, the editor should make sure that the reference is appropriate. Determine why the writer is avoiding direct mention of the person's national or ethnic background. It is better to be direct, rather than quoting broken English or imitating speech patterns in writing.

QUOTING ACCENTS.   When an accent, regionalism or dialect is quoted, the resulting transliterated writing may seem patronizing. Such quotations risk sounding like mockery and may encourage readers to look down upon the interview subject. That may be the intention of the writer, but it is a biased intention. Editors should be wary of the use of transliterated accents, regionalisms or dialects. In most cases such insulting writing should be eliminated.

Transliteration generally adds nothing but confusion and insult to the story. Readers find it difficult to decipher and many feel uncomfortable being a party to the condescending tone of the writer, particularly readers with similar accents or ethnic backgrounds.

Another reason to eliminate transliteration is because it is a very exacting science, and few writers have the ear to transliterate exactly what they hear. As a result they tend to overdramatize the speech pattern, exaggerate certain sounds, and confuse the reader with unintelligible words. In cases in which the subject is insulted by the transliteration, writers sometimes face accusations from offended literate subjects who insist that they were misquoted or claim that they "don't speak like that."

Occasionally, quoting an accent does enhance a story and provides ethnic or national "flavor" that is not insulting to the subject or the reader. In such a case (and editors are cautioned that such articles are rare), the editor should make sure the writer transliterated in a sensitive and accurate manner.

One other instance when transliteration is acceptable is when a story specifically focuses on accents, regionalisms or dialects, and the writer wants to quote these speech patterns as illustrations. Obviously, these quotations then become necessary. (See the discussion of Mispronounced Words in chapter 8, Bias Based on Appearances and Disabilities.)

CLEANING UP ACCENTS.   Journalism publications, as a rule, do not allow writers to "clean up" quotations within quotation marks. Principles of objective journalism and freedom of speech mandate that speakers' speech not be altered, fabricated, misquoted, enhanced, pulled out of context or in any other way misrepresented. However, few editors mention that there are exceptions.

Is it right to clean up someone's speech patterns in a quotation, using quotation marks? If you can do it without significantly altering the quotation, the meaning or the context, it may be mandatory to "clean up" speech in some cases. Deciding when this is appropriate, however, is a very sensitive, delicate matter. (See the discussion of Mispronounced Words in chapter 8, Bias Based on Appearances and Disabilities.)

Example.   If a person is heard saying, "I axed the president," the writers should clean up the accent. Obviously, the person quoted did not mean *axed*, and just pronounced the word *asked* in such a way that it sounded to the writer like *axed*. It would be incorrect for the editor to leave the word *axed* in the quotation, although that is the word that was actually heard. If the speaker were requested to put that sentence in writing, the speaker would undoubtedly spell the word *asked* and would say that was the word that was said.

FOREIGN LANGUAGES.   Sometimes a speaker will borrow a word from a foreign language and mispronounce it. The intention may be to impress an audience, but its mispronunciation could have the opposite effect. When a writer is unsure of what word the speaker meant to use, the writer should ask the speaker. If the speaker is unavailable, the writer should consider paraphrasing outside of quotation marks, as long as the writer is certain about the gist of the sentence. If the writer is absolutely sure what word the speaker meant to use and is sure that the speaker meant to pronounce the word correctly, the writer should just insert the word correctly spelled.

> *Example.*   Correct usage: At the pool, the film director rested on a chaise longue.
> Incorrect pronunciation: At the pool, the film director rested on a chaise lounge.

If the speaker incorrectly says *lounge,* a common English word, instead of *longue,* the correct French for part of the name for the type of chair, the writer should change the word within the quotation, because it is clear that *longue* was the word the speaker meant to say.

If an editor sees a questionable foreign usage within a quotation in a story, the editor should speak to the writer before making any changes. The writer may be unaware of the incorrect usage or spelling. But the editor should not assume that the writer used the word incorrectly. The speaker might have deliberately used the incorrect word, perhaps to make a pun or for some other dramatic effect. Always speak with the writer before changing a foreign or deliberate-sounding pronunciation within a quotation.

> *Example.*   Quoted material: If it ain't broke, don't fix it.
> Incorrect editing: If it is not broken, do not fix it.

If the speaker intentionally uses a colloquial or informal popular expression that does not follow the rules of grammar, the writer should not clean up the grammar, nor should the editor. Before cleaning up pronunciation, make sure that the speaker would prefer the cleaned up grammar or pronunciation.

Aliens

When people picture *aliens,* they often envision space creatures with antennae. When referring to people who leave other countries, use *emigrants* instead. When referring to people who arrive at a new country, use *immigrants.* Avoid the term *aliens,* as it is considered derogatory.

Chinaman, Englishman, Frenchman, Scotsman and Dutchman

Few stylebooks encourage writers to refer to a man from China as a *Chinaman,* but more permit the labeling of a man from France as a *Frenchman,* and men from England, Scotland and the Netherlands as *Englishmen, Scotsmen* and *Dutchmen.* Why these countries should be singled out, and why the usage only appears in reference to men suggests that the men of these countries are somehow different than other people.

Chinaman sounds derogatory and is not listed in many dictionaries. *The New York Times Stylebook* specifies that the term should not be used. *The Associated Press Stylebook* and *United Press International Stylebook* call the term "patronizing," but permissible when confined to "quoted matter." (Similarly, the expression *Chinaman's chance* should be avoided in reference to a doomed endeavor, as it is derogatory and gratuitously insults Chinese people.)

In the case of the other four countries, dictionaries do list *Englishman, Frenchman, Scotsman* and *Dutchman.* The usage does not sound as derogatory as *Chinaman,* partly because each compound noun is made up of an adjective and noun, in contrast to *Chinaman,* which is awkwardly composed of two nouns. (*Englandman, Franceman, Scotlandman* and *Netherlandsman* would obviously sound more awkward.) Some dictionaries list *Englishwoman, Frenchwoman* and *Scotswoman,* as acceptable terms. A man from Italy, however, is never called an *Italianman* or *Italyman.* And we don't call Canadians *Canadamen* and *Canadawomen.* For purposes of consistency, parallelism, and avoidance of subtle bias, it is better to write *Chinese man, French man, English man, Scottish man* and *Dutch man* when referring to men of these countries.

The Associated Press Stylebook and Libel Manual specifies that people from Scotland are "Scots" not "the Scotch" and people and things from Scotland may also be called "Scottish."

Foreigners

A *foreigner* is a person who is a citizen of a foreign country. Americans of foreign descent are not *foreigners.* Aside from Native Americans, all Americans are of foreign descent if the records go back far enough. This does not make all Americans foreigners, however, in common journalism style. They are Americans.

A newspaper quoting a speaker at a school board meeting who says, "There are more foreigners in our school now than regular Americans," is merely echoing the speaker's bias against immigrants, if the majority of students in the school are American citizens.

Editors should be wary of writers who classify everyone with differing appearance or customs as foreigners. When people are second or third generation, regardless of their ethnicity or racial background, they are not foreigners.

Pure-Blooded

In describing people of any nation, eliminate references to *pure-blooded*, even in quoted matter. Such usage appears most commonly in articles on patriotism, as in "pure-blooded American" or "pure-blooded Austrian." The phrase may seem like a compliment at first glance, in that nobody uses it in the negative form, describing people as "impure-blooded American," "mongrel-blooded American," or "tainted-blooded American." The seemingly positive bias, however, has deceptively negative implications. At a minimum, the usage implies that people born outside of a country's borders somehow have less pure blood or cannot be trusted. Sometimes it is used to reinforce a prejudice against marriages that occur between people of different national origins, ethnic backgrounds, and races, insinuating that their children no longer have pure blood, but instead have impure, mixed or mongrel blood. *Pure-blooded* also implies that only a certain type of patriot—supposedly a nonethnic patriot—has superior blood and is somehow a better patriot.

To use the term *pure-blooded* as a synonym for *nonethnic* in reference to Americans is an obvious oxymoron in that it implies a belief that nonethnic Americans exist. Perhaps an argument could be made that Native Americans are nonethnic Americans. If every other American (or his or her ancestors) comes from somewhere, however, no non-Native American can be called *nonethnic* or *pure-blooded.*

■ National Traits

Journalists need to be cautious to not categorize an individual's traits according to the individual's nationality. Although so-called insiders may categorize themselves in informal conversations, journalists are, by definition, outsiders, and do not have license to stereotype people by nationality. National stereotypes that appear frequently in publications include: fashionable French, unfriendly French, trendy Italians, resilient Israelis, fun-loving Irish, punctual Swiss, efficient Japanese, exacting Germans, and carefree Danes.

Chinese

In food articles, *Chinese* is an adjective, not a noun, and it should be followed by a noun. In writing about food or recipes from China, the writer should correctly refer to "eating Chinese food," as opposed to "eating Chinese" or "ordering in Chinese." (The same applies to other ethnic foods.) "Eating *Chinx*" and "ordering in *Chinx*" are never acceptable.

When referring to the people or government of China, it is correct to say *the Chinese,* using *Chinese* as a noun.

There is a tendency in some American speech to refer to all Asian Americans as *Chinese* or *Chinese Americans.* Obviously, this is wrong, because there are many other countries in Asia besides China from which Americans trace their ancestry. Likewise, it is incorrect to describe every Asian American or Asian as *looking Chinese.* Editors should watch for this incorrect usage and eliminate it. If an article focuses on an Asian or Asian American person and heritage is relevant to the story, the writer should ask the subject to specify to which Asian country he or she traces ancestry. If this information is irrelevant to the story, the subject should not be described as an *Asian American.* National heritage should be omitted from the story.

There is another tendency by some people to assume that all Asian Americans are first-generation Americans. Editors need to watch that writers do not assume that all Asian Americans are new to the United States.

There is one more stereotypical tendency to avoid, although it should seem obvious. Asian Americans are as American as other Americans. Overheard in a school newsletter discussion: "Our school is like a small-scale United Nations, populated about 30 percent by Asian Americans and the other 70 percent by regular Americans of all kinds." While the error is obvious, editors need to know not to quote sentences like that unless the intention is to address the error in an article about ethnic inequality. (See chapter 2, Racial Bias, for the section on Portrayal of Asians and Asian Americans.)

COOLIES.   The term *coolies* is derogatory and should not be used in reference to Chinese people. Originally the term referred to people who were tricked into servitude in the 19th century in the Caribbean and Latin America. Since then, the term has been incorrectly applied to Chinese miners in North America who volunteered for service, but were not forced to work.

CHINA DOLL.   Asian women should not be described as *China dolls.* The usage is considered demeaning, nationally biased, racist and sexist. *News Watch Project Style Guide* explains that the usage "reinforces stereotypes of all Asian women as exotic and submissive sex objects."

CHINESE FIRE DRILL.   Editors should eliminate references to *Chinese fire drills,* used as a synonym for *chaos,* from all copy. The expression is considered racist and anti-Chinese. According to *News Watch Project Style Guide, Chinese fire drill* "refers to a game that often takes place at a stop light. ... Involves passengers in a vehicle getting out of one door, running around the vehicle and re-entering through another door in a haphazard way."

Irish Twinkle

A politician once complained that, in an article about a speech before a group of lawmakers, a reporter described him as "smiling with an Irish twinkle." The majority of readers, he contended, probably would not notice the put-down, as the expression sounded pleasant enough. He said most would not even see that it was offensive, although he was certain that the reporter deliberately used a slur. The politician said he had two problems with the description. First, it drew gratuitous attention to the fact that he was Irish, a heritage he was proud of, but he felt that classifying him ethnically was inappropriate in a story about a speech that had nothing to do with ethnicity. His second objection, even stronger, was that *Irish twinkle* was a slur to imply a drinking problem. He said that *Irish twinkle* was being used as a euphemism for *drunkard.* What was most objectionable about this usage was that because the reporter did not directly accuse him of drinking, there was no way to fight this charge or stereotype. He said the public would not understand if he argued that he did not have an *Irish twinkle,* and such an argument would only draw attention to and possibly promote the negative stereotype.

Editors should eliminate *Irish twinkles* and similar expressions that appear pleasant at face value but have hidden meanings that insult national or ethnic groups. As a rule, no national references should be included in an article if they do not pertain to the story.

Ital-

The abbreviated prefix *Ital-* should not be used as a shortened form of the adjective *Italian*. The correct usage is *Italian American,* not *Ital-American.*

Italian Time, Polish Time, Indian Time, Mexican Time

In making excuses for lateness, speakers sometimes make ethnically disparaging remarks, usually insulting their own ethnic, religious or national heritage. (Example: "Sorry I am late. I am operating on Italian time.") Avoid quoting references that imply that certain ethnic, religious or national people are slower (or somehow in a different time zone) than other people, even if the speaker identifies with the people being disparaged.

Polish Jokes and Other Ethnic Jokes

For years, Poles became the brunt of American riddles and jokes that were otherwise unrelated to ethnicity. Polish jokes had little to do with Polish heritage, people or customs. When Polish Americans objected, sensitive humorists found that they were able to tell the same jokes without insulting any national or ethnic groups, simply by eliminating the gratuitous reference to Polish in the joke. Such ethnic bashing is not restricted to Americans or Poles. In Scandinavian countries, it is not uncommon to hear jokes about people from other Scandinavian countries. In war-torn areas, it is not uncommon to hear jokes about the "enemy."

If a writer quotes a joke that insults any nationality, the editor should question the reference and relevance of the national group to the anecdote. If there is no relevance, the national reference should be omitted from the joke. The joke can be taken out of quotation marks and rephrased substituting a more generic person (e.g., "a fool," etc.).

If the nationality is essential to the joke or riddle, the editor may want to include the anecdote in the publication, but should be cautious about doing so. First, make sure to keep the anecdote in quotation marks if it is quoted exactly, and attribute it clearly. Next, the editor should ask the following kinds of questions: Does the anecdote insult an entire nation or ethnicity? Does it belittle readers unnecessarily? Does it illustrate or enhance the information in the story? Is it essential to the story? Did the speaker intend to insult an entire population when reciting the anecdote? Does the publication want to risk insulting the same population in quoting the anecdote? If the anecdote is kept in the story with its ethnic reference, the context should be explained to the readers.

Some comedians specialize in deliberate ethnic and national jokes. A writer, particularly a theater critic or club reviewer, may want to quote some of these jokes in a review, but extreme caution is required. Just because a comedian says it does not make it funny when it appears in print for a general readership. Sometimes a joke seems funny to an ethnic audience, but the same joke may not translate well to a more general audience. One reasonable rationale for quoting an insulting joke is that the writer needs to provide a "flavor" or "taste" of the comedian's humor so the reader can make an informed decision about whether or not to purchase tickets. Editors should be careful about the context in which "off-color" humor is quoted.

Welsh or Welch on a Bet

Speakers sometimes casually accuse others of "welshing on a bet" or "welshing on a promise." Both are slang expressions based on bias against people of Wales. Writers should not include direct quotations that use *welsh* or *welch* as verbs meaning "to cheat or fail to pay a debt." Editors should eliminate references to *welshers* and *welchers*.

■ Persuasion

People do not come from different ethnic or national persuasions. It is incorrect to say, for example, that the speaker is of Latvian persuasion or Gypsy persuasion or Armenian persuasion. *Persuasion* implies that somebody has been persuaded or convinced, which does not apply to ethnicity or nationality. Persuasion is sometimes applied to religion—a religious persuasion—although it is generally not preferred usage. (See chapter 6, Religious Bias, the section on Persuasion.) *Political persuasion* is more appropriate usage.

■ Geographical Designations

The way in which a location is described in relation to other nations can reveal a writer's geographical and national bias. Editors should be wary of Eurocentric designations, or geographical descriptions that presume that any country or group of nations is at the center of the world.

Dark Continent

Eliminate any references to *the Dark Continent* as a synonym for *Africa*. *Dark Continent* is considered derogatory. The usage appears most frequently in leads in which the word *Africa* has already appeared. The conscientious writer, trying to avoid repetition in the lead, seeks a synonym for *Africa*. Instead of using *Dark Continent*, specify the country that is being described in the piece, or reword the lead.

Far East

References to *the Far East* should be avoided. Preferred usage is *Asia, East Asia* or *Southeast Asia*. The *News Watch Project Style Guide* specifies that "*Far East* ... denotes Asia, as viewed from London."

Old World and New World

In reference to Europe, use *Europe* instead of *Old World,* which implies a Eurocentric bias. In reference to North America, use *North America* or the specific name of the country discussed in the story, instead of *New World,* which implies the same Eurocentric bias. According to the *News Watch Project Style Guide,* the label "*Old World*...makes Europe the point of reference."

Third World Nations

To refer to a country as a *Third World nation* reveals a Eurocentric bias. Countries should not be classified as *Old World, New World* and *Third World,* implying that every place that is neither European nor North American fits into the catchall category of *Third World.*

The *News Watch Project Style Guide* suggests using *developing world,* in reference to locations outside of industrialized regions.

■ Most Offensive Nationality-Related Slurs

Some nationality-related slurs are considered so abusive and offensive that most editors will not permit them to appear in their publications for any reason, even if contained in an otherwise vital quotation or on graffiti. Because they are slang words, the vocabulary tends to change quickly, and editors are responsible for keeping up-to-date with the current usage. Among the more well-known banned words are *Jap* (Japanese), *Nip* and *Nippers* (Japanese) *Chink* (Chinese), *Kraut* (German), *Spic* (Spanish), *Pakis* (Pakistani), *Polack* (Polish), *Shanty Irish,* and *Wop* (Italian). (See chapter 3 on Ethnic Bias.)

5

Gender Bias

■ Gender Bias Examples

The following are examples of different forms of gender bias that commonly appear in publications or on broadcasts. Examine the sentences, and then determine how they should best be rewritten to eliminate gender bias.

The jury consisted of six ladies and three men.

The girls went out to dinner without their husbands, who baby-sat the kids.

The boss sent his boy on an errand, while his girl manned the phones.

Wearing a purple suit, she acted as cochairperson of the committee along with her masseuse, Jim Jones.

Mother Nature brought us Hurricane Gloria, and she sank our ship, leaving her at the bottom of the ocean.

■ Overview

Gender bias appears in publications in many forms, ranging from use of the supposedly "generic *he*," to job titles and other word usage that exclude women, to stereotyping personalities based on gender or physical traits, to lack of parallel treatment, to demeaning word usage and other blatant forms of discrimination.

Objective writing does not permit gender bias, and editors need to be vigilant about eliminating such bias. This chapter details some of the forms of gender bias that appear most commonly in publications.

■ Unbiased Grammar and Style

The way that sentences are constructed may reflect gender bias, and dated grammar is one of the most common forms of bias to appear in print. The supposedly "generic *he*," for example, is no longer commonly accepted as generic. Nor is *his or her* always considered an adequate remedy for *his*. *Man* and *men* are not considered generic terms for people. Editors need to monitor sentence construction to eliminate gender bias that appears as a result of arcane grammar and style.

The Generic *He*

There is no "generic *he*," when *she* is also meant. English is one of the few languages in which *he* is losing acceptance as a generic term for *he or she*. Publications are increasingly suggesting that writers avoid the generic *he*. Yet writers should not assume that the only way to remedy the generic *he* is by substituting *he or she*. Many editors and writers complain that this is an awkward construction or one that ruins the "flow" of sentences.

Fortunately, there are many creative alternatives available to a writer, leaving writers with few excuses for resorting to the generic *he*. Let's start with a sample sentence:

A good writer knows that he should strive for accuracy.

The easiest way to eliminate the masculine assumption is to shorten the sentence and make the wording more direct, possibly using an infinitive (in this case, "to strive"):

A good writer knows to strive for accuracy. Or, *A good writer strives for accuracy.*

If that does not work for the particular piece, another common method to eliminate the masculine bias is by making the subject plural.

Good writers know that they should strive for accuracy. Or, *Good writers know to strive for accuracy.*

Yet another way to handle such a sentence is to turn it around. Although this often makes the sentence longer, less direct and more passive, there are cases when this approach seems best.

Accuracy is an important goal for a good writer. Or, *Accuracy is important to good writing.* Or, *Accuracy is something for which a good writer should know to strive.*

As a last resort, if none of these approaches remedies the sentence adequately in the particular context, use the more awkward he or she.

A good writer knows that he or she should strive for accuracy.

PITFALLS.   Be careful not to mix and match a singular with a plural that does not agree. Do not write:

A good writer knows that they should strive for accuracy. Or, (more obviously incorrect) *Good writers know that he or she should strive for accuracy.*

When *his or her* is used, the grammar is more difficult for some writers. Editors should double-check this usage. The following sentence is grammatically correct, but stylistically incorrect, in that it uses the masculine bias:

Everyone should watch his diet.

It is incorrect, but a common error nevertheless, to only make part of the sentence plural in attempt to remedy the error. (Note that *everyone* is a singular, not a plural.)

Everyone should watch their diet.

A correct approach, considered awkward by some editors, however, is to write:

Everyone should watch his or her diet.

Probably the simplest remedy is to make the subject of the sentence plural:

People should watch their diets.

Editors should note that most styles do not allow writers to resort to second person usage as a means of eliminating the generic he. In other words, do not change

Everyone should watch his diet, to *You should watch your diet.*

DIRECT QUOTATIONS.   If a speaker uses the generic *he* within a quotation that the writer wants to use, there are a few ways to handle the situation. If the direct quote seems essential to the story, the writer can insert *or she* within brackets, if that seems appropriate to the speaker's statement and does not change the context.

A good writer knows that he [or she] should strive for accuracy.

Some editors would say that this approach only draws unnecessary attention to the speaker's exclusion of women. Others would argue that constant use of *"[or she]"* reminds the reader that *she* is a secondary thought, and *he* is primary. Others would argue that this insert makes the speaker's statement more inclusive, and remedies the speaker's oversight. Still others would argue that the insert tampers with the thrust of the speech: If the speaker wanted to include women, the speaker would have said "or she," without requiring an outside party to add that usage.

The preferred approach at many publications would be to rephrase the quotation, if possible, outside of quotation marks, eliminating the masculine bias.

The speaker said that good writers know to strive for accuracy.

His or Her

Editors should be careful not to overuse *his or her* in sentence constructions as a remedy for wording that previously only mentioned *his.* Constant use of this phrase in this order makes *her* sound like an appendage or afterthought. If the *his or her* construction is to be used, the editor should consider varying the order, sometimes writing *her or his.* The same applies to other similar constructions:

he or she—she or he
Mr. and Mrs.—Mrs. and Mr.
spokesmen and spokeswomen—spokeswomen and spokesmen
boys and girls—girls and boys
men and women—women and men

Some editors would argue that such alternation of *his or her* with *her or his* sounds awkward and jolts the reader, that inclusion of *her* (in any order) automatically remedies any sexism. One argument against this approach is that *her or his* is no more awkward than *his or her,* when the ear becomes accustomed to evenhandedness. Although some readers may be jolted at first, they will adjust.

Sometimes writers will insert *"[or her]"* into a direct quotation to remedy a sentence that refers to the supposedly generic *him*. If the speaker being quoted consistently restricts all statements to men, neglecting to be inclusive, the writer should probably paraphrase much of the speech, removing the quotation marks, and making the statements more inclusive. This is better than repeatedly adding *"[or her]"* to every sentence that only refers to *him*. Paraphrasing makes the quotations less choppy, and it de-emphasizes the speaker's apparent bias.

The Generic *Man*

As a rule, writers should not interpret the word *man* to be any more generic than the word *woman*. At the same time, not every word that uses *man*, but that is intended to be gender-neutral, has a gender-neutral replacement. The word *manslaughter* is a primary example. It refers to a legal term for a homicide without malice or premeditation. Most publications use the word *manslaughter*, without attempting to substitute a gender-neutral term.

Mankind and *man* in reference to all people are decreasing in usage, although both terms are acceptable in some publications. The word *humanity* is generally preferred. Other possible substitutes include *people, humans, human beings, individuals* and even *humankind*.

Manholes are still commonly referred to as *manholes*. Some editors suggest *utility holes* or *sewer holes* as replacement words. But because neither usage is readily understood by readers, both should be accompanied by an explanation.

Manmade should be replaced with either *synthetic* or *artificial*, depending upon the context and meaning.

Manpower, although permitted by some stylebooks, can easily be replaced with gender-neutral words including *workers, workforce, effort, staffing*, or *defense force*, depending upon the meaning and context.

THE 10-MAN TEAM.   Teams are not all composed of men, and writers should not presume that they are. If the writer knows that a 10-member team, however, consists entirely of men, the team may correctly be referred to as a *10-man team*. A writer may also refer to a team of 10 women as a *10-woman team*. If the team consists of a combination of men and women, however, it is incorrect style to label the team a *10-man team,* because *man* is not generic. If both men and women are on a political team, for example, the writer should refer to the team as a *10-member team* or a *team of 10.*

MAN AS A VERB.   As a general rule, *man* should not be used as a verb, when women are not meant to be excluded and when the intended meaning is either *guard, mind* or *staff.* Tollbooths are not *manned,* they are staffed. *Man your post* and *man all exits,* are phrases that should be converted to eliminate bias. Examples of acceptable alternatives: Guard all exits. Staff all exits. Guard your post. Mind your post. Staff all decks. Guard all decks.

Man your post and *man all decks* are expressions associated with the military. When directly quoted (within quotation marks) from a military official, it may be acceptable to use the word *man* as a verb. It is better, however, to paraphrase the quotation outside of quotation marks, substituting a different word for *man.*

The officer said she ordered the soldiers to guard their posts.

MANNING ALL BASES.   *Manning all bases* and *man on base* are acceptable usage by some sports writers if all of the players are indeed men. Writers should consider less-colloquial and less-biased usage, particularly if not all of the players are men and depending upon the context: *Covering all bases, playing all bases, covering the field,* etc.

Couples on Second Reference

If John Jones is an architect, and his wife Mary Jones is a butler, and an article makes reference to each of them more than once, what is the correct style in which to refer to them on second reference?

At publications where courtesy titles are used, the answer is simple. He becomes Mr. Jones and she becomes either Mrs. Jones or Ms. Jones. (A few publications are slow to discard biased second references, preferring that he be referred to as Jones on second reference, and that she be referred to as Mrs. Jones, to differentiate them. Some of these publications will even *allow* her to use Ms. Jones, Dr. Jones, or Prof. Jones, if any of those titles apply, if she specifies which one she prefers.) At publications that do not use courtesy titles, most people are called only by their last name on second reference. This makes references more complicated. It is incorrect to refer to him as *Jones* and her as only *Sue* or even *Sue Jones* on second reference. It is also unacceptable to call him *Jones* and refer to her as *his wife* throughout the piece. Likewise, it is generally against style to call him *Jim* and call her *Sue* at publications where first-name-only references are reserved for children and pets.

Typical ways that writers handle the situation:

Jones, the architect, cooked dinner, while Jones, the butler, greeted the guests.
The architect cooked dinner, while the butler greeted the guests.
The husband cooked dinner, while the wife greeted the guests.
He cooked dinner, while she greeted the guests.

If these references seem somewhat stilted, there are few alternatives for getting around this usage at publications that do not use courtesy titles. Many writers combine the four kinds of references to make the story flow more smoothly. If the article is clearly focused on one person, Sue Jones, for example, it is permissible to call her Jones throughout the piece and to refer to Jim Jones as *her husband* in a single reference. If both people are mentioned throughout the story, however, this usage is not permitted.

TITLES: MISS, MRS. OR MS.?   Many publications do not use titles on second reference before men's or women's last names. *The New York Times* is one of the publications that does use titles. *Times* style dictates that reporters should ask each woman which title she prefers before inserting a title. *Miss, Mrs.* and *Ms.* may be acceptable depending upon preference. Reporters should find out if any other titles apply that may be preferred, however, including *Prof., Dr., the Rev.* etc.

With many foreign names, *Ms.* is often preferred usage, particularly with couples in which the husband and wife have different last names.

Writers should attempt to include women's first names, even for women who choose to be called *Mrs.* in styles that use titles. Preferred usage is Mrs. Jane Jones rather than Mrs. John Jones.

■ Exclusion

One of the ways in which many general-audience publications reveal gender bias is by subtly directing the writing toward men only. An example is a headline that suggests "Great Gifts for Your Wife" presuming that the readers are all married men, or one on hair products detailing "How to Keep Your Beard from Graying." Such presumptions are acceptable in publications targeted specifically for men, a men's fashion magazine, for example, or a men's weight-lifting magazine. But when the publication is targeted for a general audience, such a bias is unacceptable.

"Dear Male Reader"

The New York Times warns in its stylebook that "in referring to women, we should avoid words or phrases that seem to imply the *Times* speaks with a purely masculine voice, viewing men as the norm and women as the exception."

■ Parallelism of Terms

As an overall principle, in order to eliminate gender bias from a publication, editors need to have a solid understanding of parallelism. In other words, men and women should be discussed and described using the same terms. If a man is described by his profession, for example, a woman should be described by hers as well. Where a man would be described by physical attributes, a woman should be described by physical features as well.

Parallelism often necessitates adopting a writing style that favors gender neutral words, rather than words that exclude men or women, or two sets of words that do not have parallel connotations. It means not making assumptions about people based on sexual stereotypes.

Instinct and Savvy

Lower forms of animal life that perform seemingly intelligent tasks are commended for their good instincts. Higher forms of animal life that perform intelligent tasks are commended for their knowledge, savvy and judgment. Editors should be wary of writing that credits a person's good instincts for a task well done.

More often than not, women are said to have good instincts, feminine instincts, nesting instincts or motherly instincts, whereas men are credited with intelligence for success with equivalent tasks. In fire stories or the equivalent, for example, a mother who rescues her children is often credited with behaving instinctively, whereas a father is said to have exercised good judgment and courage in a moment of crisis. Editors should be aware of the inconsistent usage. Constantly attributing women's savvy behavior to natural instinct may reveal a bias, and actually discredits women's intelligence. By consistently crediting instinct, the writer is affirming the notion that women react with an automatic, animallike response instead of displaying thoughtful judgment.

Catfights and Intellectual Disputes

When women disagree, writers occasionally label the dispute a *catfight*. Sometimes, the writer will hint at a so-called catfight, by describing the dispute and then commenting "Meow!" While the usage has become relatively rare and dated, the most likely places for references to so-called *catfights* to surface have been in gossip columns, fashion articles and so-called society columns.

Occasionally, a writer will insist that *catfight* refers to a specific kind of argument inherent to women, that it's not a sexist term in that not all disputes among women are automatically *catfights*. The argument wears thin. Editors should question what makes a dispute a *catfight* as opposed to an argument. If the deciding factor is the topic of the dispute, a fight over a date for example, then the same type of dispute by men should also be labeled a *catfight*. If a *catfight* only applies to a fight about a man, however, then the term is biased, unless the writer is willing to apply the same term to a dispute over a woman.

As a general rule, this kind of reference should be eliminated. Use *dispute, argument, fight, tryst, quarrel, squabble* or *spat* instead. The reference to *catfight* indicates a bias against women, whether written by men or women. The implication is that disputes among women are petty, trivial or animallike. It implies that women do not focus on larger issues and are incapable of resolving issues in a dignified way. When cats fight, they make a lot of noise and create a spectacle, but there are no intellectual issues resolved. They fight over turf or material objects. Writers never use *catfight* in reference to disputes among men, implying that men only argue over more serious or important issues.

Catfights should only be applied to fights between two felines. Women are not cats and should not be equated with animals in journalism.

Girlfriends and Boyfriends

Heterosexual women commonly refer to their female friends informally as *girlfriends*. Heterosexual men never refer to their male friends as *boyfriends*. The two words have very different connotations.

Although many grown women refer to female friends as *girlfriends,* the usage is unacceptable in journalism. *Girlfriend* connotes a girl or child and should not be used as a synonym for *female friend* or *friend* when referring to women. Preferred usage is *friend. Girlfriend* is also commonly used to mean a woman whom a man is dating. Again, most styles frown upon this usage. Use "the woman he is dating" or "companion" or "his date" instead.

Similarly, *boyfriend* is commonly used by women in reference to a man that a woman is dating. Most styles frown upon this usage, since *boyfriend* connotes a *boy* or child. Use "the man she is dating" or "companion" instead. When a man refers to another man as his *boyfriend,* it implies that both are gay, and it is not acceptable style either, since *boyfriend* connotes a child. *Boyfriend* means a friendship with a child, a boy. *Friend, companion* and *partner* are preferred.

Ladies and Gentlemen

Ladies and *women* are not interchangeable terms. In most stylebooks, *women* is the preferred term for females ages 18 and older. Some stylebooks suggest that womanhood begins at a younger age. *Ladies* may be used in quoting a speaker, as long as the usage is attributed. The term also may be correctly applied to a woman who is either married into or born into a royal family, depending upon the level of nobility.

Likewise, *gentlemen* and *men* are not interchangeable terms, and should not be used as such. In most stylebooks, *men* is the preferred term for males ages 18 and older.

For a writer seeking parallelism, "*gentlemen* and *gentlewomen*" is the correct usage, and has been gaining in popularity.

Man and Wife

"I now pronounce you man and wife," may be preferred usage at some weddings. But in journalism, traditional couples are referred to as *husband and wife,* to maintain parallelism.

Similarly, it is incorrect to write "a man and his bride." Instead the phrase should be "a groom and his bride."

Guys and Dolls and Gals

Most publications frown on usage of all three words. Favored usage is *men* and *women*. While *dolls* is obviously belittling, *guys* and *gals* appear more often. The usage is most commonly found in writing by young reporters who are uncomfortable about referring to an 18-year-old as a *man* or a *woman*. Nevertheless, *man* and *woman* are correct usage, even if the terms require some adjustment. Avoid *guy, gal* and *doll*.

Bathrooms, Washrooms and Rest Rooms

In writing about housing and public places, Americans use a multitude of euphemisms for toilet. If toilet sounds too harsh and direct, use bathroom, washroom or rest room. All three are gender neutral.

Avoid *ladies' room, gentleman's room, women's room, men's room, John, little boy's room,* and *little girl's room.* Avoid *powder room,* which according to *The Dictionary of Bias-Free Usage,* is "paradoxically sexist: The 'powder' in the phrase comes from the powder men used on their wigs in colonial times." Yet today, the book explains "the powder room is reserved for women."

WC is not widely recognized in the United States, nor are *water closet, privy* and *loo,* the British euphemism.

Coeds and Students

Male and female students should be referred to as *students,* to maintain parallelism. *Coeds,* in reference to female students, is incorrect usage. As adjectives, both *coeducational* and the shorter form, *coed* are correct. Institutions are coeducational. People are not.

To understand what is wrong with the term *coeds,* used as a noun, it is necessary to review a bit of history.

Originally, all college and university students in America were male. Harvard College was the nation's first men's college in 1636.

Separate women's schools were opened beginning with Salem Academy in North Carolina, which opened its doors in 1772, according to Kate Metzger of the Women's College Coalition. (Salem was not officially chartered as a college, however, until 1866.) In 1836, Wesleyan in Georgia became the first chartered women's college, and it eventually became the first to grant baccalaureate degrees to women. Mount Holyoke Female Seminary was founded a year later, in

1837, and began admitting students that year, although it was not chartered until 1888.

Meanwhile, Oberlin claims to be the first college in America to become coeducational, meaning both men and women attended the same institution for the first time in 1833. After also being the first college to integrate in 1835, Oberlin granted the first degree to an African-American woman in 1862. Since then, most American colleges have become coeducational, or *coed* institutions, admitting both men and women.

Over the years, as more all-male institutions became coeducational, the newly admitted female students were pejoratively referred to as the *coeds,* the ones who made the school coeducational. The implication was that they were the spoilers, or even the entertainment. The joke at some schools was that these *coeds* were only attending college to obtain their "MRS degrees." In other words, they were not perceived initially by some people to be serious students, but rather husband seekers. Many of the earliest men's schools to admit women did not allow the female students to pursue mathematics or sciences, and instead offered separate courses in the arts and education. Thus, their course load appeared "lighter," to some who viewed science and mathematics as "more serious" and demanding. *Coed,* meaning a female student, gradually became part of the popular jargon, and female college students referred to themselves as *coeds,* even years after women were admitted into all university courses at most schools. As a result, many writers may not be familiar with its origin as a biased term.

As a rule, editors should eliminate references to female students as *coeds.* In place of the word *coed,* use *student* or *female student,* if the sex of the student is deemed relevant to the story.

FRESHMAN AND FRESHWOMAN.   Nobody uses *freshwoman* for a female student or first-year member of an organization. Preferred usage, to replace both *freshman* and *freshwoman,* is either *first-year student* or *frosh,* a new word that is rapidly gaining acceptance on college campuses as a gender-neutral term.

Male and Female Jurors

Specifying the number of men and women on a jury violates parallelism, implying that the ratio of men to women inherently affects all outcomes. Such tallies can represent a form of gender bias if not justified within a particular story.

A newspaper article about a Virginia trial, for example, in which an 88-year-old woman was accused of murder, specified that the jury consisted of nine women and four men. No other description of the jurors was provided. The article did not say, for example, how many of the jurors were above retirement age, how many were unemployed, how many had disabilities, how many had been accused of crimes in the past or how many had family members who had been accused of crimes. The implication was that the ratio of men to women on a jury is a significant factor in a trial and perhaps automatically influences the outcome of the trial.

Many court stories in major newspapers make a habit of including a jury tally of men and women, without elaborating on the significance of this statistic or how it pertains to the piece. In addition, they provide no additional information about the jury beyond sex. By not justifying the inclusion of this information, they invite readers to apply their own stereotypes about men and women: Female jurors are kinder, more sympathetic, vulnerable, impressionable, and likely to be manipulated. Men are perceived as more objective, rational, tougher, and exacting.

If a writer feels that the sexes of the jurors pertain to the article, the writer should explain how it affects the story to eliminate the appearance of bias and innuendo. If the writer feels that the sex of the jurors does not add to the story, the gratuitous mention should be omitted. Editors should note that mentioning the jurors' sexes does not add flavor to a story, but encourages bias.

Criminals

To maintain parallelism, journalists should remember to be gender-neutral in reference to criminals whose identities are unknown. Presuming that a criminal is male not only reveals gender bias, but does a disservice to the public and police, who may, as a result, incorrectly seek a male suspect, when they should be seeking a female.

Radio reports and print articles occasionally refer to a *gunman,* as in the lone *gunman* theory, or a *hit man.* Journalists never write that police are seeking a *gunwoman* or *hit woman.* And they never say police are seeking a *gunperson* or *hit person*—even if the identity and sex of the shooter is unknown.

In crime stories, there is a false common presumption that all criminals are male, a bias against men. So prevalent is that bias, that relatively few editors notice it and remove it. Instead of *gunman* or *hit man,* writers should use gender-neutral words like *killer, robber, assassin,* or *gun-wielding intruder.*

Watch for revealing sentences like:

Police have no suspects, so far, but anyone with information leading to *his* arrest should call the following number.

Police suspect that there were at least two *hit men.*

Residents should stay indoors until police have a *man* in custody.

In the aftermath of the burglary, police are seeking a *man on the loose.*

Lack of Parallelism in Marketing

It is not uncommon for editors to find writers carelessly absorbing and echoing the language—especially individual words—of marketers, advertisers and publicists.

A press release, for example, calls a restaurant's offerings "exotic" and "unique." This entices a respected food critic to go to the restaurant anonymously (without accepting freebies, and without letting the restaurant know that the establishment is being reviewed) to sample a meal. After tasting the food and while writing an otherwise original review of the restaurant, the critic mentions that the restaurant's offerings are "exotic" and "unique." If this is the truth and the critic backs up the statement with examples of some of the unique, exotic offerings, then the words *exotic* and *unique* may be appropriate for the article. If, however, the only reason the word appears in the article is as a result of the initial press release suggestion—if the food in the restaurant is no more exotic or unique than the food at every similar restaurant—the editor should question the usage.

Obviously, the journalists' job is not to sell the restaurant, but to inform the public of the truth. As a result, one of the editor's jobs is to catch and eliminate unfounded promotional usage. Sometimes questioning each word seems like nit-picking, and writers complain. Ultimately, however, both writers and editors avoid embarrassment if promotional jargon is eliminated—even in reviews.

How does this relate to sexism in journalism? By echoing publicists' language, writers often find themselves sacrificing parallelism of terms. Marketers seeking to promote their product to an all-male market, for example, may invent language to help their product sell to men. In order to sell to an additional market, they create a new term for an old product, but not necessarily a new product. Journalists who then use this language, may be subtly helping the publicist to promote gender bias.

ACTION FIGURES AND DOLLS.   An article reviewing the latest toys for a holiday supplement separately discusses *action figures* and *dolls,* suggesting that action figures are appropriate gifts for boys, whereas dolls are meant for girls. The items appear under separate headings, and the reader assumes that these are two completely different types of toys.

What is the difference, though, between an action figure and a doll? Journalism students have suggested the following differences:

Action figures are male; dolls are female.
Action figures carry weapons; dolls do not.
Action figures are made of tough metal or hard plastic and are not
    made to be cuddled. Dolls are made of softer materials.
Action figures are designed to look tough, intimidating or even ugly;
    dolls are meant to look attractive.
Children play differently with action figures and dolls.

Examination of these differences, however, reveals that action figures and dolls are remarkably similar. The first observation, for example, that dolls are female, is not always true. Barbie's Ken doll is male, as is My Buddy and G.I. Joe. Would this make Ken an action figure in the eyes of most consumers? Probably not. My Buddy is hardly an action figure. G.I. Joe is the most likely candidate. Yet, wardrobe aside, the soldier doll does not look significantly different from the boyfriend doll.

The second suggestion that action figures carry weapons is not always true either. Some do come with weapons. Some do not. Dolls can be made to carry weapons. If a hunting rifle were put into Barbie's hands, would that transform the teenage doll into an action figure? Students generally say that a weapon alone would not be enough to make Barbie into an action figure.

Regarding the materials with which the toys are constructed, many dolls are not made of soft fabric or textures meant to be cuddled. Barbie, for example, is not particularly cuddly, nor are most so-called "fashion dolls," many of which are constructed of hard plastic. Although a doll made of metal is relatively rare, it is not so uncommon to see dolls made of solid materials like porcelain.

The suggestion that all dolls are meant to look attractive is also not always true. Glamour, for example, is not what sold children on Cabbage Patch Kids, once the top-selling dolls in America. The pudgy-looking toys that came with "adoption papers" had to rely on other assets for sales. Some toy writers even suggested that what appealed most to children about Cabbage Patch Kids was their homeliness.

The last suggestion that the primary difference between action figures and dolls was in the way children played with them, only confuses the distinction, as different children handle toys differently. Many children play with fashion dolls by dressing and undressing them, but many others use such toys for games of pretend. Action figures are generally used for pretending, as are baby dolls and other dolls. Some games of pretend are violent. Some are nonviolent.

What, then, is the difference between an action figure and a doll? And how do these differences affect the journalist? The primary difference is probably a matter of marketing. In much of American society, boys beyond kindergarten age are discouraged from playing with dolls. Such play is considered taboo. For this reason, parents will not purchase dolls for their sons. By calling a doll an action figure, however, the toy becomes socially "acceptable" for boys. Thus, a toy company that wants to sell dolls to boys—a significant portion of the toy market—can do so without breaking a societal taboo, by marketing the toy as an action figure. To some companies, this means adding a toy weapon to the packaging of the doll, in an attempt to differentiate it. Some clothe the doll in a military-style uniform, or add an alien-looking body part or robotic physical features.

The reason this bears significance in the editing process is that objective journalists should not base their word choice on marketers' promotional usage. Because a marketer calls a doll an *action figure* to sell it, should not mean that the journalist automatically calls the doll an *action figure*. The journalist should not be promoting marketing illusions. Is there a real difference between action figures and dolls? If not, should journalists distinguish between dolls and action figures to help sell toys, while promoting the barrier between "girls' play" and "boys' play"?

Toys.   Most publications prefer that toys not be assigned sexes, even when the portrayed sex of the toy is obvious. Dolls are generally referred to as *it* on second reference. Barbie is not a *she* but an *it* in journalism. Marketers may feel otherwise.

COLORS.   Colors do not have sexes. Although marketers may use color to sell redundant products to women and men, pastel colors are not feminine or masculine. Primary colors are not feminine or masculine. Editors should eliminate references that equate colors with sex. (Examples: *Her dress was a feminine pastel pink. The bold colors of his bedroom were very masculine.*)

If marketers want to increase their sales by encouraging parents with boys and girls to buy the blue version as well as the pink version, journalists do not have to help them sell this color concept to the American public. Such references appear most commonly in fashion and decorating articles.

UNDERWEAR.   Men's underpants are commonly called *drawers* or *shorts,* sturdy-sounding conservative clothing. In contrast, women's underpants are commonly referred to as *panties,* a more childish sounding word, that some would argue lacks dignity. Is there a need for two different terms for *underpants*? One can argue that drawers and panties are shaped differently and therefore require different words. Or one can argue that both are names for *underpants,* and do not require separate language. A label on a pair of women's boxer shorts calls them "boxer panties." How does this differ from boxer shorts? An editor should look carefully for such usage and evaluate it in the context of the story and the style of the publication. The question that the editor should ask: Is the writer buying into a biased notion, by incorporating the marketers' terminology?

■ Assignment of Sexes to Inanimate Objects

People and animals can be described as male or female. Parts of plants can also be described this way. Inanimate objects do not have sexes, however, and as a rule should not be described as *he* or *she* in journalism. Nor should inanimate objects be characterized as behaving like a man or woman.

She-Ships, He-Ships and Other Transportation

Sea vessels do not have sexes and should not be referred to as *he* (as in the *Poseidon*) or *she* (as in the *Queen Mary*) in the majority of journalistic publications. Although many sailors call their ships *she,* this is not considered acceptable style within much of journalism.

As a rule, inanimate objects do not have sexes in journalistic style. In quotations, the portion of the sentence that refers to the ship as *he* or *she* can be rephrased outside of quotation marks. The rest of the sentence can then be kept within quotation marks. Each ship is an object and should be referred to as *it* on second reference, or *the ship,* regardless of the name of the vessel. The same applies to other vehicles: cars, trucks, trains and airplanes.

Oceans and Seas

The sea should not be referred to as *she.* Oceans and seas obviously do not have sexes, and referring to the sea as *she* is not accepted style at most journalism publications, although some sailors may describe the ocean or seas this way.

Mother Nature

As a general rule, nature should not be referred to as *she.* There is an exception, however: If a feature writer is using the term *Mother Nature,* instead of nature, *she* becomes appropriate usage in the personification. Capitalize the *M* and the *N* in this usage, treating the term as if it is a name.

Hurricanes, He and She

Hurricanes do not have sexes and should not be referred to as *he* (Hurricane Gilbert) or *she* (Hurricane Gloria) in journalistic publications. Years ago, all hurricanes were given women's names. Although hurricanes now are given men's and women's names, the storms are still not called *he* and *she* in journalism. The hurricane should be called *it, the storm* or *the hurricane.* (Example: *Hurricane Gloria did extensive damage as it moved up the East Coast*).

Dogs and Cats

Writers should not assume that all dogs are male and all cats are female, an obviously flawed stereotype. If this were the case, neither animal would be able to reproduce. Yet many writers persistently use *he* on second reference to the family dog, and *she* on second reference to every cat. Editors should watch for this usage. Make sure that Spot is a he, by double-checking with the writer, if the writer seems to assume that Spot is male.

As a general rule, writers should not randomly assign sexes to animals. Animals on second reference are not to be called *he* or *she* in most publications, even if the sex of the animal is known. In some publications, however, if the sex is known by the writer, or indicated by the animal's name, using *he* or *she* on second reference is permissible. In general, the preferred style is to call the animal *it* on second reference. (Example: *The fish swam toward me when it spotted the bait.*)

Countries and Sex

Nations do not have sexes and should not be referred to as *he* and *she.* Although many people refer to their homelands as the Motherland or the Fatherland, American journalism publications do not. Preferred usage is *it, the nation, the home country* or *homeland.* (Example: *The United States offers spectacular scenery, and it contains many national parks.*)

■ God

Should God be referred to as "He"? A lot depends upon the religion discussed in the particular article and also for whom the article is being written—a religious publication or a secular newspaper. Writers should not assume that all representations of God are male in every religion. Not all religions believe in one God. Of those that do, not all believe that that God is male or even of one sex. The issue becomes stickier in that within some religions, often not all people necessarily agree on one particular image or usage. Some writers prefer to hedge by referring to God as *God* on each additional reference, rather than assigning a sex to the reference. (Refer to God in chapter 6, Religious Bias.)

In secular journalism, when publications refer to God as a male, common style practice is to lowercase the first letters of the personal pronouns referring to God: *he, him, thee* and *thou*. In religious texts, these pronouns generally start with a capital letter.

■ Gender-Neutral Job Descriptions

Many job titles traditionally ended with the suffix *-man*. As more women have been entering the workforce, many jobs that were previously monopolized by men are requiring new or updated nomenclature. A woman who delivers mail, for example, cannot accurately be called a mail*man*, just as a man who delivers mail most likely would not want to be called a mail*woman*.

Publications are increasingly using neutral titles that may be applied to men and women, rather than adding the suffix *-woman* to the old male titles. Thus instead of *fireman* and *firewoman*, the job title *firefighter* is generally preferred usage. In some cases, however, adding *-man* and *-woman* is still preferred usage.

Old Usage and Preferred Usage

Many terms used in the past to refer to people or occupations were masculine. Some are gradually being replaced by gender-neutral terms. Here are some examples:

Ad man becomes *advertiser, ad seller, ad executive*

Anchorman becomes *news anchor, anchor, anchorman and anchorwoman*

Bellboy becomes *bellhop*

Businessman becomes *business executive, manager*

Cameraman becomes *camera technician, camera operator, camera crew, camera engineer*

Caveman becomes *cave dweller, prehistoric people*

Common man becomes *ordinary people, common folk*

Congressman becomes *representative,* or *congressman and congresswoman*

Copyboy becomes *copy clerk, editorial assistant*

Doorman becomes *security guard, valet, butler*

Fireman becomes *firefighter*
First baseman becomes *first base*
Fisherman becomes *fisher, fish catcher*
Foreman becomes *supervisor*
Gal Friday/guy Friday becomes *office assistant, administrative assistant*
Garbage man becomes *garbage collector*
Ice cream man becomes *ice cream vendor*
Mailman, postman becomes *letter carrier, postal worker*
Milkman becomes *milk delivery*
Newsman becomes *reporter, correspondent, writer*
Policeman becomes *police officer*
Publicity man, PR man becomes *publicist, publicity officer*
Repairman, handyman becomes *repairer*

Middleman

Newsday's stylebook specifies that *middleman* is a term "with a specific meaning in the language," and is therefore acceptable usage, "although *agent, processor, distributor* or *packager* are [also] acceptable." In most cases, the gender-neutral alternatives are preferred. Do not use *middlewoman.*

Spokesperson, Chairperson and Salesperson

Although gender-neutral terminology has been gaining acceptance, not every gender-neutral word is widely accepted. For a limited group of job titles, most stylebooks favor maintaining the suffix *–man,* and for women holding the same job title, the ending *–woman* is preferred. Few stylebooks favor the more generic *–person* suffix.

Most of the time, when the words *spokesperson, chairperson* and *salesperson* appear in an article, the writer is referring to a woman. These are not the parallel terms for *spokesman, chairman* and *salesman.* By calling men *spokesmen, chairmen* and *salesmen* while labeling women *spokespersons, chairpersons* and *salespersons,* the implication is that using the word *woman* is bad, as if there is something wrong or shameful about being female. To keep the style consistent and unbiased, editors should note that there are two ways to achieve parallel construction: either use *chairman* and *chairwoman* for men and women, or use *chairperson* for both men and women. Using *chairman* and *chairperson* in the same publication is not parallel construction.

Most publications do not use *chair* as an acceptable alternative for *chairman, chairwoman* or *chairperson.* If the person in the article contends that his or her actual title is *chair* and not *chairwoman* or *chairman,* and does not want to be referred to as *chairwoman* or *chairman,* the editor may use the word *chair* as a verb to maintain style. (Example: *Mary Jones, who chairs the committee ...*) Do not use *chair,* however, as the female equivalent of *chairman.* (Do not write "*Chairman* John Jones along with *Chair* Mary Jones ...") To do so, again implies that there is something wrong with being a woman, unless both men and women are referred to as *chairs.*

Occasionally, a writer attributes a quote incorrectly to a *spokesperson* at a publication where the style specifies against use of the word *spokesperson.* If the editor is unsure if the speaker is a man or woman, ask the writer and change the word to *spokesman* or *spokeswoman.* If the editor is unable to contact the writer, *spokesperson* should be changed to *representative, advocate* or *publicist,* depending upon what term is applicable.

Saleswoman is always preferred over *salesgirl* or *saleslady.* Do not use *chairlady, lady chair, lady chairman* or *Madam chairman.*

-ix, -ette and -ess

American writing is moving away from *-ixes, -ettes* and -e*sses.* Although many publications still accept *waitress* and *actress,* some prefer *waiter* for both men and women, and *actor* for both men and women. But few would still refer to Amelia Earhart as an *aviatrix,* or a female hotel director as the *proprietress.*

The trend is to use a neutral word or the masculine word for both men and women.

Authoress becomes *author*
Aviatrix becomes *aviator*
Hostess becomes *host,* particularly when used as a verb (Women do
    not *hostess* events; they *host* events.)
Majorette becomes *major*
Poetess becomes *poet*
Priestess becomes *priest*
Sculptress becomes *sculptor*

Seamstress becomes *tailor*
Stewardess becomes *flight attendant*
Usherette becomes *usher*

Following the same principle, although not ending in an *-ix, -ette,* or *-ess,* the word *comedienne* is gradually fading from use. Publications are increasingly using *comedian* for both male and female comic entertainers.

EXCEPTIONS.   In titles of nobility, *-ess* endings still prevail for women. *Princess* is still universally accepted, as are *duchess, baroness* and *countess.* In addition, there are *marchioness* (the wife of a marquess, but note that the masculine title ends in an *–ess* as well) and *viscountess* (wife of a viscount). *Governess* is sometimes used, particularly within a quotation, although a gender-neutral word like *tutor* is often preferred.

In legal writing, *executrix* is still used for a female executor. In journalism, however, executor is generally preferred for both men and women.

Woman Doctors and Female Doctors

Women who are doctors are *female doctors, not woman doctors* and *not women doctors.* In the same way, men who are doctors are *male doctors,* not *man doctors* or *men doctors. Male* and *female* are both adjectives, and *man* and *woman* are nouns. (Ignoring parallelism, there are some dictionaries that define *woman* as both a noun and an adjective, although they specify that *man* is always a noun.) While writers rarely incorrectly use *man* as an adjective when referring to men who work, the usage is prevalent in writing about working women. The implication is that the phenomenon of working women is so odd that even the grammatical construction needs to be awkward. The usage comes across as gawking in disbelief that women hold positions of authority.

If an adjective is required, use *male* and *female.* In most cases, however, writers should not indicate *male* or *female* directly before a person's job title, unless the sex of the person is a major element of the piece.

Changing the commonly used form to the correct form:

Woman administrator becomes *female administrator*
Woman astronaut becomes *female astronaut*
Woman athlete becomes *female athlete*
Woman business executive becomes *female business executive*
Woman dentist becomes *female dentist*
Woman doctor becomes *female doctor*
Woman firefighter becomes *female firefighter*
Woman lawyer becomes *female lawyer*
Woman pilot becomes *female pilot*
Woman pitcher becomes *female pitcher*
Woman president becomes *female president*
Woman professor becomes *female professor*

Man nurse becomes *male nurse*
Man secretary becomes *male secretary*

There is one exception—when writing about an organization that uses *woman* or *women* as an adjective as part of its name (the League of Women Voters, for example). In quotations, when quoting someone who uses *woman* incorrectly as an adjective, it is generally better to paraphrase outside of the quotation marks, using *female* instead.

Newsday's stylebook recommends against using such modified titles as *female doctor* and *male nurse,* since "terms such as doctor and nurse include both men and women." Specifying the sex of the professional implies that there is something unusual or wrong about that person's sex. *Newsday* specifies that "A gee-whiz attitude toward competent women is unacceptable, but breakthroughs in formerly all-male areas are legitimate news."

Workers

Secretaries, clerks and messengers who are adults should not be referred to in copy as *boys* and *girls.* If an employer uses this language in a quotation, remove the statement from quotation marks and paraphrase to eliminate the usage.

In keeping with this policy, we do not say:

The *girls* in the office...
Send *your boy* over to pick up the package.
I'll have *my girl* type that up for you.
I'll send over *my boy* to drive you.

Employees should not be referred to as *servants* or *subservient workers.* They are *employees.*

Office employees also should not be referred to as "the help." (See discussion of *the help* under Household Employees later in this chapter.) Such references are demeaning and tell little about what tasks the person performs. For the sake of accuracy as well as clear writing, writers should specify job titles when referring to office workers: *secretary, clerk, custodian, janitor, transcriber, messenger, receptionist,* etc.

If the head of the corporation refers to a secretary as a "girl" or hedges the reference by calling her a "gal," this reference should not be parroted by the writer. If the quotation is important to the story, take the statement out of quotation marks and paraphrase it to eliminate the inappropriate use of *girl* or *gal.*

In certain fields, it is more common to hear men and women referred to as *boys* and *girls.* For example, it is not unusual to hear adult ballet dancers refer to each other as boys and girls, or for their directors and choreographers to refer to them that way. This is not license, however, for the writer to pick up that usage when writing about the dancers. To a writer and editor, dancers who are adults are *men* and *women.*

COPY BOYS AND COPY GIRLS.   Most publications no longer refer to beginning journalists as *copy boys* and *copy girls,* although these workers are often the youngest members of the staff. The preferred usage is *copy clerk* or *editorial assistant.*

Beauticians and Barbers

At many publications, the correct term for one who cuts hair is *haircutter,* rather than *beautician* or *barber,* since many people who cut hair are trained to cut both long and short hair, men's and women's. *Beautician* and *barber* are generally considered outdated terms; however, if a piece refers to an old-fashioned barber who cuts men's hair only and offers a shave along with the haircut, *barber* may be correct usage. Similarly, if a piece refers to an old-fashioned beautician who offers facials and other beauty treatments, *beautician* could be justified. The editor should examine the usage in context.

In keeping with this style, a place where hair is cut should be generally referred to as a *haircutter* or *stylist,* rather than a *beauty parlor, beauty shop* or *barbershop.*

When one goes to a *haircutter* or *stylist,* one gets a *haircut* or even a new *hairstyle,* not a *hairdo.*

Masseuse

Contrary to the way many people speak, *masseuse* refers specifically to a woman who gives massages. *Masseur* is the masculine version. There is no gender-neutral job title. *Massager* would work, although many people use *masseuse* to mean both male and female.

Men at Work

For years, construction signs along public highways specified "Men at Work." When women in different parts of the country objected to this sex limitation, particularly when more women were getting jobs in construction, some signs were changed to "People at Work." Some regions introduced signs that showed a picture of a generic worker or group of workers working. Preferred usage within articles about highway or other construction is to refer to the area as a "Construction Zone," rather than a "Men at Work" area.

The Men

People who do physical labor or traditionally male jobs are not necessarily men and should not be presumed to be men. If the writer mentions that "The men were expected to arrive by 9 a.m. to fix the plumbing system," for example, the editor should confirm that the plumbers in the piece were indeed all men. It would be better usage, however, to change *the men* to *the plumbers.* Here is a better way to word the sentence: *The plumbers were expected to arrive by 9 a.m. to fix the system.*

Likewise, painters should not be referred to as *the men,* nor should electricians, construction workers, roofers, chimney cleaners, appliance repairers or other physical laborers.

Within a quotation, if an interview subject refers to laborers as *the men,* it is generally better to remove the quotation marks and paraphrase. This can also help tighten the writing.

Direct quotation: *The witness said, "She was already gone when the men arrived to paint the house."*

Preferred·usage: *The witness said she was already gone when the painters arrived.*

First Lady

Most of the major stylebooks do not recognize *first lady* as a formal job title. *First lady* is not an elected position, nor is there a formal job description associated with the title. AP style specifies, "Do not capitalize, even when used before the name of a chief of state's wife."

The New York Times has a different policy: "Capitalize when used in reference to the wife of a President of the United States or of a foreign country where the term is used, or the wife of the governor of a state." *First Lady* should only appear after the name, according to *The New York Times* style.

Household Employees

Household employees are not *boys* and *girls*. A woman who cleans houses for a living is a *cleaning woman* or *housekeeper* (preferred usage), not a *cleaning lady, cleaning girl* or *the girl*. A man who cleans houses for a living is a *cleaning man* or *housekeeper*. The terms *maid,* which implies servitude, and *household servant* are fading from usage in favor of *housekeeper.*

In the context of housecleaning services, however, the word *maid* may be used as an adjective without being pejorative. A cleaning service may be referred to as *maid service,* as long as the individual workers are not referred to as *maids.*

Although many hotels use the term *chambermaid* for the person who cleans, these so-called chambermaids are generally dispatched through the hotels' housekeeping units or offices. As a result, hotels are increasingly referring to the room cleaners as *housekeeping.* Likewise, writers should refer to hotel cleaners as either *housekeepers* or *housekeeping.*

In actual households, many people commonly refer to household employees as *the help,* but the usage is often considered demeaning. (Refer to the discussion of *the help* under *Office Employees.*) Journalists should avoid references to *the help.* Individual job titles that more accurately describe the worker's task are more desirable, since they are more revealing. In addition, such titles imply more responsibility. Most publications prefer that writers specify the job title: *housekeeper, butler, tutor, chauffeur* (usually spelled this way in English when referring to male or female drivers), *driver, gardener,* etc.

Best Man for the Job

Seen on a bumper sticker: "The best man for the job may be a woman."

The expression *best man for the job* is at best, a dated cliché. Writers should strive to eliminate clichés from their writing, particularly when the clichés are biased, in this case, against women.

Obviously there are many more suitable ways to say the same thing. Preferred expressions include: *the best person for the job, the best worker for the job, the most qualified person, the best one for the job, the most qualified, the most qualified one for the job,* or simply, *the best for the job.*

If the expression appears within a quotation, it is better to rephrase the quotation outside of quotation marks. If it is somehow essential to the story or context to keep the expression within quotation marks, the writer can insert *or woman* in brackets: *the best man [or woman] for the job.* If inserting *or woman* seems inappropriate in context, the writer should explain, if it is not evident in the story, why the job is only suited to men, according to the speaker.

In general it is better practice to paraphrase an unintentionally biased quotation than to include women in a parenthetical or bracketed afterthought within someone's careless quotation. Although brackets may seem adequate to remedy a discrepancy or two, constant use of brackets (to insert references to those excluded from quotations) becomes a crutch, and only emphasizes second-rate treatment of a population by the speaker or speakers.

■ The Women's Perspective

There is an old maxim that suggests that if you gather three leaders in a room, you might hear six different views on any given issue. Each leader may bring two views, sometimes two seemingly opposing perspectives, to the discussion.

The same holds true for any group of thinking men and women. There is no uniform "men's perspective" or "women's perspective," regardless of the issue. Publications that suggest that they are being fair by interviewing a token woman or "sampling" of women in order to present the "female perspective" or "women's perspective" are misleading readers.

Women who claim to represent *the women's perspective* are false representatives, unless they are elected to do so by a group of women, in which case they are not offering *the women's perspective,* but rather their group of women's perspective. There is no universal women's perspective. To claim to represent *the women's perspective,* even with the best intentions, is to do a disservice to thinking women, in that it implies that while men have many thoughtful perspectives, women's thoughts can be summed up by a single spokeswoman.

Years ago, newspapers had separate "Women's Pages," where *the women's perspectives* were supposedly presented to female readers. Some of the articles on those pages contained what was considered "fluff": gossip, fashion, recipes, household cleaning tips, and family health. Some of the articles, however, dealt with "hard news" about a particular female newsmaker or an item that affected women's rights, safety or politics. Most major publications gradually eliminated Women's pages, as the designation increasingly became viewed as sexist. In place of designated Women's pages, publications specified Fashion pages, Food pages, Society pages, Home pages and either Family or Health pages, still targeted largely for women, but without a label that restricted the audience to women. This allowed the publications to continue to offer the same categories of articles without offending readers.

What confused some editors, however, was lack of an official department for the editorial discussion of "hard news" that was about women or affected mostly women. While the news itself could be integrated into the rest of the publication with other hard news, there was no designated space for thoughtful critique and dialogue of "women's topics" (which they did not want to integrate with other critique and dialogue). In response, many major publications introduced columns that specifically focused on so-called women's issues, in some cases, women's perspectives.

Was this an appropriate response? The new packaging of the same dated concept is obviously a contradiction. But many publications report that these columns and pages are popular among readers. Editors should monitor these columns. Each column should stipulate that it is one woman's opinion, if that is what it is, rather than presumptuously suggesting that it somehow represents the views of all or most women.

At some publications with histories that excluded women, the "female space" is provided as a means to help remedy previously discriminatory hiring practices. In some cases the "women's column" may be a matter of trying to correct an image problem, of not providing enough attention or credence to women.

Is there room for a "women's column" at a modern unbiased publication? Yes, if the column is clear about not pretending to represent any woman but the writer, and if the column deals specifically with issues that potentially have specific ramifications for women. A "women's column" that deals with planning a wedding, finding suitable child care, and making chocolate-covered strawberries may be insulting to readers who resent the designation of these tasks as of interest to women only. All of these advice pieces could appear in sections that are not exclusively for women ("Social Pages," "Family" sections and "Food" sections). The need to cover issues that range from overcoming sex discrimination in the office, to health situations unique to women, to legislation specifically involving women, provide better justification for inclusion of a separate women's column.

As a rule, editors should remember that good editing means understanding that not all women are the same, and not all share a common perspective. Writing should not even suggest that most women share a common perspective unless most women are interviewed for the piece, a task that would obviously be impossible.

■ Feminists

Feminism may be defined as the pursuit of equal rights and opportunities for women. It is an ideology and a social movement that embraces women of many varying political perspectives. It is not tied to any one agenda, and many people with varying views on particular issues and differing approaches to achieving equality consider themselves to be feminists.

Male Feminists

Feminist is not a term that is exclusive to women. Men who support equal rights and opportunities for women may also correctly be referred to as *feminists*. But many men are uncomfortable with the label, probably because the term itself does not sound gender-neutral. As a result, *feminists* is generally applied to women.

Card-Carrying Feminists

There are no cards issued to feminists declaring one a feminist. Therefore, there are no card-carrying feminists, and the cliché serves no purpose but to reveal the writer's bias against so-called *feminists* or equal rights for women. Although the expression is meant to be figurative, references to *card-carrying feminists* are generally meant to be pejorative and should probably be eliminated by the editor. Even self-disparaging remarks made by women ("Granted, I'm no card-carrying feminist") should probably be eliminated, since such remarks are generally meant to undermine those who favor equal rights for women.

Post-Feminists

The designation *post-feminist* first appeared in publications in the 1980s, in reference to young women who were growing up in what was perceived by some to be the aftermath of feminism. The implication, although not necessarily intended, was that feminism was over. The terminology appeared to be a post-mortem declaration. The references to *feminism* and *modern-day feminism,* however, seem to have outlived the reference to *post-feminism,* which is no longer widely recognized.

Gender Barriers

Writers should not imply that the opposite of *feminist* is *male,* or that men are somehow the main obstacles for feminism. This is a biased notion. Many men consider themselves ardent feminists or supporters of feminism.

OLD BOYS' NETWORK.   There is nothing wrong with referring to *the old boys' network* in text, as long as there is some explanation of context and meaning accompanying the reference. Originally, *the old boys' network* referred to British alumni of preparatory schools and universities, who collaborated to further their business connections and careers. In the United States, the term has been applied to the white working male establishment that for decades monopolized government and major industry. The term has been used disparagingly by women and minority groups excluded from leadership positions, in reference to perceived bias and career barriers.

GLASS CEILINGS.   *Glass ceiling* is a figurative term referring to the seemingly invisible barrier that prevents groups of people from achieving promotion and success, usually career success. The usage refers to a difficult-to-detect bias that often limits women's career movement, but also targets minority advancement.

Glass ceilings may be as difficult to document as they are to detect. In pieces about disgruntled employees, writers should attempt to be specific and to document wherever possible any evidence of a glass ceiling, lest the writer be accused of subjective reporting or a bias against the employer.

■ Describing Women

Editors should be wary of reporters who constantly find women's appearances relevant to their articles, but find men's achievements, not appearance, relevant.

A major daily newspaper described in detail the outfit of one of the witnesses at a major trial: purple sweater, plaid slacks and even silver earrings. The same article did not mention the attire worn by any of the men in the room, nor did it tie in the relevance of the woman's clothing to the trial. No doubt the reporter felt that describing the woman's clothing added "flavor" to the story, but what flavor did it add? Would it add the same "flavor" if the readers were told what color suits each lawyer wore? What was the jury wearing? Does anyone care?

The implication was that because a woman was testifying, her outfit somehow would be of interest to the readers. In contrast, the men were only described in terms of what they said and how they said it. If the reporter had been trying to say that the witness was a break in the drab courtroom sea of gray suits, that should have been spelled out, particularly if it influenced the proceedings in any way. Perhaps the writer was trying to imply that the witness seemed indifferent to usual dress codes and formalities—that too should have been pointed out, if that were the case.

The reader was left to think that women's appearances count more than men's, as well as that women's appearances are more interesting than their speech or actions. The other implication was that women are still considered an oddity in a courtroom, so much so that their appearance needs to be described to people who might not have ever seen a woman in court before. Obviously this is a false notion. An editor should have caught the inconsistency and lack of parallelism and either qualified the description with an explanation (showing its relevance to the story) or omitted it.

This should not mean, however, that journalists should never mention a person's appearance. There may be nothing wrong with describing a woman's appearance, as long as the appearance is relevant to the story and as long as the men in the story are also described by their appearances. If the article is about women's clothing trends in Brazil, for example, there is nothing wrong with describing women's appearances. If the story is about a female secretary of state touring the Middle East, clothing discussion is probably inappropriate. An exception would be if the secretary of state is wearing something outlandish or shocking, particularly if this clothing might have some impact on negotiations.

Physical Descriptions

Editors should also note that certain descriptive terms are viewed as particularly offensive. As a general principle, no personality traits should be automatically assigned to a person based on physical body features.

BUXOM.   The word *buxom* probably has no place in any piece that is not a fashion story. (Refer to the section Flat-Chested in this chapter.) To some people, the word is a euphemism for *fat*. To others, it connotes *sexy, voluptuous, promiscuous* or even *motherly, grandmotherly* and *nurturing.*

The reporter should not assume that a woman with large breasts is the "reticent nurturing type," or the "aggressive promiscuous type" or the "matronly overbearing type." Nor should the reporter assume that large-breasted women are not athletic—many are. All of these biases assume that *buxom* women are not "office material" and suggest that large-breasted women are too encumbered or obsessed with their bodies to be energetic businesswomen and leaders.

Also, in articles about parenting or infant nutrition, writers should not assume that large-breasted women are better breast-feeders than smaller-breasted women. According to La Leche League, there are no advantages in ability to nurse a baby associated with the size of a woman's breast.

FLAT-CHESTED.   Again, a woman's breast size has no place in a story that is not a fashion story. (Refer to the section Buxom in this chapter.) Writers should not assume that it is every woman's dream to have large breasts, or that women who have smaller breasts are less motherly, less sexy, less mature, less feminine or more athletic. Writers should avoid assigning personality traits to their interview subjects based on bodily features.

Although in some years, discussions and jokes at the Academy Awards have focused on breast size and artificial implants, journalists should not assume that smaller-breasted women are less happy about their physiques. Nevertheless, the term *flat-chested* is generally considered insulting usage.

FRAGILE.   Writers should beware of wording that describes women stereotypically as fragile and needy. Among the terms to watch are *dainty, petite, slight, pixielike* and *delicate,* although there may be instances when such words are appropriate. While some may perceive such fragility to be flattering, others view such usage as an excuse to limit the responsibilities of women, claiming that they are too frail or needy to be useful.

HAIR COLOR.   Women are blondes. Men are blonds. Women are brunettes. Men are brunets. But when using both hair colors as adjectives before a noun, use *blond* and *brunet* for both men and women. (Example: *The blond models showed the clothing styles.*)

According to *The Associated Press Stylebook and Libel Manual,* red-haired, redhead and redheaded "all are acceptable for a person with red hair."

Writers should not assign personality traits to article subjects based on their hair color. Common American stereotypes dictate that blond-haired people are less intelligent ("dumb blonde"), more fun loving, sexier, and more attractive. Brown-haired people are described sometimes as uninspiring, average and even "mousy." Redheads are vibrant, energetic, sometimes bold and even bossy. Black-haired Caucasians are wild and exotic or morbid. Editors should watch for these biases on the part of the writer. Hair color does not determine personality.

STURDY.   Women who are strong should not be described as an aberration, thus implying that most women are fragile. Among the terms to watch are *overly muscular, sturdy, substantial, masculine* and *matronly.*

Behavioral Descriptions and Stereotypes

Some writers inadvertently use biased adjectives to describe women's behavior, promoting stereotypes and revealing chauvinism. In selecting proper adjectives, writers and editors should consider whether or not the same adjectives could be applied (and are applied) as often to men. If not, the writers should question the fairness of the adjective, determine if it is insulting and examine the adjective's appropriateness.

GIRLISH. Women are adults and should be treated as adults in copy. In referring to a woman, writers need to select appropriate adjectives that do not diminish the woman's maturity or compare her to a child. Just as the word *girl* is inappropriate when referring to a female who has reached her 18th birthday, adjectives that equate *women* with *girls* are also not acceptable.

As a rule, it is better to avoid the clichés and stereotypes of girlhood—even when writing about girls. Avoid using *girlish, coy, giggly, shy, timid, sweet, dainty, petite, prim, ladylike* and *fickle.* If any of these words seem vital to the story, editors should consider the relevance on a case-by-case basis.

In the same way, nouns should be selected carefully, if the word *woman* does not fit in a particular context. Eliminate terms that equate women with baby animals like *chick, kitten* and *pet.* If such terms are used within a quotation that is vital to the story, remove the quotation marks and rephrase the statement, using more appropriate language.

INNOCENTS. In war stories, battles, violent confrontations, hostage situations, and even ship sinkings, there are occasional references to "innocent women and children." Editors should probably eliminate all such references. The expression has become a cliché, but more offensively, the usage implies that women and children are all innocent, whereas men somehow deserve to die. Some gender-neutral possibilities include *civilians, bystanders* and *victims of circumstance.*

NURTURING. Writers should not imply that women's temperaments are the same or even similar, and that all women are naturally nurturing in personality. Writers should avoid labeling women who care as *mothering, coddling, nurturing* and even *smothering.*

PANIC AND HYSTERIA.   *Henny-Penny* is the story of a hen who believes that the sky is falling. To refer to a woman as *"Henny-Pennyish"* or *"a Henny-Penny,"* is to promote the stereotype that women worry excessively and irrationally. Because the name comes from the word *hen,* it is typically only applied to women.

Women's voices are typically higher than men's. That does not mean, however, that when women with high-pitched voices speak that they are panicking or behaving irrationally. When a writer mentions a high voice, the implication is that the speaker is overly excited or panicking. Gratuitous references to a woman's shrieky, squeaky, or shrill voice, when it bears no relevance to an article, should be eliminated, as they are inappropriate.

Editors should watch for the words *hysterical* and *hysteria* in copy. Both words tend to be applied only to women and convey strong bias.

PETTY.   Writers should not presume that women are unable to see the "big picture," and as a group focus on trivial details. Ability to care for details, observe accurately and work efficiently are positive traits in both men and women. As a rule, writers should avoid labeling efficient and observant women as *trivial, detail-oriented, petty, frivolous, catty, gossipy, mindless* and *clueless.* These words, seldom applied to men by writers, reveal strong bias.

SUPERSTITIOUS.   Writers should not assume that older women are ignorant, out of touch with modern reason or superstitious. When discussing superstition, do not use the expression *old wives' tale,* thus encouraging continuation of the stereotype. Inaccuracies and misinformation should not be senselessly blamed on old married women. The usage is gender-biased, family-biased and age-biased. Instead, describe the so-called tale as a *superstition, rumor, irrational outcome* or *a superstitious story,* depending upon the reference, meaning and context.

TEMPTRESSES.   Writers should not assume that women who look attractive are trying to be seductive. Labeling a woman *seductive, foxy* or *sexy* may seem like a compliment, yet all three terms can easily be construed as pejorative in inappropriate situations. As a rule, a writer should not be measuring the attractiveness or seductiveness of an interview subject unless such a yardstick is required in the story: a fashion piece on clothing that is meant to be seductive, for example. Writers should also avoid labeling women *voluptuous, feminine, soft-skinned, zaftig, buxom, developed, sexy, hot* and *suggestive*.

WICKED.   Writers should not imply that women who take strong stances on controversial issues are being irrationally mean, stubborn, manipulative or wicked. Avoid labeling outspoken women as *overly aggressive, domineering, controlling, matronly, marmish, spinsterish, butch, bitchy, tough cookies, witches, nagging* or *feisty*.

In Relation to Others

Women are often described according to their relationship to others: wife of, mother of, daughter of, granddaughter of, grandmother of, sister of, etc. In contrast, men are rarely defined in news stories by their family relationships, but rather in context of their careers. The implication is that women succeed only as appendages to other relatives or are only valued as family members.

Editors should omit such references to relationship, when the woman identified in the piece is the primary newsmaker in her own right. However, when a family member is the primary reason that the story is newsworthy, it becomes acceptable, and even essential, that if the female relative is mentioned, the relationship be specified. At the same time, editors need to be very careful not to overcredit a famous relative, thus degrading the efforts or newsworthiness of the woman being discussed.

Newsday's stylebook specifies that "irrelevant references to or unnecessary emphasis on a person's marital status is unacceptable. The number of children a person has should not be mentioned unless it is relevant to the story."

APPENDAGES.   Editors should eliminate words that imply that women are appendages of men, or ones that are patronizing in attempt to compensate. Among the expressions that demean women's independence: *my better half, the Mrs., my assistant* (in reference to a spouse), *my scout* and *my right arm*.

Similarly, men should not be referred to as *the boss* or *the chief* in copy.

Squaw.   Editors should watch all uses of this word, since it is generally used in a way that is offensive to Native Americans as well as to women. *The Associated Press Stylebook* includes the words in a list of Indian-related disparaging words to be avoided. (Refer to the Native Americans section in chapter 3, Ethnic Bias.)

Medical Descriptions

When female or male body parts are discussed in health, science, medical or disaster articles, the usage should be scientific, specific and mature. Editors should watch for flowery or euphemistic terms that reveal the writer's discomfort with terminology. Such euphemisms are generally considered tasteless and more confusing to the readers.

Body parts should only be mentioned in copy if such references are vital to the story. Gratuitous references should be omitted.

■ Nontraditional Sex Roles

Tomboy and Boyish

A *tomboy* years ago meant a girl who wanted to be a boy and supposedly behaved like a boy. As many taboos and restrictions have been lifted for girls, much of society has come to recognize that there are few behavioral traits that are inherently exclusive to boys. As a result, the notion of *behaving like a boy* has become dated. Increasingly, girls are being raised to be bold, athletic, curious, aggressive, intellectual and happy to be girls.

Writers should not assume that because a girl is athletic, she wants to be a boy. Nor should athletic or aggressive behavior be labeled *boyish* or *tomboy* behavior. Editors should watch for this usage to make sure that a writer's own biased notions about gender-appropriate behavior are not revealed. Generally avoid both terms.

Effeminate

The word *effeminate* reveals similar sexual biases to the word *tomboy.* The *Dictionary of Bias-Free Usage* specifies that effeminate, "... in its most commonly understood sense ... is pejorative and sexist, loaded with cultural stereotypes about what it means to be a man or a woman today." The book suggests the following alternatives, depending upon intended meaning and context: *passive, gentle, timid, weak, agreeable, docile, fussy* and *particular.*

PLAYING LIKE A GIRL.   There is no one way that girls or boys play any game. Boys do not all throw balls one way or catch one way. Girls do not all run the same way. Editors should eliminate suggestions in copy that all boys or girls play one way. If the material appears in a quotation, the editor may rephrase the comment outside of quotation marks. Ask the writer what was meant by the comment. Did it mean that the athlete was not coordinated? Did it mean that the player was a good catcher or was not afraid to get dirty? Then ask the writer to be specific rather than quoting someone else's stereotype about boys' play and girls' play.

Sexual Orientation

As a general rule, sexuality should not be mentioned in a piece if it does not specifically pertain to the piece. If the piece is not about sex, sexuality, sex discrimination or sex-related diseases, the mention of sexuality is probably inappropriate.

How publications refer to people of differing sexual "preferences" or orientations often depends on whether the policy-making editors believe that sexual behavior is genetic, learned or elected behavior. As a result, any approach is vulnerable to accusations of bias.

Writers and editors who contend that sexual orientation is genetic or congenital are more likely to favor treating homosexual causes like any other civil rights challenges. Editors should be cautioned, however, that although such equal treatment may seem universally fair by some standards, this approach may be perceived as biased by those who believe that homosexuality is learned or elected behavior, particularly by those who believe that homosexuality is wrong (philosophically, religiously or medically).

At the same time, writers and editors who believe that homosexuality is learned or elected behavior (particularly those who believe it is wrong philosophically, religiously or medically) are less likely to treat homosexual causes and news like other civil rights causes. They might ignore or give less space to such stories. Or they may show partiality to those who oppose homosexuality. This in turn may be perceived as discrimination and bias by those who believe that homosexuality is genetic or congenital and that society is victimizing people born with this orientation.

SEXUAL PREFERENCE.   The expression *sexual preference* is viewed as biased by those who contend that homosexuality is not chosen, but rather congenital. According to the *News Watch Project Style Guide,* the term *sexual preference* should be avoided. It "implies a choice to stray from the straight and narrow. Use *sexual orientation*" instead.

OPENLY GAY.   The term *openly gay* is preferred over *self-avowed, self-admitted, self-confessed* or *practicing,* in instances where the sexual orientation of an individual pertains to a story, according to *News Watch Project Style Guide.* The guide says *acknowledged* is acceptable if appropriate to the context. The example cited in the guide is, "A person accused of being gay *acknowledges* it."

HOMOSEXUAL.   The term *homosexual* is preferred over *gay* in the *United Press International Stylebook. The Associated Press Stylebook and Libel Manual,* however, specifies that *gay* is acceptable as a "popular synonym for homosexual," both as a noun and an adjective.

Many homosexual rights organizations use the word *gay* within the names of their groups and prefer to be called gay instead of homosexual.

LESBIAN.   The word *lesbian* is acceptable usage in reference to homosexual women, according to both United Press International style and the Associated Press style. The two stylebooks specify that *lesbian* should be "lowercase in reference to homosexual women, except in names of organizations."

Although the word *lesbian* is acceptable in its proper context, certain usage of the word is not. To refer to someone as "a real lesbian," for example, is meant to sound derogatory and should not be used.

SLURS.   Editors should beware of writers who use slurs in reference to homosexual men or women. Among the words to avoid are: *butch, dyke, fag, faggot, fairy, homo, queen* and *queer.* Even when these words appear in quotations, on signs or graffiti, they should be avoided. When quoting speakers who use any of these words (even if they use it about themselves), writers should rephrase the quotation outside of quotation marks, substituting words that are not offensive, attributing the remarks and explaining the context.

Occasionally insiders, meaning people who claim to be homosexual, will use these words in reference to themselves or others. While the insider may presume license to use the word, journalists do not have such license. Working journalists are by definition outsiders—regardless of whether they support or identify with the people about whom they are reporting.

6

Religious Bias

▪ Religious Bias Examples

The following are examples of different forms of religious bias that commonly appear in publications or on broadcasts. Examine the sentences, and then determine how they should best be rewritten to eliminate religious bias.

The neighbors were told that they should wear their usual church clothes to the annual town party.

The children were taught religious music as well as secular Christmas songs for their public school holiday concert.

The guest speakers included the reverend of a Seventh Day Adventist church, a Catholic minister, and a priest from the local Quaker parish.

The robbery suspect belonged to the same mosque as the terrorists who were recently convicted in the bombing.

She was of Buddhist persuasion, but dressed like a JAP and belonged to a WASPy country club.

▪ Overview

A group of professionals were having a discussion over dinner. One quoted a newspaper columnist.

"You read that paper?" someone at the table challenged. "I find it very anti-Semitic."

"Anti-Semitic?" another laughed. "They are primarily anti-Catholic. They're always saying bad things about the Pope and the Catholic Church."

"I don't think it's just the Catholic Church," someone else countered. "It's all of Christianity."

"Have they ever said a nice thing about the Muslims?" another asked.

Contrary to what many readers contend, much of the religious bias that appears in the American press is not against one particular religion or another, but against religiousness instead. Writers tend to tread carefully and sensitively when discussing particular religions or religious groups. When discussing religion, however, as an institution, or issues that affect religion, more bias is revealed.

Probably the most obvious example of this bias appears in articles about people who believe strongly in any religion, particularly those who prefer to go back to the original texts and interpret them literally. They find themselves labeled as *fundamentalists, extremists* and *fanatics*. If this were not offensive enough, many publications go on to essentially equate or attempt to link all so-called religious fundamentalists, extremists and fanatics with terrorists and violence.

For writers seeking to eliminate religious bias from their work, most of the major stylebooks detail the practices and principles of each major religion. Although explanations are generally limited to a few paragraphs, enough information is provided for a novice reporter to write intelligently about religions with which he or she is not very familiar. If a reporter were to cover a piece about the Jehovah's Witnesses, for example, *The Associated Press Stylebook* devotes seven paragraphs to an overall summary of the history and teachings, which the reporter could read before attempting to report.

What becomes confusing, however, are the terminology differences that are accepted within different religious environments. Use the wrong term, and you are accused of religious bias, whether or not such bias was intended. There are few generic terms when it comes to religion, and certain terms have become buzzwords that reporters should avoid.

This chapter discusses the language used by some of the major religions, and examines some of the anti-religious language and stereotyping to help journalists eliminate religious bias from their writing. Editors should note that individual entries vary in length, and that this space allotment is not proportionate to any religion's influence or following. Instead the amount of space is roughly based on frequency of bias that appears in publications and the perceived need to clarify terminology.

The listings do not provide an extensive theological discussion or comparison of the different beliefs, nor is every religious group covered, a task that would require volumes. (It has been estimated that more than 1,500 different religious faiths exist in the United States, including 75 varieties of Baptists, and 360,000 houses of worship.) Instead, the listings are meant to offer quick references to supplement and complement the major stylebooks as well as religious texts. Thus, this section should not be used as a replacement for a stylebook or reference book on religion.

■ Generic Religious Terms

Before editing a piece about a religion or religious event, an editor should read the summary of the religion in a stylebook and become familiar with the religion's (or denomination's) unique terminology. Do not assume that every Christian group refers to its leaders or place of worship the same way, for example, or that the worshippers refer to themselves in the same way.

The Church

A church is not a generic term for "place of worship" for all religions. Some religions use *mosque, temple, synagogue,* or *meeting house,* and may be offended by the use of *church* in reference to their place of worship, if they have a place of worship. Not all religions do. Some believe that home is the only true place of worship. Some worship outdoors. Some believe that worship is not a collective activity, but should remain very personal and private and therefore do not believe in gathering as such.

If the subject of an article says, "Every American should attend the church of his or her choice regularly," such a quotation is perceived as biased by religious people who do not worship in churches. Before using a direct quotation, the writer should ask if the speaker specifically meant *church* or the more generic *place of worship.* If the speaker meant to be generic, the writer should paraphrase such a sentence outside of quotation marks. (Example: *The speaker advocated that every American should attend a place of worship regularly.* Second example: If the gathering place was not essential to the essence of what the speaker meant, the writer might state, *The speaker advocated that every American worship regularly.* Third example: *The speaker advocated that every American should attend religious meetings or services regularly.*) If the speaker did not intend to be generic, but specifically wanted to tell Americans that only churches are acceptable places of worship or places to pray, this bias should probably be explained in the article. Editors should watch for the usage of the word *church.*

Obviously, in reference to a specific church, there is nothing wrong with the word *church.* Editors need to understand that the word is not generic, however.

Churchgoers

The people that gather at religious institutions are not to be generically referred to as *churchgoers, congregants, the church body, believers, followers, ward, minion, flock, parishioners* or *the parish.* When referring to specific religious establishments that use these terms, writers and editors may use the words that apply. When referring to the more generic group of people who attend places of worship, however, *worshippers* is probably a less-biased word.

Editors should also make sure that writers do not assume or imply that people who do not attend churches are not religious people. Again, some may believe in worshipping at home. Others may attend mosques, temples, synagogues, prayer groups, and meeting houses.

Denominations

The word *denominations* is not generic to every religion. Judaism, for example, uses the word *movement* (as in Reform movement or Conservative movement) to describe its various branches and approaches to observance. Other religious institutions refer to *branches* or *sects,* rather than *denominations.*

The Sabbath

The Sabbath may refer to Friday, Saturday, Sunday, or Monday depending upon the religion. Writers should not assume any one day is the Sabbath.

Religious Communities

It is correct to refer to a *religious community,* when describing a group of people who attend the same religious institution, know each other and act as a community together. Just being affiliated with the same religion, does not constitute being part of the same religious community, however. Editors should be wary of this usage, since writers sometimes use it to generalize about all people affiliated with a given religion.

Religious Leaders

Minister is not a generic term. Nor are *pastor* and *preacher.* Some religious establishments are led by priests, rabbis, parsons, imams, vicars, bishops, deacons, practitioners, lecturers or gurus. Editors should check with each religious listing separately to make sure that the writer uses correct terminology. In addition, editors should make sure that writers do not assume that all religious leaders are male.

The Rev. is an adjective, although many people use the term incorrectly as a noun, referring to a person as *the reverend.* Use it only as an adjective before a name.

Holidays

Editors and writers who are sensitive, insightful and meticulous about eliminating ethnic bias, sex bias and age bias, are sometimes oblivious to issues of religious bias and biases that confront members of minority religions.

A major issue for some minority religions, for example, is what constitutes a religious holiday. By some definitions, a religious holiday is one where the primary focus is worship and prayer. By others, a religious holiday is any celebration or commemoration that has religious origins—regardless of whether the resulting observances involve worship or prayer. Editors need to be very careful in characterizing holidays that have known religious origins. To label such holidays *secular* is often considered biased by religious groups that have different religious traditions. Even if national offices are closed, or public schools participate in the festivities, if the holiday has religious origins, many would argue that the holiday is religion-based.

Editors need to be sensitive to these issues if they don't want to be put in the biased position of determining which holidays are secular and which are religious.

CHRISTMAS.   Christmas celebrations and traditions are often characterized as nonsecular events in the media, although the holiday, a celebration of the birth of Jesus, is definitely tied to Christianity.

Is Christmas a religious holiday? Depending on whom you ask, the answer will vary. Many Americans who do not come from Christian backgrounds or heritage would say that although national offices are closed in observance of Christmas, the holiday is a religious one. They would argue that there is no such thing as a secular Christmas song, a secular Santa Claus, a secular Christmas tree or a secular wreath. They would argue that these are all symbols of a religious holiday, whether or not they are used during worship.

Christmas Music.   In a court ruling, a public school was told that at holiday concerts, religious Christmas music could be performed as long as an equal amount of secular holiday music was performed in the same concert. A radio report discussing this issue declared that "We Wish You a Merry Christmas" was clearly a secular song, and could provide the proper balance to "Oh Holy Night," which was deemed a religious song. What the writer did not realize, however, was that for many Americans who are not of Christian ancestry, any Christmas song is by definition religious, whether it is a children's song like "Rudolph the Red-Nosed Reindeer," or a more spiritual work like "Silent Night." Both are about Christmas, a Christian celebration. The fact that Santa Claus was an American creation, does not make "Santa Claus Is Coming to Town" any less religious for non-Christian Americans than "Little Town of Bethlehem."

Some schools have pursued so-called balance by performing other religions' holiday songs in equal doses. For each Christmas song performed, for example, a Jewish Chanukah song is also sung. This obviously does not represent all of the religious diversity in major city schools, whose populations include Hindus, Buddhists and Muslims. Some people would argue that neither Christmas nor Chanukah is secular, and that neither holiday tradition should be promoted or even discussed in public schools.

Reporters covering issues of religious music should note that the topic is considered highly controversial. Characterizing any Christmas music as secular is considered biased by many. Writers seeking to be objective should avoid such characterization.

Trees.   Is a Christmas tree an American tradition or a religious symbol? Within neighborhoods that consist mostly of Christians, the

Christmas tree is often perceived to be an American tradition, a secular seasonal decoration. In neighborhoods where other religions dominate, the Christmas tree is often perceived as an exclusively Christian symbol, and not a generic American holiday symbol. Editors need to be cautious in characterizing Christmas trees as American institutions. Such characterizations are viewed as biased by many non-Christian religions.

Wreaths.   A Catholic student from Ireland who arrived in the United States during Christmas was taken for a drive to see the local holiday decorations. She suddenly became worried.

"Who died?" she asked.

Her hosts were puzzled. "Nobody," they said.

"Why does everyone have a wreath on the door?" she asked. "In Ireland, wreaths are only used when someone dies."

The wreath is an American Christmas decoration, the Americans explained. In the United States, wreaths are part of Christmas, although now flower wreaths and harvest wreaths are being used to celebrate spring and fall as well.

Is the wreath a religious symbol? If it is a Christmas wreath, many would say that it is tied to Christmas, a religious holiday. Many non-Christians would argue that all wreaths are religious symbols. It is not customary for non-Christians to display wreaths on their doors. Wreaths are associated with Christmas, a Christian holiday. Editors need to be careful in characterizing wreaths when writing about decorations and holiday symbols. To characterize a wreath ornament as secular would be considered biased by many non-Christians.

HALLOWEEN.   To many, Halloween might seem like an indisputably secular American holiday. After all, Halloween began in the United States. And children of many ethnic backgrounds and religions participate in trick or treating and the other seemingly secular Halloween rituals.

But this inclusive philosophy is not shared universally. Editors should be aware that writers who insist that the holiday is a secular celebration would be viewed as biased by religious minorities who feel that the holiday either contradicts their beliefs or is religiously inappropriate. According to *Holiday Symbols,* "Halloween came to America with the Irish immigrants of the 1840s." The book says the holiday began in the 4th century as All Hallows' Eve, a Christian attempt to "stamp out [Celt] pagan festivals like Samhain."

Some non-Christians argue that because Halloween's origins are traced to All Hallows' Eve, Halloween is inherently a Christian holiday. In many neighborhoods that are primarily non-Christian, Halloween is not observed at all. Children do not trick or treat, attend parties, or dress in costumes. In some Christian communities as well, parents discourage the holiday, arguing that its origins are pagan.

ST. VALENTINE'S DAY.   St. Valentine's Day, February 14th, is widely regarded as a secular salute to romance. Greeting cards, love notes, chocolates and red roses are exchanged by children and young romantics.

But once again, the celebration is rooted in a Christian observance, and editors need to be aware that not all Americans consider Valentine's Day a secular celebration. According to *Holiday Symbols,* St. Valentine's Day was originally meant as a Christian means of distracting Romans from celebrating Lupercalia, a lover's holiday, on February 15th. According to the book, "In 469 C.E., Pope Gelasius set aside February 14th to honor St. Valentine, a young Roman who was martyred by Emperor Claudius II on this day in 270 C.E. for refusing to give up Christianity. Because of the proximity of the two dates, many customs associated with the Lupercalia were carried over to the Feast of St. Valentine."

As a result, many of the same Americans who do not celebrate Halloween, do not observe St. Valentine's Day. Some non-Christians argue that the Christian-rooted tradition, although not laden with religious overtones, is inherently a Christian holiday. And some religious Christians argue that St. Valentine's Day's origins are pagan and therefore inappropriate.

■ Buddhism

Buddhist gathering places are generally called *temples,* and that is the preferred usage. Some Japanese-American Buddhists, however, refer to their gathering places as *churches,* according to the American Buddhist Congress.

Temple ceremonies are led by an *abbot* or *abbess* and generally take place on Sundays, although scheduling often varies by institution. There is no one Sabbath day in Buddhism. Temples may have monks and nuns, who wear robes and answer to a preceptor. The temple congregation is called a *sangha,* which originally referred only to the gathering of ordained monks and nuns, but has come to mean a gathering of all people engaged in practice and following traditions, according to the American Buddhist Congress.

Buddhism consists of three main traditions: Thervada, Mahayana (which includes Zen) and Vajrayana (which includes Tibetan tradition). In addition, there are subtraditions. All are based on the same original text called Tripitaka, written in the Pali language.

■ Christianity

Christianity includes many branches, denominations, sects and independent worship groups with wide variations in beliefs and traditions. Thus, editors should be careful of writing that purports to focus on "true Christians" or those who claim to be the only real Christians. Obviously such labels become offensive to those Christians who are excluded from the category, and they may perceive the writing as biased.

Editors need to be familiar with the language of each individual Christian group (or at least have good reference materials in which to look up terminology). Different Christian groups have different titles for their leaders and different terminology for their places of worship, rites, members and texts. Writers often are unaware of the lack of uniformity within Christianity. This section does not attempt to offer an exhaustive study on terminology. (Editors—particularly religion editors—are advised to use religion reference books.) But it aims to acquaint editors with some of the variations, to sensitize editors to the complexity of usage.

Churches of Christ

This church consists of independent congregations that do not consider themselves a Protestant denomination. The leader is referred to as *brother,* and ministers do not use clergy titles, according to UPI style.

Interfaith Churches

Interfaith churches generally refer to places of worship that welcome many Christian denominations. Writers should not assume, however, that interfaith churches, ecumenical churches, ecumenical prayers or interfaith church services honor all religious traditions or are perceived as welcoming to those of non-Christian faiths.

INTERFAITH PRAYERS.   Prayers, by definition, are connected with religious customs and traditions, thus, no prayer can be entirely interfaith. Where one tradition may require that heads be bowed during a prayer, another may require that heads not be bowed, or that prayers be said without shoes on, or with a mandatory head covering, or with no head covering. One tradition might dictate that any prayer must mention God, whereas another does not permit the mention of the holy name. To write about an interfaith prayer is contradictory. Editors should watch for this usage.

Jehovah's Witnesses

Jehovah's Witnesses are a Christian group, but they do not consider themselves Catholics or Protestants and should not be classified among either religion by journalists. *Minister* and other titles are not used. The organization is run by a director.

Mormons

The correct name for the Mormon Church is the Church of Jesus Christ of Latter-day Saints, but Mormon is acceptable in all uses. The church is Christian, but does not consider itself to be a Protestant denomination. Members are referred to as *Mormons.* Members belong to a *ward,* a congregation based on geographical location. The head of each church is called a *bishop* who leads along with a *first* and *second counselor; minister* and *the Rev.* are not used.

Mormons attend church services called *meetings* for three hours on Sundays at *meeting houses.* Mormons also say they are "going to church." Meetings include hymns, talks and classes. A Mormon *temple* is a separate building, where weddings and other rites are performed, and only Mormons may enter. Temples are closed on Sundays and Mondays.

Orthodox Christians

Orthodox Christians are members of the Eastern Orthodox Church. They should not be referred to as Protestants.

Eastern Orthodox churches are led by nine equal-level patriarchs according to nation: Turkey (Constantinople); Egypt (Alexandria); Greece (Antioch); Israel (Jerusalem); Russia (Moscow); Georgia; Serbia; Romania; Bulgaria. Russian Orthodox churches outside of Russia are led by metropolitans. Individual churches are led by *priests,* who are referred to as *the Rev.* (followed by the name of the priest) on first reference.

Writers should be aware that Orthodox Christians celebrate many of the major holidays on different days than other major Christian faiths.

Protestantism

The major American journalism stylebooks provide brief histories of the largest Protestant denominations, along with limited style information on how to refer to religious leaders, membership and religious gathering places.

Editors need to note that not all Protestant denominations use the same vocabulary in describing their practices. Most places of worship, but not all, for example, are led by *ministers,* who are called *the Rev.* (followed by a full name) on first reference. In most cases the title *the Rev.* is dropped on second reference, with only the last name used. But not all places of worship are called *churches.* And not all churches are led by ministers, and not all ministers are correctly referred to as *the Rev.* Editors need to be aware of these differences when handling religion stories.

BAPTIST.   Baptist clergy members are referred to as *ministers.* The leader of a congregation is called a *pastor* or *the Rev.* on first reference. Baptists worship in *churches,* and members of the church are called *Baptists.*

CHRISTIAN SCIENCE.   The Christian Science Church may also be referred to as *Church of Christ, Scientist.* Do not use *pastor, minister* or *the Rev.* in reference to leaders of this church. The leadership positions include *reader, practitioner* and *lecturer,* offices that may be held by women and men. All members of the church are lay members and may be called *Christian Scientists.*

CONGREGATIONALIST.   Clergy members are referred to as *ministers*. Those who lead congregations may also be referred to as *pastors*. *The Rev.* appears before a minister's name on first reference.

EPISCOPAL.   The Episcopal Church is a member of the Anglican Communion.

Episcopal is an adjective. It may refer to an Episcopal church, an Episcopal priest, an Episcopal parish, etc. *Episcopal* is not a noun, however, so a person cannot be an *Episcopal*. One who belongs to an Episcopal church is an *Episcopalian*.

The people who attend an Episcopal church are referred to as a *parish*. And they are led by a *rector* or *vicar* (both of which are never capitalized), but not a pastor or minister. Other leaders include *bishops, priests* and *deacons*.

LUTHERAN.   People who attend a Lutheran church are referred to as the *congregation*. A minister who leads a congregation is called a *pastor* and is referred to as *the Rev.* Other members include ordained *bishops and lay elders, deacons* and *trustees*.

METHODIST.   People who attend a Methodist church are referred to as the *congregation*. Ordained clergy members are referred to as *bishops* and *ministers*. Ministers who lead churches are called *pastors* and are referred to as *the Rev.*

PRESBYTERIAN.   Presbyterian leaders are referred to as *ministers,* or *the Rev.* on first reference. The leaders of a congregation include a *pastor* and *ruling elders* selected by the congregation (capitalize the *E* in *Elder* before a name). Ministers and representative elders report to a *presbytery;* presbyteries together form a *synod.* The leader of the denomination is the *stated clerk;* capitalize before a name.

QUAKERS.   Members of the Religious Society of Friends are known as *Quakers.* Quakers gather in *meeting houses,* rather than in churches.

The UPI stylebook specifies that "There is no recognized ranking of clergy over lay people," among the Quakers. "Unordained officers are called elders or ministers [always lowercase] ... some ... describe themselves as pastors." Some use *the Rev.* The *E* in *Elder* should be capitalized when appearing before a name.

Quakers are not part of congregations or parishes, but instead are part of *monthly meetings, quarterly meetings,* and *yearly meetings.* The *New York Times Manual of Style and Usage* specifies that *"Monthly Meeting, Quarterly Meeting, [and] Yearly Meeting ..."* are capitalized in references to specific organizations.

SEVENTH DAY ADVENTISTS.   Friday evening to Saturday evening is the Sabbath for Seventh Day Adventists. The religion teaches vegetarianism, abstinence from alcohol and tobacco and observes Old Testament requirements. The leaders are referred to as *elders* and *pastors,* but not *the Rev.*

Roman Catholicism

The *pope* leads the church from the Vatican, and beneath him are *cardinals, archbishops, bishops, monsignors, priests* and *deacons.*

POPE.   Pope is capitalized only when it precedes the name of a specific pope. When referring to a pope or popes, however, without specifying which one, the *p* is lowercase.

PONTIFF.   Pontiff is not the preferred term, according to *New York Times* style. In general, use *pope* instead. If the writer uses *pontiff* in reference to a specific *pope,* capitalize the *P* in *Pontiff.* When referring to a *pontiff* or *pontiffs,* the *p* should be lowercase. AP and UPI styles specify that *pontiff* is not a formal title, and therefore should always appear lowercase.

VATICAN CITY.   The pope resides in Vatican City, which is located within Rome, but is an independent state, not Italian territory. Therefore Vatican City stands alone in datelines and is not followed by *Italy* or *Rome* within the text of articles.

■ Hinduism

Hinduism is one of the world's largest religions. Hindus believe that there is one supreme being and many gods and goddesses.

Hindu gathering places are called *temples,* not *churches.* Temples do not have formal clergy. *Hindu* is the religion. The followers are called *Hindus. Hindi* is a language.

■ Islam

Islam is the name of the religion, and its followers are called *Moslems* or *Muslims*. Followers of Islam pray to Allah in *mosques,* not churches or temples. The Sabbath is observed on Fridays.

The religion began when Allah revealed the *Koran* (the religious book) to the prophet Mohammed in Mecca. The *Koran* is in Arabic, and the religious code of law is called the *Shariah.*

There are two major groups within the religion: Sunni and Shiite. Sunni is the larger group and includes the majority of Muslims in most Arab countries. Iran is the only country where Shiites are in the majority, and significant Shiite populations also exist in Iraq and Lebanon.

The leader of prayer is called an *imam* in the local community. The imam is not formally ordained, and there is no organized priesthood.

Islamic

Islamic is the proper adjective describing that which relates to the religion of Islam. Do not use *Muslim* or *Moslem* as an adjective.

Moslem, Muslim and Black Muslim

Whether a follower of Islam is correctly called a *Moslem* or a *Muslim* depends upon the particular stylebook. The *United Press International Stylebook* prefers *Moslem,* but permits use of *Muslim* within the names of organizations that prefer *Muslim.* UPI cites the Black Muslims as an example, but the Associated Press notes that *Black Muslim,* in reference to "a member of a predominantly black Islamic sect ... is considered derogatory by members of the sect, who call themselves *Muslims."*

The New York Times used *Moslem* previously, but now specifies that *Muslim* is the preferred form. *The Associated Press Stylebook* also prefers *Muslim.*

Mohammed

Mohammed is the preferred spelling for the name of the founder of the Islamic religion, according to the Associated Press, *The New York Times* and the *UPI Stylebook.*

■ Judaism

Jew is correct usage. Do not substitute *Hebrew* or *Israelite* when writing about a modern-day Jewish person.

To call a Jewish person a *Jew* is not offensive or derogatory. It is no more offensive than calling a Catholic person a *Catholic* or a Protestant person a *Protestant.*

Some writers suggest that it sounds more polite to write, "He is of a Jewish background," "of Jewish faith," "of Jewish descent," "of Jewish persuasion" "a follower of Judaism," "a Jewish person," or "a member of the Jewish community." Such phrases are not more polite, and instead reveal that the writer is uncomfortable about calling a Jewish person a *Jew,* thus implying that the writer has some kind of anti-Jewish bias.

The leader of a Jewish congregation is a *rabbi,* not a minister or priest. Jews observe the Sabbath from sundown Friday night to sundown Saturday, and they worship in a temple or *synagogue.*

Jewishness

There are no different degrees of Judaism, although there are people who claim to be more Jewish than others. The preferred usage is *observant.* Some people are more religiously observant Jews than others. Whether or not it is correct to say that some Jews are more religious than others is disputed. Many Reform Jews would say that they are just as religious as the most Orthodox Jews, but not as observant.

Jewishness is not necessarily inherited. People can become Jewish by conversion.

When Jew Is Derogatory

Jew, used as a verb, is derogatory, as in *to Jew somebody* or *to Jew somebody down.* Editors should eliminate such usage from the copy. The exception is when the verb appears in a quotation, if the editor feels that the quotation is needed in the story to demonstrate, in the speaker's own words, the speaker's degree of anti-Semitism.

Calling someone *a real Jew* in a piece is also derogatory. It obviously is not meant to imply that there are some real Jews and some fake Jews, but rather it is meant to be used as an insult and implies that there is something wrong with being Jewish.

Two dictionary publishers that included derogatory definitions of the word *Jew,* are correcting the listings in their new editions, according to the Anti-Defamation League. Oxford University Press, publisher of the *Oxford Spanish Dictionary,* and Ediciones Larousse, publisher of *El Pequeno Larousse Ilustrado,* respectively, used the offensive terms *miserly, tight-fisted* and *usurer* to define *Jew.*

JEWESS.   *Jewess* is considered derogatory, largely for its sexist connotation. A woman who is Jewish is a Jew, not a *Jewess,* in the same way that a woman who is a Lutheran is not a Lutheraness and a Buddhist woman is not a Buddhistess.

JEWFISH.   A large grouper fish classified technically as *Epinephelus itajara* is more commonly known as the *jewfish.* The fish is not known for its aesthetic appeal, and many consider it particularly unattractive and the name offensive. *Merriam Webster's Dictionary* describes the fish as "usually dusky green, brown or blackish, thickheaded, and rough-scaled." A major U.S. aquarium that had such a fish on display recently relabeled the tank, *Epinephelus itajara.*

Old Testament and New Testament

In discussing biblical references and the Scriptures, many writers specify Old Testament or New Testament for the sake of accuracy. What they do not realize, however, is that such terminology reveals a pro-Christian bias. Judaism does not refer to the first books of the Bible as the *Old Testament,* for example, which connotes *worn, outdated,* or *primitive* and would imply recognition of an additional testament. In place of the name *New Testament,* Jews would generally refer to the *Christian Bible* instead.

Jewish Accents and Religious Accents

Jewish is not a language, dialect or region. Hebrew is the national language of Israel. Yiddish is a language spoken by Jews from central Europe, and Ladino is a language spoken by Jews who trace their roots to Spain and Portugal.

Because there is no language called *Jewish,* there is no Jewish accent. If a writer mentions a Jewish accent, the editor should ask the writer what accent is meant. Should it be a New York accent, for example? A

Brooklyn accent? Polish accent? German accent? Israeli accent?

There are no religious accents. There is no Catholic accent, Protestant accent or Muslim accent.

Reform Jews

Jewish synagogues and organizations that are affiliated with the Reform Movement of Judaism are called *Reform temples* (and groups), not *Reformed temples* (and groups).

Religious or Observant?

Orthodox Jews are commonly considered more religious than Reform Jews. But many Reform Jews find the term *religious* to be judgmental and offensive. They would say that they are just as religious—just as committed to their own beliefs—although less observant, meaning they do not believe in participating in all of the same rituals. *Observant* is considered a more objective term to describe the difference between the Orthodox and Reform Jews.

Zionism

The AP stylebook defines *Zionism* as "The effort of the Jews to regain and retain their biblical homeland." The term is traced to Mount Zion, location of the ancient temple in Jerusalem. UPI describes it as "The movement ... supporting the biblical homeland, Israel, as the Jewish national state."

Editors should be wary of definitions that stray significantly from *"preservation of a Jewish homeland,"* as a definition, particularly when the altered definition is used to promote anti-Semitic bias. In the past, some non-Jewish organizations have redefined Zionism in a strategy to gain permission to distribute anti-Semitic literature on college campuses. Such groups contend that they are not anti-Jewish or anti-Semitic, only anti-Zionist (as defined by them).

■ Sikhism

The Sikh religion is a monotheistic faith based on the scripture called Sri Guru Granth Sahib. The *sangat* (congregation) worships in temples called *gurdwaras* ("door or home of the Guru"), where two services are held daily. In the gurdwaras, the use of chairs is not permitted. Non-

Sikhs entering a Sikh temple must cover their heads with a *capor* (handkerchief).

There is no priesthood, but a *Granthi* or *Sewadar* (caretaker) may be employed by the sangat to read the scripture, perform ceremonies or help in the free kitchen. The gurdwara is managed by a committee, elected by the sangat annually.

■ Religious Fundamentalists

Because the journalism media so often equate religiousness with violence, journalism students who are asked to define *religious fundamentalist,* often describe a terrorist or militant instead of referring to a person who follows the back-to-basics fundamentals of any particular religion.

In journalism, *fundamentalist* has incorrectly become a buzzword for *lunatic* or *violent fanatic.* Newspapers commonly use the phrases *Muslim fundamentalist, Jewish fundamentalist* or *Christian fundamentalist* to connote *terrorist.*

Fundamentalist is not a synonym for terrorist and should not be used that way. A fundamentalist is a religious person who believes in the fundamentals and original texts of a religion, sometimes interpreting them literally. Most people who are committed followers of fundamentalist teachings do not commit violence. In many cases, fundamentalists are committed pacifists, opposed to violence because it violates their religious beliefs. When the terms *fundamentalist* and *terrorist* are used interchangeably, the reader is asked to swallow the anti-religious bias.

Writers should avoid labeling people *fundamentalists.* The exception, however, is if a religious group uses the term to describe itself.

■ Extremists

Otherwise objective journalists often seem comfortable labeling people as *Muslim extremists, Jewish extremists, Buddhist extremists* and *Christian extremists.* These terms should be avoided for the same reason that *religious fundamentalist* should be avoided: They imply a bias against religion. The implied message is that religion is good to a certain point, but if one becomes too religious or extremely committed to one's own beliefs, terrorism is the automatic outcome.

Editors should be careful with articles that label people *extremists,* even when violence is committed in the name of a religion, particularly if the religion as a whole does not endorse violence as an acceptable approach. If an individual resorts to violence, *militant* or even *terrorist* may be a more appropriate label. *Extremist* obviously implies that a person goes to extremes. What is an extreme in one reporter's eyes, may not be an extreme in another person's eyes, particularly when it comes to religion.

Be particularly wary of writing that labels people as *religious extremists.* Many religions and religious groups do not allow for partial or supposedly moderate belief, with the philosophy that either you believe or you do not. This should not be interpreted to mean that all followers of such religions are *extremists,* even if they view themselves as extremely devout. Most religions advocate peace. (Refer to the Extremists section in chapter 1, Political Bias.)

If the pope is extremely devout and religious, does this make him a religious *extremist* or a Catholic *extremist*? Obviously, no, according to most publications. Editors need to understand what constitutes *extreme.* The word should not be used as a euphemism for *terrorist* or *militant.*

■ Guilt by Association

An article in a respected newspaper pointed out that the subject of the article, a murder suspect, was a member of the same Harlem mosque as a well-known terrorist. A good editor should have caught the error. It seems obvious that being a member of the same mosque, church, temple, synagogue or meeting house does not make one a criminal. Often, in larger institutions, the people who attend regularly do not even know each other. Being a member of the same institution does not mean that the people mentioned are in any way collaborating. How many people could say with certainty that their own religious institution, should they belong to one, is free of criminals or people with previous criminal records?

This reference should be eliminated, unless the writer is able to establish a more specific relationship between the two people. There are exceptions. If, for example, the religious institution were known to be a front for a bomb factory or something similar, the reporter would be justified in mentioning the link. In such a case, however, good journalism would require that the reporter do more research to establish this fact, and then add that background information to the story.

■ Persuasion

Referring to people as members of a religious persuasion, may seem correct, in that the reference implies that the people have been persuaded or convinced to change their religion or religious philosophy. Often, *persuasion* is used euphemistically in reference to people who belong to cult groups or minority religions. Although the intention may be politeness, the usage is generally considered patronizing. Instead of writing that the person is of the *Buddhist persuasion,* write that the person is *a Buddhist,* assuming that the religious angle is relevant to the story. Likewise, instead of *Catholic persuasion* or *Jewish persuasion,* write that the person is *a Catholic* or *a Jew* or is *Catholic* or *Jewish.*

■ Religion and Politics

Occasionally religious groups stick political labels on other religious groups, particularly those that they oppose on controversial issues (church and state, homosexuality, etc.). Editors should be cautious about writing that adopts this language. Just as pigeonholing is bad practice in writing political stories, such labeling should be avoided in religion stories. Political labels may seem convenient to the writer, but they tend to promote generalizations, reveal writer bias and do the readers a disservice.

Liberal Religious Groups

Religion writers sometimes describe some congregations as *liberal* churches or *liberal* temples. These are not terms that are always acceptable. In fact, some groups find the label offensive and do not feel that their interpretation of their religion is liberal at all. They would argue that their interpretation is correct, and it is the other groups (the name callers) that are backward, perhaps, or out of touch. As a rule, editors should eliminate this usage, unless the religious organization labels itself *liberal* or includes the word *liberal* in its name.

The Religious Right

Editors should be wary of writing that labels advocates of religious causes *the religious right.* Instead each individual, group and cause should be afforded enough respect to be examined separately. Some groups find the label offensive and do not feel that their interpretation of their religion is rightist at all. They might prefer to describe themselves as conservative, moderate or traditional. Or they might argue that their interpretation is correct, and it is the other groups (the name callers) that are hypocrites, materialists, *leftists* or not committed. As a rule, editors should eliminate this usage, unless the religious organization identifies itself as part of the so-called *religious right,* or includes the reference to *religious right* in its name.

■ Capitalization

Most publications have specific styles on capitalization of religious references. The *G* in God is generally capitalized, for example. The Associated Press and United Press International also specify that the proper names of all monotheistic deities should be capitalized. Capitalized names include *Allah, Jehovah,* the *Father,* the *Son, Jesus Christ,* the *Son of God,* the *Redeemer* and the *Holy Spirit.* Both stylebooks lowercase the words that are derived from God and related pronouns. (Examples include *he, him, godfather, thee* and *god-given.*) Both stylebooks lowercase plural references to the gods or goddesses in polytheistic religions, but capitalize the first letter for names of individual gods and goddesses. (Examples include *Venus, Neptune, Janus.*)

Bible begins with a capital *B,* and Scripture and Scriptures begin with a capital *S.* Use lowercase *h* for heaven.

Writers should note that stylebooks do not leave capitalization to writers' discretion, depending upon individual religious affiliations and bias. At any publication, writers should check capitalization policy in the appropriate stylebook.

■ Mythical Gods and Superstitions

Writers should be careful about labeling others' deities *mythical,* particularly if there is any chance that any of the readers worship these deities. Calling others' deities *mythical* reveals an obvious religious bias.

Editors should also be wary of writing that labels other people's beliefs as *superstitions,* particularly religious beliefs that do not coincide with the dogma of "mainstream religion." Using the word *superstition* reveals a bias against the person's beliefs and is equivalent of labeling someone's convictions primitive, ignorant, or simple-minded.

Rituals

An article in a major New York daily newspaper described Santeria as "the religion that combines African rituals with elements of Catholicism." Looking at this description, the reader could guess that the writer was not African or a follower of Santeria.

Although there is nothing wrong with the word *ritual,* and although most religions have rituals, writers should be careful about how the word is used. When the word appears up front in the definition of a religion, especially a lesser-known religion, the image may be one of primitiveness, a ritualistic group, or a backward group. Few religious groups would feel comfortable about being defined by their rituals. Most would prefer to be defined by their beliefs, their following (population), their mission and their geography. By focusing first on rituals, the writer reveals an obvious bias, separating him- or herself from the religion. Before attempting to define any religious group, imagine describing one of the major religions in one sentence, and apply similar language.

Cults and Cult Groups

A *cult* is loosely defined as a religious group, and as such may sound like an objective usage. But the term has a pejorative connotation that means unapproved religion, unorthodox religion, fringe group, or fake religion. Editors should be wary of writing that definitively pronounces any religious group a *cult,* even if the group is not considered to be part of the so-called mainstream of a major religion by leading members of the larger religion. *Cult* may be perceived as an insult or slur, and editors should not judge which groups are cults and which groups are "respectable."

Cult may be used in quoted material, however, if the word appears within a quotation (or paraphrased), the quotation is attributed and the writer explains the context of the usage. If a religion authority or religious leader, for example, labels a particular religious group a *cult,* the writer may quote this information, attributing the charge to the authority or leader.

■ B.C. and A.D.

Calendar years are generally described as either *B.C. (before Christ)* or *A.D. (anno Domini*: in the year of *the Lord*) in the major stylebooks. If no designation appears after the year, it is presumed to be *A.D.* Obviously, these abbreviations are both Christian designations. Many religious groups that do not believe that Jesus Christ is synonymous with *the Lord* would say that the A.D. designation is biased and prefer to use C.E. (common era) instead of A.D., and B.C.E. (before the common era) instead of B.C.

■ Pejorative Abbreviations

Abbreviations and acronyms sometimes seem like convenient ways to communicate images, particularly in headlines where space is very limited and editors are faced with the task of trying to cram in information. Editors should be wary of abbreviations that attempt to sum up or define religions or those associated with religions based on acronyms that stereotype.

WASPs

The acronym stands for White Anglo-Saxon Protestant but tends to be used pejoratively, sometimes implying blame for discrimination or inequality. As an acronym, it promotes inappropriate bias and stereotyping. This usage should be avoided. If religion is vital to a description of a person, specify which religion or denomination applies. If skin color is pertinent, specify skin color. If the ethnic element is the important factor, specify ethnicity. It is rare that all three elements pertain to the same story. If none are vital, do not specify the person's racial, ethnic or religious roots.

Within a quotation, WASP may be used if the quotation is vital to the story. The writer should only use the word within quotation marks, however, attributing the sentence and explaining the context.

JAPs and CAPs and B.A.P.S.

JAP, with uppercase letters, refers to "Jewish-American Princess." *CAP* refers to Catholic-American Princess. And "B.A.P.S." was the title of a 1997 movie about "Black-American Princesses." All three designations are derogatory and biased, and should not be used by journalists. The implication is that young Jewish, Catholic and black women are demanding, materialistic, lazy, valueless and perhaps "clueless." The terms are ethnically offensive, two are religiously offensive and all three are sexist.

If the usage is deemed essential to the story within quoted material (including the name of the film, in a review of the film, for example), the words may be used with attribution and an explanation of context.

7

Age Bias

■ Age Bias Examples

The following are examples of different forms of age bias that commonly appear in publications or on broadcasts. Examine the sentences, and then determine how they should best be rewritten to eliminate age bias.

The elderly woman appeared very energetic for a 55-year-old senior citizen.

The boy, age 14, responded to the emergency very responsibly, and not like a typical teenager.

The girls played bridge together, while their husbands went bowling for a boys' night out.

An adult video store that opened in the residential district caused an uproar by local homeowners.

The new film at the festival was recommended for mature audiences only.

■ Overview

A student was describing a particular TV commercial to the class. "You know the commercial," she said. "It's the one with the old lady." The other students, all younger than 24, seemed to know the so-called old lady. The professor did not know the commercial. Finally, flustered, the student said, "You know the one with the woman in her mid-forties or something."

Age is relative. What is old to some people is young to others. So-called generation gaps are not new to contemporary generations.

Socrates worried about the next generation. So did Shakespeare. Throughout time, older people have complained that "the young people of today" compare unfavorably to those of previous generations. And as older people complained, some of the young people argued that older people just do not seem to understand them or their values.

Our legal system considers age in evaluating crimes, and our society uses age to assign privileges. There is a drinking age, a voting age, an age when one is eligible to drive or to serve in the military, an age when one may be tried as an adult depending upon the crime committed, and an age when one may legally cease to be a dependent. In some institutions, there are legal retirement ages and minimum ages for employment. There are age requirements for certain medical insurance benefits. And for a variety of ages, companies offer incentive discounts to promote their products: children's tickets at the movie theater, senior discounts, children's train fares, etc.

Although age plays a significant role in society, incorporating age bias in writing is not acceptable style in objective journalism.

■ Youth Culture

Many social scientists contend that our contemporary society is based largely on a so-called *youth culture*. Advertisements show clear biases toward looking younger, feeling younger and even acting younger. Youth is equated with goodness or the most desirable state of being. Editors need to be cautious that writers are not automatically parroting this idolizing and idealizing of youth in their work.

Illustrations and photographs accompanying articles, for example, should not be limited to depictions of young people. Youth should not be portrayed as the norm and aging as the aberration. Nor should middle age be excluded in illustrations and photographs. In the same way, writers should strive to include a variety of age groups in copy.

Specifying Age

Many publications dictate in their style that age should not be mentioned in the headline, news lead or feature "nut graph" unless age is a major element of the piece. At such publications, reporters need to ask themselves how vital the age element is to the story.

Following are some examples of articles where age is a major element:

A 10-year-old scores a 1600 on the SATs.

A 98-year-old wins the New York Marathon.

A 3-year-old rescues a friend by dialing 911.

A 17-year-old gets computer access to top-secret government information.

A 70-year-old gives birth to triplets.

A 50-year-old ballet dancer makes a debut with a major company.

A 13-year-old flies a plane to Europe.

A 22-year-old wins the state lottery and retires from working.

A woman in Siberia is found to be 128 years old.

A 34-year-old is elected president of an organization whose next youngest leader was 64 years old.

Although age is not to be specified in the lead of most articles, there is no reason to avoid mentioning age in the continuing paragraphs of these articles if age pertains. The style on inclusion of age varies slightly from one publication to another.

Typical examples of the styles are:

John Smith, 48, was convicted yesterday.

John Smith, age 48, was convicted yesterday.

Forty-eight-year-old John Smith was convicted yesterday. (Some publications prefer that writers avoid putting ages before names of people.)

When writers insert the word *age* (as in example 2), editors should make sure that the word is *age* and not *aged*. It is incorrect to write, "John Smith, *aged* 48, was convicted yesterday."

A major exception: In obituaries, most publications require mention of age in both the headline and the lead. Readers look for the age immediately in obituaries.

■ Old People

What is old often depends on the age of the writer. If the writer is a 4-year-old, a 25-year-old nursery school teacher may seem just as old as the 16-year-old high school intern who is volunteering part time at the nursery school and the 60-year-old director of the program. They are all adults to this child and are all therefore old.

Writers should be very careful about labeling people *old*, lest they give away their own age and bias. Better practice is to specify the age of the subject, if age is pertinent to the article, rather than merely describing someone as *young* or *old.*

Stereotyping Old People

Editors should be alert to stereotypes that are age-related. Writers should not assume, for example, that because a person is old, the person is also lonely, sad, bored, immobile, unproductive, forgetful, ill or old-fashioned. Many older people lead very successful, happy, active lives.

Writers also should not assume that all elderly people wear thick glasses, walk with canes, wear hearing aids, or require wheelchairs, or that any of these devices are bad. All of these tools encourage independence for those who use them.

When writing an article about an old person who is a pioneer or innovator, and who is leading an active life, writers should not respond with a "gee-whiz attitude."

OLD WIVES' TALES.   Do not use the expression *old wives' tale* as a substitute for the term *superstition.* Inaccuracies and misinformation should not be blamed gratuitously on old married women. The usage is gender-biased, family-biased and age-biased. Instead, describe the so-called tale as a *superstition, rumor, irrational outcome* or *a superstitious story,* depending upon the reference, meaning and context.

What Is Elderly?

College students have suggested that age 55 is elderly. A 75-year-old suggested that 90 constitutes *elderly.* A 100-year-old said that he considered himself elderly. *Old* and *elderly* are not necessarily the same. *Elderly* implies weakening or frailty along with aging. Thus, there is no specific age at which one becomes elderly. An athletic 75-year-old, who plays golf and tennis regularly, should not be described as elderly.

Instead of labeling someone *elderly,* it is generally better to cite specific disabilities if this pertains to the subject of the article. If such disabilities or age do not pertain to the article, omit gratuitous references to age.

The Associated Press Stylebook warns writers to "use this word carefully and sparingly." The term is more acceptable, according to AP, "in generic phrases that do not refer to specific individuals: *concern for the elderly, a home for the elderly,* etc."

Other stylebooks find the term more acceptable, and apply it to younger people. Whereas the *Broadcast News Writing Stylebook*, for example, suggests caution in using the word because it "may be viewed as negative or simply inappropriate," the book advises writers to "use only in relation to people 65 years of age and older—and even then, carefully."

Senior Citizens

Is it more polite to call an older person a *senior citizen*? Many publications frown on this usage, contending that *senior citizen* is a euphemism for *old* and that there is nothing wrong with being old. As a rule, if the age of the person described is known, and if this age is relevant to the piece, it is better to specify an age than to label the person *old, elderly* or a *senior citizen*.

Some publications prefer *senior* to *senior citizen*. Other publications would argue that this is still a euphemism and only confuses the readers. When shortened to *senior,* the term is sometimes confused with high school or college students within an article. (Example: *Jane Jones, a senior, enjoyed computer classes.*)

Never specify *senior, senior citizen* or *Senior Citizen* before a person's name, implying that it is a title. (Example: *Senior Citizen Jane Jones enjoyed computer classes.*) *The Associated Press Stylebook* advises writers to "use the term sparingly." The *New York Times Manual of Style and Usage* suggests that writers "avoid the term whenever possible."

There are times, however, when most publications would permit references to *senior citizens* or *seniors.* If the usage appears within the name of an organization (Example: *Senior Citizens* for a Clean Environment), it is acceptable. Also, when it is part of a civic or corporate program that uses the word *senior* (Example: *Senior* discount, *senior* fare, *senior* tours, *senior* center).

Retirees

Do not assume that all older people are retired, and do not assume that all retired people are old. Do not use the term *retiree* as a euphemism for *old* or as a hint to inform the reader that the person in the article is old. Also *retiree* should not be used on first reference as a means of defining the article subject. When retirement pertains to the piece, mention it after the second reference. (Example: *Jones, who retired from a career in a textile factory.*)

When discussing retirement or retirees, the writer must mention from where the person retired. What sort of work did the person do? Where did the person do it? Without this information, *retiree* becomes a flippant and meaningless label. Do not write, "The retired man went to the park," because the implication is that the retiree is no longer a man, or retired from manhood. It is better to write "The *retiree* went to the park," or better yet, "The *retired swim instructor* went to the park."

Golden-Agers and 70 Years Young

Avoid patronizing euphemisms for old people. The *Media Writer's Handbook* recommends that writers avoid both terms entirely.

Mature

Writers occasionally use the word *mature* as a euphemism for *old*. Most publications prefer the word *old*, since *mature* has a different meaning and is not necessarily synonymous with *old*. Also, when *mature* is used as a euphemism, it has a patronizing connotation.

Widows, Widowers and Dowagers

Despite possible associations with black widow spiders or "The Merry Widow," there is nothing wrong with using the terms *widow* and *widower* in reference to a person whose spouse has died. But these labels should only be applied to individuals whose marital status or widowhood is relevant to the piece. The reporter should not flippantly or gratuitously label someone a widow or widower if it bears no relevance to the story.

In any case, the term should not appear on first reference to a person as the defining feature of that individual (as in *widow Jane Jones*). If the widowhood pertains to the piece, it may be mentioned on second reference after the person's name, by inserting: "who became widowed in 1995," "who has been widowed for five years" or "who is a widow."

Widow refers to a woman whose husband has died. *Widower* refers to a man whose wife has died.

Unlike *widow* and *widower*, the word *dowager* may be distasteful. Not only does it categorize a person by marital status, but it also hints at both economic and sex bias. *Dowager* means a woman who holds wealth as a result of her husband's death. While some definitions say the term connotes stately dignity, others say it implies stuffiness, pretentiousness, and even greed or parasitism. Because it emphasizes a person's financial assets, it is probably tasteless in most contexts. Avoid this term.

Words to Avoid

Codger should be avoided. Although few writers will call an elderly person an *old codger,* the person might refer to him- or herself that way in a humorous but self-deprecating way. This is not license for the reporter to quote the term or label the person as such. Do not use *codger,* even in quotations. If the quotation seems pertinent to the piece, rephrase it removing the quotation marks and removing the word *codger,* and attribute it.

Old maid refers to an older woman who never married. Use it in reference to the card game only (capitalize the *O* and the *M*), and not as a label for an unmarried woman.

Other derogatory words to avoid merit less discussion. Do not use the labels *marm, old school marm* (in reference to older female teachers), *fuddy-duddy, gray, dentured, fussbudget, stodgy, stale, over-the-hill, decrepit, feeble, confined to a nursing home, crotchety* or *wrinkled.*

Frail may be used in describing a person who has become weak, but the term should not be applied as a label before a name (as in *frail* John Jones) and should be avoided on first reference. If the term is vital to the subject of the piece, it may be used following the second reference, using the following kinds of phrases: "who is *frail,*" "who recently became *frail* as a result of an injury," or "who was able to compensate for his *frailty* by taking vitamins."

■ Young People

Just as there are many negative stereotypes about older people, many biases exist against youth as well. To say, for example, that a child acts young for his or her age is an insult. (To say that someone looks young for his or her age is a compliment, however.) *Childlike behavior* tends to be equated with *bad behavior,* as does *teenage behavior* (or behaving like a *typical teenager*). *Mature behavior* equals *good behavior.*

Objective writers should be conscious of their own usage, and should not presume that young people behave badly or even that there is some collective behavior that can be called *childlike behavior.*

Boys, Girls and Youths

Boys and *girls* become *men* and *women* at age 18, according to most popularly accepted journalism styles. Some publications, however, prefer to make the distinction at ages as young as 13. Others feel more comfortable with 21 as the age that establishes adulthood.

Both *The Associated Press Stylebook* and the *United Press International Stylebook* specify that *boy* is "applicable until 18th birthday is reached. Use *man* or *young man* afterward." For *girl,* the same applies. After the 18th birthday, "use *woman* or *young woman.*"

Many writers feel uncomfortable referring to 18-year-olds as men and women. They attempt to hedge by calling 18- and 19-year-old men *youths* (rarely applying the term *youths* for young women), particularly in crime stories. (Example: *An 18-year-old youth was arrested yesterday in a car theft.*) This is incorrect usage at most publications. *The Associated Press Stylebook* says *youth* is "applicable to boys and girls from age 13 until 18th birthday," and again emphasizes that writers should "use *man* or *woman* for individuals 18 and older." The *UPI Stylebook* states the same policy.

Teens, Teenage and Teenagers

Some writers who feel uncomfortable referring to 18- and 19-year-olds as *men* and *women* attempt to hedge by calling them *teenagers* instead. This violates United Press International style, which dictates that *teenager* is restricted "to those 13 through 17 years old." Thus, an 18-year-old is not a *teenager,* according to UPI. This same age restriction is not necessarily the most commonly accepted style. Other stylebooks permit writers to refer to 18- and 19-year-olds as *teenagers.*

UPI specifies that the word is *teen, teenager* or *teenage,* but not *teenaged. The New York Times Manual of Style and Usage* and *The Associated Press Stylebook* hyphenate *teen-age* as an adjective and *teen-ager* as a noun, but also specify that *teen-aged* should not be used. *The Times* says that there is an exception: *Teen-aged* may be used "in quoted matter." According to *The Times* style, *teen* should not be used "by itself." *The Times* says, "*Teens* may be used in reference to a span of ages (*sons in their teens*), but not to the young people concerned, even in headlines." *Teen* is acceptable usage, however, according to the Associated Press and United Press International.

Some publications discourage use of the word *teenagers* as a noun, with the argument that it always is accompanied by negative generalizations.

TYPICAL TEENAGERS.   There is no such thing as a *typical teenager.* The common stereotype of American teenagers is that they are different from other people. According to popular myth, they are as a group less considerate, more materialistic, more self-absorbed, more self-conscious, more obsessed with fitting in, and more likely to act irresponsibly. Adults patronizingly speak of hormone imbalance, growing pains, and feeling one's oats. Intelligent writers need to recognize that just as all adults are different, so are teenagers. Writers should not stereotype teenagers on the basis of their age.

There is no ban on the word *teenager* in most publications, but the label has many negative connotations. Instead of labeling a young person as a *teenager,* it is better to specify the age if it is relevant to the story.

The most common journalistic stereotyping of teenagers appears in trends pieces. As eager to spot an emerging trend as political writers are eager to call an election, feature journalists declare that a new fashion is "typical of teenagers," or somehow endorsed by "typical teenagers." Such stereotyping only promotes lack of communication and the myth that teenagers are of some other species. This notion is fueled by parents who are occasionally quoted in articles as blaming their children's poor behavior on "typical teenage stages," or "overwhelming teenage peer pressure." Writers should be careful to avoid being goaded into stereotyping teenagers based on the complaints of parents who feel ineffective with their children.

Writers who are covering teenage trends tend to be outsiders. (Occasionally, an article is written by a teenager.) When these older writers are biased, teenage readers resent the coverage. When a writer makes a generalization about all *teenagers,* those who do not fit the trend are often alienated from the publication.

As a general rule, it is preferable to discuss a trend or fashion as popular among *many teenagers,* rather than among *all teenagers.* Writers should then try to pinpoint the group among which the particular trend is popular, rather than declaring the fashion universally accepted among teenagers.

Some sample groups include the following:

Cheerleaders at a particular high school
High school students who swim competitively
Top-achieving students in Iowa
Teenagers who spend their weekends at shopping malls
Prep school crew teams in New England
Student government leaders at large-city public schools
The drug crowd at a rural high school
The student activists who work at soup kitchens
Teenagers who perform professionally
Teenagers who work in their family businesses on weekends

Stages and Fads

The word *stage* is often applied in a demeaning or condescending way in reference to children and teenagers. When adult writers attribute what they perceive to be unusual behavior to a *stage* or *fad,* they imply that the young person is behaving automatically without thought, as if programmed for such behavior. Both *stage* and *fad* are heavily biased words that are used as a power play to demonstrate superiority. Instead of crediting the younger person for an action, the adult is implying that the action is a temporary involuntary indiscretion. Attributing a person's actions to a *stage* is a put-down, and the equivalent of calling a young person *primitive, naïve,* or *conformist.* Writers should avoid the usage. Instead of *fad,* use *trend, fashion* or *style.*

Younger Children

When it comes to writing about children, many biases are often revealed. Children are rarely looked upon as equals. For starters, most major stylebooks specify that children should be referred to by their first names on second reference, like dogs and other pets, whereas adults are generally called by their last names, sometimes with a title.

Editors should be careful about writing that incorporates bias freely in articles about children. Among the derogatory labels that should be avoided are *orphan, bastard, illegitimate child, wild child, little terror, truant,* and *runaway,* as well as milder sounding psychology labels: *juveniles* or *adolescents.*

Juvenile connotes both *juvenile delinquent* and *immature child.* And *adolescent* connotes a young person who is troubled or struggling with issues of growing up.

Instead of relying on labels to generalize about young people, the writer should describe the specific person in the story (just as the writer would do in a piece about an adult).

Adults will sometimes comment that a child is "smart beyond his or her years," or very "precocious." Writers quoting such comments should make sure that the assumption is not that children are all ignorant, thus making this child "smart beyond his or her years." If that is the assumption, it is better to omit the quotation.

■ Adulthood

Adulthood is commonly presented in publications as a privileged time when license is suddenly granted for behavior that is viewed as less desirable. Adulthood means permission to drink alcohol, for example, or to smoke cigarettes, stay out late or have sex.

To call any behavior *adult,* reveals much about the writer's own biases and values. Editors should note that when *adult* is used as an adjective, it is a subjective, editorializing term.

Adult Fiction

Adult fiction and *adult entertainment* are generally used as euphemisms for *pornographic fiction and pornographic entertainment.* Although stores that sell pornography may find this language more tasteful, appealing, or acceptable within a residential community, journalists should avoid euphemistic language. When writing about institutions or products that are labeled *adult,* the writer should ask the reason for the *adult* designation. If *adult* is used as a euphemism for *pornographic,* write *pornographic* instead of *adult.* If *adult* is used as a euphemism for *violent,* say *violent* instead of *adult.* If *adult* is used as a euphemism for *pornographic and violent,* the writer should specify *pornographic and violent* instead of labeling the work *adult.*

Labeling a film or book *adult* fiction promotes a so-called positive bias. (Refer to chapter 13, Appeals to "Positive Bias.") It promotes an allure or mystique about the product for young people, suggesting that such a product represents a rite of passage. And thus it helps to lend credence to or endorse the product.

Mature Audiences

Many films and books are supposedly targeted for *mature audiences.* *Mature* is often used interchangeably with *adult,* as a euphemism to suggest pornographic or violent content. The implication is that those who do not enjoy such fiction are somehow immature. Such a euphemism only promotes intrigue on the part of the young people excluded from books and films targeted at mature audiences only. The young people are constantly reminded by society that behaving in a mature way is good, and they equate maturity with good behavior. Thus, qualifying to be part of a mature audience is presented as if it were a milestone or positive achievement.

Do not substitute the euphemism *mature* for *adult.* If a particular movie or show is recommended for mature audiences only, find out specifically why this limit is specified and explain this to the readers. Be more explicit than the film publicists or book promoters. Instead of using the word *mature,* specify if the designation was assigned as a result of pornography, violence or foul language, or a combination of factors. (Example: *This film contains a significant amount of violent language and may be unsuitable for some audiences.*)

8

Bias Based on Appearances and Disabilities

■ Examples of Bias Based on Appearance

The following are examples of different forms of bias that commonly appear in publications or on broadcasts. Examine the sentences, and then determine how they should best be rewritten to eliminate bias.

Helen Keller was both visually challenged and hearing impaired, but she managed to live a normal life.

The professor, who was wheelchair bound, was suffering from paralysis.

In hiring an au pair, the couple sought to make sure the foreigner would be well-groomed.

At hotels, many standard-size counters, bathroom fixtures and furnishings discriminate against midgets.

The grammar teacher from an inner-city neighborhood kept saying "axed" and "exetera."

■ Overview

Aside from identical twins, triplets, quadruplets, quintuplets, sextuplets, septuplets and octuplets, people all look different. Writers sometimes reveal bias by implying that most people look generally the same, whereas a small minority of people comprises the different-looking ones, the outsiders, or freaks.

As a rule, writers should not include descriptions of individuals' more unusual features, unless those features pertain to the topic of the article. If the article is about a missing person or one who is sought by police, for example, a description is not only helpful but essential. By reading this description, more readers become empowered to help find the missing person. Likewise, if the article is about how a person succeeds despite some visible physical limitation, the writer is justified in describing that limitation. And if the article is about fashion or appearances, obviously description may be an important element to the piece. If, however, the piece is a more typical political story, business piece or human interest story, a description of the people involved may not be appropriate.

Some editors will argue that description is always relevant, that description provides more "flavor" for an article, and that this "flavor" is part of a humanizing element that makes news relevant and interesting. Many stylebooks, however, oppose this view, arguing that unless the description helps to tell the story or is a key aspect to some element of the story, the reporter's description should be minimized or even eliminated.

Are most news writers equipped to comment on appearances or fashion? Should writers describe the features they notice about a person? Should writers reveal an interview subject's blemishes and twitches? When blemishes and twitches are revealed, should the journalist be commended for astute observation or condemned for nitpicking and belittling people based on appearances?

In pleasing editors who demand "flavor" and description, writers should note that there are many ways to describe a person. Which adjectives the writer chooses and what features the writer notices reveal a lot about the biases of the writer.

A very overweight writer, for example, may be less likely to call an equally heavyset article subject *heavy* or *overweight* and may prefer to omit any reference to the person's weight. Likewise, a bald reporter is probably less likely to mention that an interview subject's hair is thin or thinning in an article.

Reporters who engage in extensive description should avoid placing value judgments in that description as much as possible. In other words, it may be acceptable to say that the witness wore a *dark brown suit,* but not an *ugly brown suit,* or a *drab brown suit* or a *flattering brown suit.*

■ Disabilities That Are Visible

Bias based on appearance is closely linked to bias based on disabilities, in that often a disability may alter one's appearance or cause one's behavior to seem unusual. Editors should be vigilant about monitoring descriptions of disabled people in articles. No description should be included unless the disability, impairment or handicap pertains to the story.

In a piece where the disability clearly is relevant, no person should be described as merely *disabled, impaired* or *handicapped* without an explanation of the nature of the *disability, impairment* or *handicap*. The more specific a writer can be, the more informative and useful the description becomes. In addition, an explanation should be included detailing exactly how restrictive this disability is and how it limits the person's work and living conditions.

Challenged

Challenged may seem like the politically correct word, but most of the major styles regard it as a euphemism to be avoided. Journalism prefers a direct approach, and using the word *challenged* spares nobody. Avoid writing *visually challenged*; write *visually impaired* or *blind* instead. Avoid writing *hearing challenged* when *deaf* is what is meant. Avoid *physically challenged* when *disabled* is what is meant. Avoid *mentally challenged* in all uses. Avoid the most obvious, patronizing euphemisms like *vertically challenged, horizontally challenged* and *follicly challenged* (bald).

Disabled or Handicapped?

In writing a piece about a person with a disability, a writer needs to understand which adjective to apply. Stylebooks offer differing perspectives. The Associated Press, for example, says writers should avoid the word *handicap,* when referring to a disability. In agreement with this policy are stylebooks that say *handicapped* tends to be used as a euphemism for *disabled,* and like all other euphemisms, it has no place in journalism.

Other reference books argue that the word *handicapped* is acceptable when used correctly, and it is not synonymous with *disabled.* According to these guides, people who have disabilities—conditions that potentially limit their activities—are disabled, but not necessarily *handicapped.* They say that the word *handicap* refers to the interaction of the disabled person and the environment. If the environment poses obstacles that act as barriers to a disabled individual, the person may then be described as *handicapped* by these barriers. If the person is disabled but is able to overcome the obstacles, the term *handicapped* generally is not used.

Individual Disabilities

Each different kind of disability is subject to different kinds of stereotyping and bias. When writing about people with specific disabilities, writers need to be informed about the nature of the disabilities and sensitized to acceptable language in describing the condition, if the disability pertains to the story.

BLINDNESS.   As with other disabilities, the fact that an interview subject is blind does not make blindness a major element of an article. As a rule, reporters should not mention a person's visual impairment within an article unless such a reference is vital to the piece. Nor should the writer hint at visual impairment by describing the clothing the person is wearing or dark glasses or a cane that the person totes.

The American Foundation for the Blind recommends relying on what is referred to as "the people-first rule." When referring to people who are blind or visually impaired in a piece where this disability pertains, do not mention the blindness on first reference. In a later reference, mention the person's name and add "who is blind."

The foundation emphasizes, "Blindness should not be the first and sole definer of the individual," just as other labels are inappropriate on first reference. It would not be acceptable, for example, to point out on first reference in today's society that the person is "Italian or Jewish or African American." In the same way, it is not acceptable to say the person is blind on first reference.

Like other interest groups, blind people can be the most lax about terminology regarding blindness. In quoting them for an article on blindness, the foundation recommends using the "insider rule." If a blind person makes a disparaging remark about blind people or blindness, do not quote the remark directly. Instead paraphrase the quotation outside of quotation marks, removing the disparaging reference. The principle is that a so-called insider has license to use language more loosely than a reporter, who is by definition always an outsider.

Avoid referring to blind people as *victims of blindness* or *suffering from blindness*. These expressions only help to promulgate a false image that blind people are helpless or pained. Many lead full, happy lives. Also, writers should not assume any single cause of blindness in the interview subject. Blindness has many causes and affects many different people in differing situations.

The Blind.   *Blind* should only be used as an adjective, not a noun or collective noun.

Among the most offensive expressions that writers use in referring to blind people is *"the blind,"* according to the American Foundation for the Blind. Writers should not refer to blind people collectively as *the blind,* and then proceed to generalize about them. (There are two exceptions: in mentioning names of organizations like the American Foundation for *the Blind,* and in carefully attributed quotations in which the context is explained.)

Images.   Blind people are often targets of humor in the media, largely because most Americans have never had contact with a person who is blind or has severe visual impairment, according to the American Foundation for the Blind. The organization estimates that there are 9.7 million Americans with severe vision impairment (unable to read, even with corrective lenses), about 2 million of whom are completely blind.

Among the common misconceptions that sighted people have are that blind people are not capable of understanding conversation, that in speaking to a blind person one must yell, speak very loudly, or have a third party translate.

Blind people are commonly depicted in cartoons as beggars, and many people assume they are unable to pursue higher education or find employment. The American Foundation for the Blind reports that contrary to popular images, there are many blind lawyers, accountants and advertising executives. They say, "Blindness in today's society should not be a barrier to achieving one's goals ... blind people are guaranteed an equal education." Advocates ask editors be alert to writing that stereotypes blind people.

Movie Images.   The American Foundation for the Blind says that many people's understanding of blindness is based on images that they see in the mass media. Movies often promote stereotypical images of blind people. "It keeps those stereotypes and myths alive," the foundation contends. According to foundation observations, blind women are portrayed as victims 95 percent of the time, "and blind men usually try to drive something [getaway cars, police cars, etc.] before the film is over." In films in which blind people are not portrayed as victims, they are generally depicted as comical.

Film critics and editors should be sensitive to the depiction of blindness in films, particularly in suspense movies and comedies. Advocacy groups would like to see more discussion in film reviews of the portrayal of blind people.

An Increasing Phenomenon.   Contrary to popular perception, blindness is not a condition that is decreasing in frequency. Instead it has been increasing steadily. Part of the increase is attributed to the aging of the American population and increased longevity. More people are experiencing macular degeneration, glaucoma and cataracts. Part of the increase is attributed to improved medicine, increasing the survival rate of babies born with an array of physical complications. Such complications sometimes include blindness and vision impairment.

The Associated Press style applies the word *blind* to total blindness only, not other visual impairment or low vision.

Expressions to Avoid.   In addition to being the brunt of jokes in the media, blindness is referred to flippantly in everyday usage. Writers should avoid casual but derogatory references including: *blind as a bat, blind to the truth, blind date* and *turning a blind eye* (or *deaf ear*). Do not quote people asking glibly, *Are you blind or something?*

DEAFNESS.   The subject of deafness may seem relevant to a reporter who would like to interview a person who is deaf, but the reporter should not then presume that deafness automatically is pertinent to the article. As a rule, do not mention a person's hearing impairment within an article unless such a reference is vital to the piece. Likewise, do not hint at a hearing disability or deafness by describing a deaf person's speech patterns or impediments in an article, unless this impairment is vital to the piece.

The major stylebooks define *deaf* as total hearing loss. The National Association of the Deaf definition is more inclusive, however, embracing those who are severely hard of hearing as well. The organization refers to people with total hearing loss as *profoundly deaf,* as opposed to *deaf.* Based on 1990 statistics, the National Association of the Deaf estimates that 2 million Americans are profoundly deaf, 26 million are either deaf or hard of hearing, and about one out of every 1,000 American infants is born profoundly deaf.

Writers should not generalize about deaf people and refer to them as *the deaf.* Deaf people should not be presumed to be less educated, less articulate, less attractive, less concerned, or less aware. Nor should writers presume that deaf people are unable to communicate. Some speak and lip-read, some use sign language, and some write notes, use computers or other communication devices.

Deaf-Mute and Deaf and Dumb.   The National Association of the Deaf says that the expressions *deaf-mute* and *deaf and dumb* should not be used. The Associated Press stylebook suggests that both expressions should be avoided, and *The New York Times* agrees, stating that both phrases "have cruel overtones." UPI also advises against using *deaf and dumb* but accepts *deaf-mute.* UPI specifies, however, that the preferred expression is *cannot hear or speak.*

Hearing Impaired.   The National Association of the Deaf does not use the expression *hearing impaired,* preferring the word *deaf.* The explanation given is that *"Hearing impaired* may sound politically correct, but *deaf* is *deaf."*

Hearing Loss.   In writing that a person experienced a hearing loss, writers should make sure that the person discussed once was able to hear. People who are born deaf should not be described as having a hearing loss.

Suffering from Deafness.   Writers should not say that a person is *suffering from deafness* or *suffers from deafness,* unless the person is indeed suffering. Absence of hearing may not be viewed as desirable, yet deaf people should not be portrayed as suffering, particularly if they are able to lead happy lives. Instead of the expression *suffers from deafness,* write *is deaf, has lost hearing, cannot hear* or *is unable to hear.*

Dyslexic

Dyslexia, an impairment that affects one's ability to read, does not make one stupid or illiterate. Many of the world's top thinkers and scholars have been dyslexic. In recent years, some historians have speculated that the great scientist and artist Leonardo da Vinci might have been dyslexic. Writers should not assume that people with dyslexia are unable to speak clearly, think clearly or write clearly.

Speech Impediments

When an interview subject has a speech impediment, the writer does not have license to draw attention to the condition. Whether it is *an inability to pronounce certain sounds, a lisp, stutter* or other obstruction of speech, do not quote the speech impediment in the article. The impediment should only be mentioned if it pertains to the story.

If it hinders the person's ability to communicate with the writer, but does not pertain to the story, the speech impediment should not be mentioned in the copy. If the impediment is so severe that the interviewer is unable to interpret what is said, the interviewer should either get a translator, have the speaker respond to questions in writing or on computer, or abandon the interview. The writer should not suggest that the speaker was not available or unwilling to communicate, however. And the writer should not transliterate the speech pattern, in any case. Such transliteration only comes across as ridicule, when appearing in print.

If the writer would like to quote the person (excluding the speech impediment) whose speech impediment is so severe that it becomes impossible to directly quote the speaker without significantly altering the quotation, paraphrasing should be used. Quotation marks should be removed, but the statement should be attributed. If the writer feels that he or she does not understand any portion of what the speaker is saying or has said, the writer should confirm (read back) any indirect quotations as well as direct quotations with the speaker.

MISPRONOUNCED WORDS.   When words or even common expressions are mispronounced, the writer should fix the mispronounced word within a quotation. If the writer is not sure what word was meant, the writer should ask the person being quoted what word was meant. If the person quoted is inaccessible or is no longer available, the writer should probably remove the quotation marks and paraphrase what the speaker was saying to the best of the writer's understanding of what was meant. If the speaker is inaccessible and the writer is no longer available, the editor should probably do the same. (See the discussion of Accents in chapter 4, Nationality Bias.)

If we were to transliterate every mispronounced word, our publications would be filled with insulting transliterations, because there are many words that are difficult to say in English. Few Americans can pronounce the word *asterisk,* for example. This is not license, however, for writers to make fun of people struggling to pronounce the word by transliterating an individual's clumsy pronunciation. In phone messages, it has become common to cleverly substitute the word *star key* so that nobody need pronounce the word.

Within a quotation, if the word *asterisk* or an equivalent word appears, it should be spelled correctly. Do not write *axkerix* or *axterix* or *asterix*, the three most common mispronunciations. Likewise, *et cetera*, seems to be difficult for a large number of English speakers. Do not transliterate with *exetera* within a quotation.

Writers who try to provide so-called "flavor" by transliterating will find that the speakers being transliterated may object to the transliteration. Many will argue that they "never said it like that" or that the writer is deliberately making them "look bad" as a result of a bias. Often, the speaker's argument is valid, in that a writer may be unfamiliar with the particular speech pattern and may not hear all of the letters being pronounced. Someone more accustomed to the particular speech pattern may know what to listen for, and would therefore hear all of the letters. As a rule, mispronunciation is never a good excuse for misspelling within a quotation.

Words pronounced incorrectly by a speaker are sometimes transcribed incorrectly by a reporter not intending to transliterate or draw attention to the subject's speech. When an editor sees a transcription error within a quotation, the quotation should be fixed. That is not considered altering a quotation, but rather editing the writing or transcription.

When the writer is quoting someone who makes the following pronunciation errors or equivalent errors, it is entirely reasonable to correct the pronunciation within quotation marks. Correcting the pronunciation here is not tampering with the quotation, and in many cases, is merely an example of fixing a writer's poor spelling.

Correct: Incorrect

Asterisk: Asterix
Et cetera: Exetera
The shop next door: The shop next store
For all intents and purposes: For all intensive purposes
In a circumscribed area: In a circumcised area
Regardless: Irregardless
That's a whole other story: That's a whole nother story
She would just as soon vote: She would just assume vote

He was supposed to go: He was suppose to go
As a matter of fact: As a matter a fact
He was matter-of-fact: He was matter-a-fact
She spoke matter-of-factly: She spoke matter-a-factly
There will be a party: There'll be a party
The attorneys general agreed: The attorney generals agreed
The brothers-in-law called: The brother-in-laws called
Her sons-in-law arrived: Her son-in-laws arrived
The suspect was age 70: The suspect was aged 70
Old-fashioned vanilla: Old-fashion vanilla
The gist is she's tired: The gist is, is that she's tired
The prospective student: The perspective student
The lawyer did not prosecute: The lawyer did not persecute

NERVOUS SPEAKERS.   The same principles apply when quoting nervous speakers. Although a nervous speaker may constantly insert "uh" or "um," these sounds should not be incorporated into the quoted material. Likewise, when quoting a speaker who tends to end each sentence on a high note, making each sentence sound like a question, a question mark should not appear at the end of each sentence, unless the speaker truly means to ask a question.

Other inserted sounds and unnecessary words, including the constant repetition of the word *like* and *really*, should be handled on a case-by-case basis by the writer and editor. Because these are words and not merely sounds, the writer should consult the speaker before omitting such words from a quotation.

Terms to Avoid

In reference to people with disabilities, avoid the pejorative words *crippled, damaged,* or *gimp*. Instead, write *disabled* or *physically limited*. In quotations, paraphrase outside of quotation marks if the interview subject uses any of these words. Although individuals may choose to use such words about themselves in a flippant or self-deprecating way, this does not give the reporter license to echo this usage in writing.

Instead of casually referring to any physical condition that pertains to an article, the reporter should always attempt to be as specific as possible in identifying the condition. Specifying *paraplegic, quadriplegic* or *amputee* is always preferred over merely indicating that a person is *disabled*.

WHEELCHAIR USERS.   People who use wheelchairs for mobility are not *wheelchair bound,* as long as they are not tied to their chairs. Many find the usage itself debilitating. They are also not *confined to a wheelchair,* and it is incorrect to use this phrase, implying that they are not permitted out of the chair.

A person who chooses to use a wheelchair for mobility may be correctly referred to as a *wheelchair user.*

■ Illnesses That Are Visible

An individual's illness should not be mentioned in an article unless the disease or illness pertains specifically to the topic of the piece. In most cases, individuals' health conditions do not pertain to articles. Writers should not presume that any disease is the primary occupation or focal point of an individual, or that individuals are unable to lead happy and productive lives because they have illnesses.

If the illness is a vital element of the piece, the illness should not be mentioned on first reference, as a label attached to the person's name, as if the person is defined by that illness. Instead, mention it on the next reference after the person's name with the phrase *who has Parkinson's disease,* or *who was diagnosed with cystic fibrosis.*

Editors should be wary of writing that incorrectly groups together people with a variety of visible mental and physical disabilities, labels them "ill" and then generalizes about their supposedly common situation.

Diseases

Names of diseases are generally lowercase in publications. The exception is when the name of a person or organization is part of the disease name. In *Legionnaires' disease,* for example, the *L* is capitalized because the illness is named for an outbreak of the disease at an American Legion convention that took place in Philadelphia in 1976. Likewise, *Parkinson's disease* starts with a capital *P,* and *Alzheimer's* starts with a capital *A.* Other diseases that begin with capitals and are named for the doctors who first reported them, include Down syndrome (note not Down's syndrome), Bright's disease, Hodgkin's disease, and Brill's disease.

Terms to Avoid

In reference to people with illnesses, avoid using the terms *fits, spells* and *attacks*. Instead write *seizures* or specify the cause of the seizure (epilepsy, etc.). In quotations, paraphrase outside of quotation marks if the interview subject uses any of these words. Although individuals may choose to use such words about themselves in a flippant or self-deprecating way, this does not give the reporter license to echo this usage in writing.

When a person has an illness, it is better to spell out the name of the illness, the degree (or stage) of the illness and any impact it has on the person, assuming that discussion of the illness pertains to the piece.

SUFFERING FROM ILLNESS.   When an illness does pertain to the topic of the article, do not write that the interview subject *suffers from* or is *suffering from an illness,* if the person does not appear to be suffering or is trying to assume a normal lifestyle. Do not say the patient *is suffering from cancer* or *suffers from AIDS,* but rather the patient *has been diagnosed with cancer* or the patient *has AIDS.*

Although nobody wants an illness, people often make adjustments of varying degrees, depending upon the severity of the situation. Writers should not assume that people who have illnesses are in a constant state of suffering. A writer should ask the following questions:

1. Is the person in pain?

2. Is the person really suffering? Or is the person feeling milder discomfort?

3. Is the person constantly aware of the illness? Or does the pain flare up occasionally?

4. Is the illness being treated? Is the person undergoing physical therapy or taking medication?

5. Is the illness acting as an unsurpassable obstacle that is causing psychological torment? Or is the person able to battle the obstacle?

Likewise, avoid describing the individual as a victim. Do not write that the person was a *victim of allergies,* or a *victim of HIV* or a *victim of an ear infection.*

■ Bias Based on Notions of Appearance

People should not be described by their supposed physical attributes or imperfections, unless such physical features are vital to the story— even if an editor argues that such descriptions inherently provide needed "flavor." Not every man or woman who appears attractive to the reporter, for example, should be described as such in an objective article. Nor should every person who has imperfections face the reporter's judgment.

As a principle, journalists should not be judging or weighing the beauty or physical faults of people discussed in copy. In describing people, writers reveal bias as they subjectively choose the physical features upon which to focus. (See chapter 5, Gender Bias, for discussions of Describing Women and Physical Descriptions.)

What is unattractive to one writer may be gorgeous to the next. Non-fashion writers need to be careful in writing or editing pieces that judge "attractiveness," as if reporters are authorities on appearance.

Obviously, when covering a town council meeting, for example, there is little justification for including an evaluative description of each speaker's weight, complexion condition, posture, attire, hairstyle, dandruff problems, body odor, speech deficiencies, hemline, stammering problems, stuttering, mumbling, nervous laughs, twitches and "ums" or "uhs." Yet if the same meeting is about how the nearby water pollution is causing all of the men in the neighborhood to go bald, baldness of the speakers becomes relevant to the article. Likewise, if the meeting is about how the schools need to introduce more public speaking courses, mentioning the speakers' speech deficiencies, stammering problems, stuttering, mumbling, nervous laughs, twitches and "ums" and "uhs" may be justified.

As a general rule, reporters are expected to be polite listeners at meetings, although they are often afforded the opportunity to ask questions to increase their understanding of issues or to learn more facts. Objectivity often means being nonjudgmental. Pointing out deficiencies obviously requires that the writer first notice these deficiencies, which suggests an impatience and bias against the people being described. Although a reporter might notice a nervous laugh, the reporter's job is not to publicize each speaker's shortcomings, but rather to report on the content of what the person said. If the nervous laugh is indicative of some other aspect of the story, however, the reporter may justify mentioning it.

Height Bias

People who are significantly shorter than average or significantly taller than average should be treated like every other interview subject. When writing about people of unusual height, writers should ask themselves if height is a vital element in the story. If not, a discussion of height should be excluded from the copy.

LITTLE PEOPLE.   If height is pertinent to the story, the writer should specify the height of the interview subject instead of labeling the person a *midget, dwarf* or *little person,* terms that often offend, particularly when applied incorrectly. Specific height is much more informative and descriptive in a story where height pertains. If the writer is unable to establish a specific height in a story where height is relevant, the interview subject should be described as *of short stature,* although this phrase is obviously a euphemism, and euphemisms are to be avoided wherever possible.

Writers should not assume that because a person is extremely short, that height automatically becomes relevant to the story. Sometimes a tall writer who has never encountered an extremely short person may find it difficult to get beyond the height observation. This bias should not be carried into the writing. Because a person is short does not make height a topic of discussion.

Examples of stories where height is vital:

1. Coverage of a convention of the Little People of America

2. An article about Hollywood film roles for people of short stature

3. An article about discrimination against or challenges facing people of short stature

4. An article on medical breakthroughs for people of short stature

5. An article on new products available specifically for people of short stature

Little People of America.   For journalists seeking information about little people, dwarfism and midgets, information can be obtained from Little People of America, National Headquarters, P.O. Box 9897, Washington, DC 20016.

Dwarfism.   A dwarf is generally defined as an adult who, when standing, is less than 50 inches tall. Dwarfism should not be labeled a *disease* by writers. Nor should writers refer to adult dwarfs as *cute* or *childlike*. More than 200 medical conditions may lead to dwarfism; there is no one singular cause.

Midgets.   *Midget* is considered a pejorative term by some. It is used in reference to the circus and in demeaning jokes. It refers to dwarfs who are in similar physical proportion to taller people. Do not use the word *midget* in articles.

TALL PEOPLE.   Just as height is not relevant to every story about people who are shorter than average, it is also not pertinent in every piece about unusually tall people. As a rule, a person's tall stature should not be discussed in a piece unless height is a vital element of the story.

Reporters should not assume that every tall person is comfortable about discussing height. Nor should reporters joke about height or ask gee-whiz type questions of every tall person like, "Do you play basketball?" Or mocking questions like, "How is the air up there?" Writers do not have license to nickname tall people with labels like *Gulliver, Big Foot, Giant,* etc.

When height is relevant to a story about a tall person, the reporter should inquire about the specific height and use that number as part of the description, rather than describing an individual as *an extremely tall person.* Somewhere within the piece, the writer should explain how height relates to the story.

Weight Bias

Every year new statistics are released about the percentage of Americans who are overweight by medical standards. Every year, the figures seem to change, but what remains constant is the fact that studies continue to find that a significant portion of Americans are overweight.

In articles about weight problems and health, weight may be a vital element to the story, and therefore may merit a lengthy discussion. In most other stories, however, individuals' body weight does not pertain. As a rule, reporters should refrain from describing weight, unless they can justify how such a description enhances a reader's understanding of the story.

When weight is deemed essential to the story, writers should attempt to be specific, not by estimating weight, but by asking for numbers. For example, in a piece about a weight-loss clinic, it is better to specify that a customer lost 80 pounds, after weighing in at 230 originally, than to say the customer lost a lot of weight, or started out heavy and now looks average. If weight is vital to the story, so are numbers. Otherwise, the story becomes subjective and less informative.

WHERE WEIGHT IS VITAL.   There are many cases when an individual's body weight is pertinent to a story and must be mentioned in the piece. The following are some examples.

1. Profiles of athletes who do sports that classify "players" by weight

2. Review of a diet clinic or diet camp

3. A profile of a new model who is heavier than traditional models and is promoting a new heavier look

4. A piece about how weight became an obstacle and how a very heavy person overcame that obstacle and succeeded despite the odds

5. A piece about how weight became an asset on a very windy day

6. A health piece on the dangers of being overweight or underweight

7. A piece about someone whose weight breaks records

8. A piece about cures for anorexia or bulimia

9. A how-to piece about controlling weight

10. A profile of a person who was unable to gain weight, who finally succeeded

11. An article about a discrimination suit filed by an airline passenger who required two seats in order to be comfortable on a plane

12. A piece about a dancer forced to retire from the ballet as a result of a weight problem

IN SEARCH OF A EUPHEMISM.   If the piece is about weight, and a person is overweight, then the right word to use in describing the person is *overweight*. If the piece is about weight and a person weighs too little, then the right term is *underweight*. Editors should note that in most cases, where weight is a vital element of a piece, it is the weight (measured numerically and objectively) that is essential, not the fat or appearance.

Assuming this to be true, exact numbers tell more than vague descriptions of a person's weight. Weight is a measurement that is dependent on gravity. Words relating to weight tend to be more acceptable in descriptions than words relating only to appearance. The more acceptable list includes *heavy, heavyset, weighty* as well as *overweight*. But a specific number should be supplied, if at all possible, to underscore that this *heavy* designation is not a mere value judgment.

The words to avoid are the ones that subjectively focus on physical appearance, including *fat, stout, chunky, chubby, bulging, doughy, obese, flabby, stuffy, meaty, pudgy, fleshy, wide, oversized, extra-large* and *hefty*.

Some words do not sound as offensive, but they are basically euphemisms. Good journalism favors directness and frowns upon euphemisms as a means to report truths.

These euphemisms include *broad, broad-shouldered, hardy, husky, stocky, solid, man-sized, portly, women's-sized, full-figured, curved, developed, substantial, robust, voluptuous* and most obnoxiously *pleasantly plump*.

WEIGHT AND INTELLIGENCE.   People with weight problems sometimes complain that writers show bias against them, assuming that increased weight means decreased intelligence. Writers obviously should not make any such assumptions. People have weight disorders for many reasons, ranging from gland problems to allergies and eating disorders to physical immobility. Writers should not presume that an overweight condition signifies a lack of self-discipline.

Editors should watch for other personality stereotypes. Why, for example, does the adjective *jolly* (synonymous with merry and joyful) tend to be reserved for people who are overweight, as does the verb *chuckle*. Santa Claus chuckles. Don't thin people chuckle too?

ANOREXIC.   Anorexia is a serious condition. Writers should not use the terms *anorexic* or *bulimic* lightly to describe the appearance of a thin person, if the person does not have either anorexia or bulimia.

Well-Groomed

Well-groomed sounds harmless enough when it is used to describe a puppy or a pet. When used in reference to people, it can imply certain biased values, particularly relating to appearance. *Well-groomed* is rarely used to describe a person's cleanliness or how often a person showers. Instead, some writers would describe a male as *well-groomed* if he has no facial hair, as if facial hair makes one poorly groomed, or if he wears a suit and tie to work. Other writers use *well-groomed* as a euphemism to describe a woman who shaves her armpits and legs, whose nails are manicured, whose hair stays in place or is straight, and who wears delicate makeup but not heavy makeup.

While there is nothing technically wrong with describing one as *well-groomed,* editors should note that *well-groomed* is a value judgment and could reveal some of the writer's subtle biases. For example, crew cuts, while considered well-groomed in the American military, are not considered well-groomed within some religious communities where men are required to wear their hair long. In other words, what is well-groomed to one person, is not necessarily appropriate to another.

In determining whether or not the use of *well-groomed* is appropriate in an article, editors should ask the following questions: Is grooming relevant to the article? Is the writer biased against facial hair or make-up or some other cosmetic feature? Is the writer revealing some other bias by describing someone as *well-groomed?*

An example of grooming used as a euphemism for other bias: In an interview, an American woman described a household employee she had fired as "poorly groomed." The writer asked the employer what constituted poor grooming. The employer said the woman did not shave her armpits or legs. "Her grooming was very primitive," she elaborated. When pressed, the employer whispered that the employee was foreign-born and did not learn proper American habits. When the writer asked if the employee bathed and washed regularly, the employer said she had. The writer realized that the question was not one of grooming, but rather of bias against the culture from which the employee came. The employer was using grooming as an excuse.

Writers should be cautious about quoting bias against foreigners that gets hidden in issues of proper grooming. Acceptable appearance and attractiveness vary by custom. Writers who quote such bias become guilty of promoting the same bias.

9

Bias by Economic/Social Class

■ Economic/Social Bias Examples

The following are examples of different forms of economic and social class bias that commonly appear in publications or on broadcasts. Examine the sentences, and then determine how they should best be rewritten to eliminate bias.

Although they were on welfare and lived in the urban ghetto, they seemed to know how to read and write.

The upscale resort attracted high rollers, accustomed to comfortable living and expensive taste.

The coupon clippers fit in well among the mobile home set, since they loved to buy clothing at bargain prices.

The broadcasters were accountable to their immediate superior as well as their boss.

As a society woman, she knew it was important to have her wedding announcement appear in the Sunday newspaper.

■ Overview

Welfare recipients complain that journalists assume wrongfully that people without jobs must be less educated or less intelligent than other people. Similarly, writers sometimes assume that wealthy people know more, which is obviously faulty thinking. Journalists should not judge people, their expertise, or their value based on income.

As a general rule, writers should not discuss a person's income, finances, or assets unless their money pertains to the story. If it does pertain, writers need to be careful in how they discuss finances. People should not be categorized or labeled according to income.

Editors should also note that money does not equal expertise. Editors should ask what makes the interview subject (or the person quoted in an article) an authority on the issue discussed. If the article is not about money or business and the interview subject has no credentials beyond wealth, the editor should suggest that the writer pursue a new "expert."

■ "Expensive Taste"

Editors should be wary of writers who automatically equate affluence with taste. Because people are wealthy does not mean that they are authorities on home decoration, art, architecture or fashion. The editor should make sure that the writer's interview subject has expertise beyond living in attractive houses, buying expensive art works and wearing attractive clothes.

When selecting interview subjects or consulting with so-called experts for a piece on interior design, for example, the writer should determine whether or not each interview subject actually played a significant role in decorating a home or office. In making this determination, the writer should inquire about and specify the actual role played by the interview subject. Did the interview subject do the actual decorating alone? Did the interview subject hire a professional decorator to do the decorating? Did the interview subject merely select the wallpaper, while leaving the rest to professionals? Did the interview subject meet with a series of decorators before settling on one or two, who did most of the work? Did the interview subject do most of the decorating with only minimal consultation with professional decorators? Did the interview subject only participate in decorating by exercising veto power or approval of other people's ideas?

The writer should establish the interview subject's credentials early in the interview. Does the designer have a university degree or certification in interior design, for example? What design skills does the interview subject claim to have? What experience does the interview subject have in interior design? This information should then be specified in the article to enhance the credibility of the advice.

When seeking expert opinions, writers often find that even the least qualified people willingly offer advice. Establishing credentials early in the interview allows the writer to better evaluate the advice. If it is learned that the interview subject contributed relatively little to the decorating process, the writer might want to interview the actual designer instead. Editors should be ready to question the expertise of the writer's interview subject, to make sure that the subject was not selected on the basis of economic bias. An article written about a knowledgeable designer is much more informative to a reader seeking to learn more about design than an interview with a wealthy person living in a pretty house.

Fashion editors and art editors should follow the same basic guidelines, applying the same "expensive taste" rule: Because a person wears an attractive outfit or buys a famous painting does not mean that he or she is an expert on fashion or art. Some of the most influential people have no time for shopping. Instead, they hire fashion consultants who recommend or dictate what they should wear. A fashion story is generally stronger if the clothing designer or fashion consultant is interviewed, rather than the wearer of the clothing.

■ Words That Reveal Bias

Certain words can reveal hidden economic bias, depending upon how they are used by the writer. While some economic bias terms are obvious buzzwords, others are used more subtly. Some reveal economic bias in an office setting, others reveal bias in terms of social class. Although not all of the following words are inherently biased, all merit double-checking in context.

Affordable

Obviously, what is affordable to one person may not be affordable to everyone. General interest publications that are not targeted for specific economic groups should assume that their readers range economically from welfare recipients to billionaires, and therefore should not flippantly deem anything *affordable.* Affordability is relative to how much money a person has or earns and how much that person is willing to allocate to different priorities. As a result, editors should be wary of articles that discuss "affordable housing" without specifying to whom it is affordable. In fact, any article that pronounces any product or service *affordable,* should also specify to whom it is affordable.

Among the most frequent violations in newspapers and magazines: *affordable child care arrangements, affordable vacations, affordable homes, affordable loans, fashion that's affordable, affordable private schools* and *affordable colleges.*

Bargains and Budgets

Because readers spend their money differently, items that may easily fit into one reader's budget may not find a place in the next reader's budget, even if their incomes are equal. As a result, what may seem like a bargain or budget item to one consumer may be expensive to the next.

In editing consumer pieces, editors should make sure that the writer does not callously declare price-reduced items to be *bargains.* A dress that sells for $2,000 in a trendy boutique may be on sale for half price. But that may not make the dress an automatic *bargain* to many of the readers, who would not consider $1,000 a budget price.

Editors need to be sensitive to the different economics of different households. In declaring something inexpensive or budget-priced, the writer loses credibility with readers who have less discretionary income and among those who may feel the writer is extravagant, biased and more interested in promoting products than informing readers.

Boss

Not every office consists of a boss and a group of employees. Reporters should not assume that administrators are all *bosses* for the people whose paperwork they manage or oversee. In an article about a hospital, for example, it would be incorrect to refer to the physicians as *employees* and the hospital administrators as *the bosses.*

Writers should not assume that every worker has a *boss.* In many contexts, particularly when professionals are involved, the term *boss* is considered insulting, belittling and unprofessional. In some offices, workers report to a supervisor. In some, workers report to an administrator or a business manager or an editor. In some, all workers handle their own administrative paperwork, and there are no supervisors, bosses, managers or administrators. Writers should be sensitive to the office language of any office they are covering, as well as the individuals within it.

At a publication where journalists consider themselves professionals, many would say they report to an editor rather than a boss. *Boss* indicates a blue- or white-collar orientation, rather than a professional perspective.

Classes: Lower, Upper and Middle

According to popular wisdom, most Americans think of themselves as middle class, whether they live on $15,000 per year or earn six figures. Some see themselves as lower middle class; some identify themselves as upper middle class. But few speak of themselves, at least openly, as either lower class or upper class.

Editors should beware of writing that labels people as *upper class* or *lower class,* revealing the writers' economics positions relative to the people in their articles.

Collars: White and Blue and Professional

Be careful not to label people white-collar workers who might view themselves as professionals. In general, collars should only apply to jobs (*white-collar jobs* and *blue-collar jobs*), rather than people. But even with jobs, it is better to use other, more precise terminology. If a job description is an important part of a story, be specific. Mention the job title and describe the work that the person does, rather than pigeonholing the person's job as *white-* or *blue-collar.*

Comfortable

What is comfortable for one is not necessarily comfortable for others. *Comfortable* is sometimes used as a euphemism for *rich* or *well-to-do* by affluent people who want to sound modest. *Comfortable* is also used by people who are content to have just enough on which to live. *Comfortable* is most commonly used by retired people, in describing their own living conditions. Reporters should be cautious about picking up this language in their writing, since it does not contribute much to an understanding of anyone's economic situation and only sounds evasive. If economics do not pertain to a particular story, it is better to omit any mention of how *comfortable* the interview subject is. If economics do pertain, it is better to ask more questions and detail more specifically the economic situation, without resorting to euphemisms like *comfortable.*

If *comfortable* is to be used, perhaps within a quotation, the writer should attempt to get more specifics. What is meant by *comfortable* in context?

Coupon-Clippers

On occasion, arrogant writers have been known to ridicule people who clip coupons as a means of economizing. These writers refer to people as *coupon-clippers* or even *the coupon-clipper set*, incorporating a negative bias. Such labels are insulting in two ways: They suggest that people who use coupons are trivial, implying that cutting coupons is a waste of time. They suggest that people have nothing better to do with their time than clip coupons. In addition, they belittle the work that people who clip coupons do. They imply that the kind of work for which *coupon-clippers* are qualified pays so little money that clipping coupons becomes a time-efficient way to economize. (Many of these coupons, incidentally, are clipped from newspapers and magazines.)

Expensive

In editing consumer pieces, editors should remember that *expensive* is a relative term, depending upon how much money one has and can or is willing to spend. What is expensive to one person, may be viewed as a bargain to the next, depending upon their values and their budgets. Writers who declare everything *expensive* lose credibility with more affluent readers, who detect a low-budget bias.

Writers should not declare something *expensive,* without explaining where the reader can get the identical product, with the same quality for less money. A writer should not compare an orange that sells for a dollar at a roadside stand (freshly picked, organically grown, perfectly sweet, and easy to peel) with a similar looking fruit sold at a supermarket for 25 cents (refrigerated, sprayed with pesticides and painted orange to look appealing). The two products are not identical, and the writer therefore loses any license to dub the first one *expensive.*

Mobile Home Set

Writers sometimes snobbishly generalize about people who live in mobile homes or trailer parks, referring to such residents as the *mobile home set.* Some editors are slow to send reporters to cover stories that take place in trailer communities, contending that such stories are not as important, since the homes are worth less money and the people are not as connected with the general community. In addition, residents are reputed to be transient, unstable, unreliable, less educated, less articulate and less able to earn a living.

Mobile home communities include a wide variety of people, some of whom can afford fancier lifestyles, but prefer a more pared down way of living. Writers should not imply that people with less money or those who prefer a simpler lifestyle, are less interesting, or unworthy. References to the *mobile home set* are demeaning and generally indicate economic bias.

TRAILER TRASH.   Eliminate the label *trailer trash* in reference to poor people who live in mobile homes or trailers. It is heavily biased. If the usage appears in a quotation, remove the quotation marks and rephrase the statement, eliminating *trailer trash.*

Society

Years ago, many newspapers had "Society" pages, where engagements, births and marriages were officially announced and where parties and charity balls were described in detail. "Society" in that context meant *high society,* and the implication was that *high society,* or affluent society, was all the society that mattered or was of interest to readers. To social climbers, having a mention on the Society pages meant having arrived. Thus, people whose announcements did not make the Society pages felt snubbed or overlooked.

Many publications still announce engagements, marriages and births, but the pages where they appear tend to have less economically-biased headings: Community News, Social Announcements, Congratulations, etc.

Society columns are often referred to nowadays as social columns, or less politely, gossip columns.

Superiors

The word *superior* is not an acceptable synonym for *boss* in an unbiased publication. It is incorrect to write, "The workers were told to report to their *superiors.*" The reasoning is obvious: If workers have superiors, then by definition, they must be the inferiors. If they hold others to be superior, they must hold themselves to be inferior. Individuals may speak this way and perceive themselves this way, but the editor should not let a writer impose such status on the subject of a story. The usage should not be quoted within a story. If an employer refers to him- or herself as a *superior* and the statement seems essential to the story, remove the quotations and paraphrase the essence of the quote.

One exception is in a story about the military, where certain officers are designated as *superior.* The other rare exception would be in a story about hostile or offensive work conditions, where the employer claims to be a superior. In this context the writer should let the employer demonstrate through language his or her degree of disrespect for employees.

Upscale and Downscale

Upscale is a euphemism that does not exist in many dictionaries, but it appears commonly in real estate pieces, travel articles and crime stories. Writers sometimes use *upscale* in place of *affluent, rich, expensive, upper class,* or *upper crust,* sensing that it somehow sounds more polite and less class conscious. Some editors specify that the word should not be used, however, because it is a euphemism. If using the word *upscale* does not violate editorial policy or style, editors should monitor the usage carefully to determine why the euphemism is needed. Depending on the context, *upscale* can also be interpreted as a euphemism for *white, exclusive, upper class only* or even *segregated.*

Upscale implies the existence of *downscale,* another adjective that does not appear in many dictionaries. Use of *downscale* is less common, probably because it implies snobbery and bias. Few writers feel comfortable using *downscale* in describing a neighborhood or resort.

■ Economic Bias Disguised as Geographic Bias

Writers sometimes introduce economic bias disguised as geographic bias. They comment about where people live or come from, knowing that that location may be perceived as economically inferior or even embarrassing. Economically inferior, incidentally, does not necessarily mean poorer. It could be a put-down of affluence as well.

A writer described a senior prom that took place "deep in the rich folks' ghetto." The implication was that the prom and those in attendance were decadent, materialistic and devoid of wholesome values. The use of the word *ghetto* implies that these people are trapped in their conspicuous consumption, confined to this valueless lifestyle.

Ghettos

Most of the major stylebooks specify that the word *ghetto* should not be used lightly in reference to neighborhoods inhabited by poor people or minorities. The Associated Press stylebook suggests that *"Ghetto* has a connotation that government decree has forced people to live in a certain area." A ghetto's inhabitants are unable to leave by law.

In contrast, the *United Press International Stylebook* defines *ghetto* as "the section of a city to which minorities or the poor are restricted by economic pressure or social discrimination."

The New York Times Stylebook advises writers not to "overuse [*ghetto*] in its newer, non-historical sense in referring to the areas of cities inhabited by minorities or the poor. That usage has become established, but it is not required, or justified, in every instance."

All three stylebooks suggest that writers should mention the specific neighborhood or neighborhoods by name, if it is known by a name, to avoid the word *ghetto*. AP and UPI cite Harlem and Watts as examples. As alternative words, AP and *The Times* stylebooks recommend using *section, district, slum, area* or *quarter.*

INNER CITY.   References to *inner city* conjure up stereotypical views of poor, supposedly crime-ridden urban nonwhite neighborhoods, according to the *News Watch Project Style Guide*. The guide suggests that *inner city* would only be acceptable "if it were also used to refer to wealthy neighborhoods in central cities."

Victim of the Projects

Building projects are generally intended as improvements on living conditions. As a result, the expression *victim of the projects* would appear to be a contradiction. If the article subject is indeed victimized by some problem or negative condition within housing projects, the writer should specify what that problem is, rather than blaming the building development itself. *Victim of the projects, victim of the ghetto, product of the mean streets,* and *victim of the slums* have all become euphemisms. As always, writers should try to avoid euphemisms, and instead aim to be more specific in isolating what element within one's particular living conditions contributed to or caused a given situation.

Not Far from the Slums

Locating a person not far from the slums within an article is tantamount to locating the person within the slums. Although this may sound like a geographical designation, writers should be careful about casting judgment on where people live, particularly if it seems that the person mentioned in the piece would not identify his or her living conditions as being slumlike or comparable to slums. Do not mention a location gratuitously in any story if the location does not pertain to the topic of the piece.

Downtowners

Writers should not stereotype individuals according to the neighborhoods in which they reside. In a time when communities are becoming increasingly mixed, where boundaries are stretching to encompass new neighborhoods, where integration is steadily increasing, and exclusion is not being tolerated, generalizations about Uptowners, Downtowners, Eastsiders, Westsiders, Left Bank and Right Bank residents, lose their meaning. Such designations only suggest that the writer is unwilling to let go of old biases.

Rural Residents

People who elect to live in rural areas or own vacation homes in undeveloped areas should not be labeled *hillbillies, hicks, country boys, simple folk, farmers' daughters* or *cowboys* (in a pejorative sense). Editors should not assume that residents of rural areas are any simpler or less educated than people who live in major cities.

10

Lifestyle Bias

■ Lifestyle Bias Examples

The following are examples of different forms of lifestyle bias that commonly appear in publications or on broadcasts. Examine the sentences, and then determine how they should best be rewritten to eliminate bias.

In the average American household, the older brother does not help his younger sister with homework.

The inventor, who had grown up an only child, was hailed for his success.

The girl was rescued from the fire by her adoptive mother, as her real mother lived in another state.

The criminal, who had been an adopted child, refused to tell police his Christian name.

While the head of the house brings home the bacon, the lady of the house likes to shop.

■ Overview

There is no such institution as the typical American family or even the average American household. Families and households differ greatly in the United States. Writers should avoid comparing every family to television's "Donna Reed" and "Ozzie and Harriet." Many young readers have not seen either show, and the supposed charm of that style of living is a vision not necessarily shared by all readers, including the ones who have seen both shows.

Many homes in America are run by single parents. Some families have in-house relatives who are handicapped, elderly, new immigrants or cousins. Some families have one child, some have many. Some couples have no children and prefer to have no children. Some households are run by two adults of the same sex. Writers should be careful not to equate the words *household* and *family*. Not every household houses a family.

Not every American family is a single ethnicity, race, religion or religious denomination. When writing about a family, reporters should not assume sameness of all members. Ask about each individual mentioned in the piece, if ethnicity and religion pertain to the story. If they do not pertain, do not mention ethnicity or religion in the piece.

Editors should be cautious about writing that assumes that only one style of living is normal or preferable. As a rule, lifestyle should not be mentioned in a piece or even hinted at, unless it specifically pertains to the piece.

■ Children

There is no correct formula for the all-American family. Families vary tremendously. Reporters should not imply that there is a correct number of children or a best ratio of boys to girls or a preferred order of birth in the family. Editors should watch for stereotyping of families, particularly in feature stories that require hypotheticals. Every hypothetical family or "average family of four" should not consist of two adults and two children: an older brother and younger sister.

Adoption

Sometimes publications reveal a subtle prejudice against adoption that adoptive parents, in particular, find disturbing. A dramatic example was the Lisa Steinberg death in 1987, when newspapers referred to Hedda Nussbaum and Joel Steinberg as "Lisa's *adoptive* parents." After it was revealed that Lisa was never in fact legally adopted, newspapers continued to refer to the couple as "*adoptive* parents," casting a bad light on adoption. Many references to the case still refer to Lisa as the *adopted daughter.*

ADOPTED CHILD.   A child who has been legally adopted is an *adopted child.* This status should not lead to any generalizations about the child by the writer. Children are put up for adoption for many reasons, including death or illness of parents or other physical inability of parents to adequately care for a child. An adopted child should not be portrayed by the writer as an *unwanted child* or *inherently sad child,* and no assumptions should be made about the child's biological parents or reason for adoption.

The fact that a child is adopted should not be mentioned in the article unless the adoption specifically pertains to the topic of the article. Many writers gratuitously mention a child's adoption in pieces where such personal information does not pertain. Some justify the inclusion by saying they just find it "interesting," others contend that such biased detail adds flavor. Some writers make a point of emphasizing adoption in crime stories, if the victim or perpetrator was adopted, whereas they would find it inappropriate to other stories. Adoptive parents argue that as a result, references to adoption appear disproportionately in crime stories, leading some readers to infer that adopted children are involved in more crimes than other children or are in some way troubled as a result of adoption.

Editors should eliminate such flippant mentions of adoption, just as they would eliminate other references to the way a child was born or joined a family. Adoption status becomes relevant in pieces about adoption or about hereditary diseases. In general, it does not pertain in stories about a child's accomplishments, indiscretions, school environment, social life and family.

Editors should be careful to make sure that writers do not include this information unnecessarily, as it implies that there is something very wrong with or different about being adopted, a theme that many adoptive parents feel is neither constructive for their children nor informative to the public.

ADOPTIVE PARENT. A parent who adopts a child is an *adoptive parent,* not an *adopted parent.*

Articles referring to families that have adopted children should not refer to the parents as *adoptive parents* throughout the piece. In fact, it is generally inappropriate to point out the fact that the child is adopted within the piece, if the piece is not about adoption. Adoptive parents should be called *parents,* unless the article is specifically about adoption, just as biological parents are called *parents,* in articles that are not about giving birth.

There is a tendency among journalists in stories about child abuse to point out if the abusive parents are adoptive parents rather than biological. This has the impact of sounding biased against adoption, in that when the abusive parents are biological parents, the writers rarely point out that the parents are biological. The end result is that readers get the impression that a majority (or at least a significant percentage) of the child abusers are adoptive parents.

If adoption is an important aspect of the story, then it is acceptable to point out the fact that the abusive parents are adoptive. But if that is to be mentioned, the writer must clearly justify within the piece why that aspect is important to the story. Did the couple make a habit of adopting children in order to have someone to abuse? Did the adoption agency knowingly or negligently give out babies to hardened criminals?

If adoption has no bearing on the story and the writer is unable to substantiate a good reason to include the mention of how the child came into the family, a gratuitous mention of adoption is biased and should be omitted by the editor.

BIOLOGICAL PARENT.   Biological parents are fathers and mothers who physically contribute to the birth of a child. The biological parent should not be referred to as the *real* parent, implying that there is also a fake or unreal parent. If the biological parent raises the child, the biological parent should be referred to as *the parent* (no need for *biological* to precede the word *parent* each time). In the same way, if an adoptive parent raises the child, the adoptive parent should be referred to as *the parent* (no need for *adoptive* to precede the word *parent*). The exception is when the article is specifically about physically giving birth or about adoption, or when either of those acts become significant elements of the story.

BIRTH PARENT, BIRTH MOTHER.   Biological parents may be referred to as *birth parents*. But the birth parent should not be referred to as the *real* parent, unless the birth parent raises the child. If the birth parent does raise the child, then there is no need for *birth* to precede *parent*.

NATURAL PARENT.   A natural parent is someone who seems to be talented at parenting, as in "He was a real *natural,* when it came to calming the baby." But *natural parent* should not be viewed as synony-mous with *biological parent*. To call a biological parent the *natural parent,* implies that the adoptive parent is either unnatural or supernatur-al, hinting of bias against adoption.

REAL PARENT. The parent who legally raises the child is the real parent—whether this is the biological parent, the adoptive parent or both. In general, writers should avoid using the term *real parent,* because it implies that there are also fake parents or unreal parents. The term is confusing to the reader and hints at a bias against adop-tion.

Childless Couples

Not every couple wants to have children. Writers should not presume in their writing that childless couples are *lonely, barren* or *desiring chil-dren* in their life. If a writer is interviewing a married adult who has no children, the writer should only inquire about children if the focus of the piece is lifestyle. If the person is being interviewed for a non-lifestyle piece (about business, politics or a profession, for example), asking about children is inappropriate. Writing about lack of children is even more inappropriate in a nonlifestyle piece.

Editors may notice that some writers have the tendency to ask every female interview subject about her desire to have children or about her status as a parent. The same writers might interview male business executives or lawyers, and the thought would not even occur to these reporters to ask about children. Writers should not assume that women want children more than men do, or that women think about children more than men do. Editors need to be alert to writers who only ask female interview subjects about their interest in having chil-dren and ignore the topic with men. The decision to have children obviously involves both men and women, and writers should not assume that children are exclusively or even predominantly a women's topic. The same rule applies for columnists.

Infertility and Sterility

The Dictionary of Bias-Free Usage specifies that *infertile* may be used "for both men and women, although most often it modifies 'couple.'" According to the dictionary, the term refers to "the lack of offspring in people who have been having unprotected intercourse ... *Sterile* usually indicates that a cause for the infertility has been found. Infertile people are not necessarily sterile. Sterile people are always infertile."

Only Children

Writers should not assume that "only children" are lonely children, or that they need a sibling. To suggest that a family is somehow incomplete with only one child is to impose the writer's values on the interview subject. Not every family that has one child wants or has a second child, although some do. Some couples choose to have one child. Some couples who have one child are unable to have a second child and are happy to stop at one.

Writers should also note that not all only children are spoiled or overly protected. Never assume that only children are all brought up in the same way or share the same experiences.

Place in the Family

Writers should avoid stereotyping children by their place in the family. Oldest children should not be presumed to be the most likely to succeed. (Wilbur and Orville Wright, as just one example, were third and fourth in the family.) A prominent science contest asked each competitor to indicate on the application his or her place in the family, as an indicator or predictor of how successful the student would be in the competition. The implication was that firstborns were more likely to become leaders of science. While statistics may seem to support this bias, there are many cases of second- and thirdborn children also becoming extremely successful. Editors need to recognize that although some families devote the most resources to their firstborn children, many others do not.

For the same reason, journalists should not assume that middle children are all troubled, overlooked and ignored. Granted, there may be many documented cases in which middle children feel that they need to compete harder for parental or societal attention. In many other cases, however, middle children are well-adjusted.

Writers should not presume that second-born children are usually second best academically or professionally to firstborns. Nor should writers assume that ability decreases as the place in the family increases. (In other words, that the oldest is always the wisest, the second-born is second wisest, etc. in descending order.)

Youngest children are not all accustomed to being babied. Writers should not presume that youngest children are spoiled, cute, or the most wanted or least wanted by parents. They should not presume that the fourth son in a family with four children was supposed to be a girl or that the fourth daughter was supposed to be a boy. And children who come from large families should not be stereotyped as attention seeking, love starved or neglected.

Likewise, siblings do not all perceive each other as rivals, and rivalry should not be presumed by the writer.

Right Number of Children

Editors should watch for value judgments by writers on how many children a family should have. There is no "right" number of children. Families come in all sizes.

Writers should not impose their own ideas by asking the following kinds of inappropriate questions:

1. Why do you have so many children?

2. Do you find that you are unable to give your children all the attention they need because you have so many children?

3. Have you ever heard of birth control?

4. Are you able to support all those kids?

5. Were you originally planning to have all these kids, or were some accidental or serendipitous?

6. Did you have all of those kids for religious reasons?

Sons and Daughters

Writers should not presume that parents with sons only are luckier than parents with daughters only, or that those with daughters are luckier than parents with sons. Likewise, writers should not assume that parents with both sons and daughters are luckier than parents with only sons or only daughters. All families are different. Different situations make different families happy.

Writers should not assume that boys are easier to raise than girls or

that girls are easier to raise than boys. Every family has its own situation and a unique set of personalities. Some families find some children difficult to raise, but this should not be elevated to the point
where a generalization is made by the writer that boys are easier than
girls or girls are easier than boys.

■ Children's Care

America is very divided when it comes to defining proper child care,
and many otherwise objective writers reveal strong biases on this issue
through their writing. Some contend that when children are young, at
least one parent should stay home to care for them. Others suggest
that every child should have two working parents to adequately provide for them and also create a home where everyone feels challenged
(and possibly invigorated) by his or her work. Within this group, some
argue in favor of day care as the only truly stimulating environment
for a young child, whereas others contend that baby-sitters allow
young children maximum time at home and more one-on-one attention while parents go off to work.

Writers covering home and education topics need to be vigilant
about maintaining objectivity when writing about child care. Many
different patterns are successful for many different family situations
and needs.

Baby-Sitting and Sitting

Baby-sitters are people other than parents or legal guardians who care
for children for short periods of time. Many people feel uncomfortable
calling a caregiver a *baby-sitter* when the child is no longer a baby. It is
a generally acceptable style to call the caregiver a *sitter,* particularly for
an older child, a 9-year-old, for example.

Because fathers are parents, they cannot *baby-sit* their own children
while mothers go out. Instead, they *care* for their children or *supervise*
their children or *watch* their children. If the father is the parent of the
children, he is not a *baby-sitter* but a father watching his own children.

Day Care

Day care has received bad press in recent years. Most pieces that mention day care refer to it in a negative context—when there is a scandal,

accident or dangerous situation—leading many to believe that all children who attend day care are either molested, neglected or underprivileged. Obviously this is not the case.

Writers should not assume that all children in day care are underprivileged, poor or in some way disadvantaged, or that day care itself is cruel treatment or a last resort. In a society where the majority of children's primary caregivers work outside the home, day care is often the child care option of choice. Families that can afford full-time housekeepers or baby-sitters, often opt for day care programs instead, contending that such programs provide more stimulation, opportunities for socialization and safer environments. Even families in which one parent is home full-time sometimes enroll their children in day care programs for additional stimulation.

Day care centers range in amenities and facilities, and some charge more tuition than the most selective private high schools in America. Some provide minimal baby-sitting services, whereas others are far more elaborate, with well-equipped nurseries, nutritionists on staff, state-of-the-art learning tools, formal curricula and licensed teachers.

In editing a piece about day care, editors should make sure that the writers do not approach the piece with preconceptions and biased assumptions about day care, the children who attend the programs, or the kind of parents who send their children to such programs.

Full-Time Mothers

A *full-time mother* is a misnomer, since it implies that working women (women who work outside the home) are only part-time mothers. *Full-time mother* is a euphemism that refers to a mother who does not work outside the home, and instead devotes all of her working time to caring for her children. Many women prefer calling themselves *full-time mothers* instead of *homemakers,* and it is perceived as a bolder career title. The implication is that less time is spent cleaning the house or housekeeping, and more time is spent creating quality time and raising children. The aim of the euphemism is to present a positive image of full-time parenting, and it supposedly elevates at-home women from a maintenance job image to educator, health provider and caregiver.

Of the various euphemisms and labels for *homemaker, at-home mother,* and *soccer mom,* this is probably the most popular, although women who work outside the home often find it offensive. In general, editors should eliminate any of these job labels from an article if no such job title is required by the story. If, however, a job description is vital to the article, a writer could replace the job title by inserting the phrase *"who works at home full-time,"* after the person's name.

Latchkey Kids

In many American towns, public after-school day-care style programs are referred to formally or informally as *latchkey programs.* The concept is aimed at enhancing community safety by discouraging children and teenagers from going home to an empty house while their parents are still at work. The name is somewhat of a misnomer, however, in that the purpose of the program is to eliminate latchkey situations and to provide a supervised place for young people to congregate safely after school. *Anti-latchkey programs* would be a more appropriate designation.

Latchkey kids generally is used to mean children who are left on their own, unsupervised, in an empty house, where the only protection they have from the outside world until their parents arrive home is the front door latchkey. The image is one of vulnerability of the children, as a direct result of supposed negligence on the part of the working parents. The implication is that mothers (more often than not the ones held accountable for their children's welfare by society) are irresponsible parents if they are not home when their children arrive from school each day.

A child who attends day care or after-school care is not a latchkey child. A child with two parents who both work outside the home or a single parent who works outside the home is not a latchkey child if there is a baby-sitter, grandparent, neighbor or other adult in the house taking care of the child in the absence of the parents.

The usage is laden with bias in a society that often demands that mothers work full-time while being responsible for their children's health, safety, education, transportation and social arrangements full-time. Referring to a child as a *latchkey kid* is pejorative and offensive to over-burdened parents who may not have many alternatives. The term should be used very sparingly. When used, it should be reserved for situations where young children are left unattended regularly and without protection or supervision.

Nannies

In American dictionaries, *nannies* are goats. *Nanny* is the British term for *baby-sitter* or *sitter,* and writers often find the term classier or more endearing. Parents who would be reluctant to leave their toddler with a baby-sitter for nine hours a day, are charmed at the prospect of the child spending this time with a *nanny.* There is no real difference in the job description or the expertise required, however. Some parents argue that a *nanny* refers to someone who is mature, more experienced and sometimes even credentialed by a local child care agency. But the same credentials can be applied to the terms *baby-sitter* and *sitter.*

A more significant difference is the fact that *nanny* denotes a female baby-sitter, and excludes men. A man is not referred to as a *nanny,* although he can be called a *baby-sitter,* a *sitter* or, more awkwardly, *a child care provider.* Thus *nanny,* despite its appeal, is a biased job title.

Some publications specify preference for the terms *baby-sitter* or *housekeeper,* if keeping house is included in the job description. At publications with no written style on this usage, writers should use *baby-sitter* or *sitter* because both are less biased.

Soccer Moms

Soccer mom is another euphemism for *full-time mother* or *homemaker,* but it presents a more aggressive image. The image is one of a fun, active mother who drives kids to soccer games in a recreational vehicle and sits on the sidelines, handing out bottled water, cheering and coaching her offspring. Mothers whose children play other sports besides soccer often refer to themselves as *soccer moms* as well—it is not the sport, but the image that gives the term meaning—or occasionally as *baseball moms* or *hockey moms,* etc.

The term is obviously reserved for women, an indicator that the so-called job description is biased, despite any trendiness. To apply the test of parallelism, note that few men, when asked what kind of work they do, would feel comfortable saying that they are full-time *soccer dads.*

Soccer mom is acceptable within an attributed quotation. Outside of a quotation, it has become a cliché and a euphemism for mothers who do not work outside the home. Although the term may sound trendy to some, reporters should not label at-home mothers as *soccer moms.*

■ Divorcées

Women who are divorced should not be casually referred to as *divorcées,* just as men who are divorced should not be referred to as *divorcés.* In most stories individuals' marital status is not relevant to the piece, and mentioning marital status is therefore inappropriate.

In articles where marital status is vital to the piece, however, the nouns *divorcée* and *divorcé* should be eliminated as well. Both sound pejorative or flippant at best. In most cases, it is better not to mention any divorce in the lead of a piece, unless the divorce is one of the most important elements of the story (a piece about divorces, for example). If the divorce is vital to the story, it is usually better to mention the divorce later in the piece, using the phrase *who is divorced* after the name of the person.

■ Family Bureaucracy and Division of Labor

As a general rule, reporters should not assume that most couples or families conform to any one model, when it comes to division of labor, keeping track of finances or taking charge.

Breadwinner

The *breadwinner* refers to the member of the household who traditionally earns most of the money that supports the household. While the usage is considered acceptable in most publications, reporters should be careful about designating the breadwinners in their writing. In a large percentage of American households, two adults share the breadwinning responsibilities. In such households, it would be incorrect to designate only one of the working adults as the official *breadwinner,* even if one of two adults in the household earns more money than the other.

As a result, the concept of a breadwinner is considered dated at many publications. The usage implies that only one adult in a household provides meaningful financial support. If the other spouse works outside the home and is not also described as a *breadwinner,* the usage becomes insulting. The implication is that the second working spouse bears less economic value to the family, and his or her financial contribution is viewed by the writer as less significant.

The traditional notion was that the husband was the official bread-winner, and the wife stayed home and took care of the house. Writers who use the word *breadwinner* should no longer assume that winning bread is a male task, or that men are the presumed breadwinners within traditional-style families or couples. In single-parent households, where women are the single parents, obviously the women become the breadwinners. But in many cases, women are also breadwinners in families with two parents.

BRINGING HOME THE BACON.   *Bringing home the bacon* means acting as a breadwinner, but it is a cliché. Good writing means avoiding clichés.

Head of the Household

Households are not business or political institutions. As a result, very few have one designated *head of the household.* The 1950s notion was that the father is the head of the household, and in the absence of a father, the mother became the head of the household.

Although some writers may think that the usage is nonsexist and nonpresumptuous, the designation is generally considered outdated. Ask a child who the head of their household is, and the result is usually a puzzled look. Ask a parent who the head of their household is, and the parent may point to their most demanding child or children tongue-in-cheek. Instead of referring to a *head of the household* in an article, the preferred usage is *parent* or *guardian.*

Helping Out

A man who is working in the kitchen of his own home is not helping out in the kitchen. *Helping out* implies that the kitchen is not part of his home or that he is somehow secondary in that room of his home. This usage reveals a bias in that it connotes that women *work* in the kitchen, men only *help out.* If he is working in his own kitchen, he is not *helping out,* he is *working* in his own kitchen. The same applies to other household chores. A man who does laundry is not *helping out* with the laundry but doing the laundry. A man who cleans dishes is not *helping out* with the dishes, but washing dishes. A man who takes care of his children is not *helping out* with the children, but taking care of his own children.

Similarly, when women work outside the home, they are not merely *helping out* with the family income. They are *working.*

Homemaker, Housewife and Househusband

People who work at home full time focusing primarily on cleaning, cooking, shopping and raising a family are *homemakers.* The term applies to both men and women, and is not restricted to the chores mentioned. Homemakers may also be involved as volunteers in politics, education, community service projects and fund-raising, as part of their daily commitment, and still be considered homemakers. Homemakers focus primarily on the needs of home, family and community. A person who runs a commercial business from his or her home and therefore works from home full time would not be considered a *homemaker* if the focus of the business is not the individual's home and family.

Housewife is a dated term for *homemaker* that presumes that the job of homemaker is restricted to married women. In a quotation, *housewife* may be used, but the writer should explain the reason for the usage. If there is no worthy explanation for why the term is chosen over *homemaker,* it is better to rephrase the quotation, removing quotation marks and replacing the word *housewife,* with *homemaker,* the preferred usage.

Househusband, although it is rarely used, is generally meant disparagingly in reference to a male homemaker, implying that men should be working outside the home and not focusing primarily on household chores and family. It not only belittles the man described, but it demeans the job of homemaker, suggesting that such an occupation is somehow beneath a man or not a respectable enough profession for a man. *Homemaker* is the preferred, unbiased usage. In a quotation, *househusband* may be used, but the writer should attribute the quotation, and explain the reason and context for the usage.

Housekeeper

A person who cleans and tidies up a house is a *housekeeper,* not a *maid* in current usage. The term *maid* has come to imply servitude, whereas *housekeeper* connotes an independent contractor or employee.

A family member who works at home full-time, focusing primarily on cleaning, cooking, shopping and raising a family is not a house-keeper, but a homemaker. *Housekeeper* generally refers to an outsider, or nonfamily member, who either lives in or comes to the house regularly to clean.

Lady of the House

Lady of the house, a sales euphemism, should be eliminated from copy. The preferred usage is *mother, wife, companion, parent,* or *guardian,* depending upon the context in the story. Using *lady of the house* has become "sales speak." It implies that the person at the door is afraid to inquire whether the woman who lives in the house is the wife, mother, daughter or mistress of the person who answered the door, and safely asks for the *lady of the house* instead.

Mothers

Writers should not assume that mothers are necessarily the volunteers of the family, food providers, child care supervisors or permission givers. Such stereotypes appear most often in school-related stories. In covering a school event or function, do not assume that participating parents are class mothers, when some might be class fathers, grandparents or other guardians. Use the gender neutral terms *class parent* or *adult volunteer* instead.

Watch for references that specify *mother* unnecessarily and inappropriately. If a teacher asks that children bring clothing donations to school and requests that the children "ask your *mothers* to send in a donation," reporters should feel free to paraphrase outside of quotation marks, stating that children were asked to bring in donations. There is no need to specify *mother, father* or even *parent.*

UNWED MOTHERS.   Writers rarely refer to *unwed fathers,* yet *unwed mothers* is used commonly. Obviously, for every unwed mother, there is an unwed father. Avoid this terminology, since it tends to blame the mother for not being married to the father of the child, regardless of the circumstances. Use *single mother, single father* or *single parent* instead.

Out of Wedlock.   Do not refer to children as *born out of wedlock,* since the usage stigmatizes children for their parents' decision not to marry.

As a rule, when writing about children, do not discuss the parents' marital status unless it specifically pertains to the story.

■ Alternate Lifestyles

Alternate lifestyles is a euphemism for *aberrant lifestyles,* and can be perceived as biased usage. Although the terminology may appear tolerant of diversity, it implies that certain lifestyles are normal and others are deviant. Because each household and family has a different lifestyle, writers should not presume that any one approach is normal or typical. (See chapter 5 on Gender Bias.)

■ Names

What is in a name? Sometimes bias. Editors should be aware of some of the bias associated with name terminology.

Christian Names

An application form required that an applicant neatly print his Christian name. But the applicant was puzzled since he was Hindu and did not have a *Christian name* as such. He ultimately guessed that the form was requesting his first name, since there was another space where he was requested to list his last name.

Was the form biased? Although the creator of the application probably believed *Christian name* to be a generic term, the presumption was made that all applicants were Christians. A *Christian name* generally means one's first name, as opposed to one's family name or last name. Among families of Chinese descent, however, where the family name may be written first, the so-called *Christian name* would be the last name.

Requesting a Christian name on a form or in an article sends an unwelcome biased signal to those who are not Christians and are not familiar with the terminology. Most styles prefer *first name* or *given name.*

Family Name

Refer to a *last name,* rather than a *family name* in writing. Not everyone in a modern American family necessarily shares the same *last name.* Reporters need to inquire about each person's full name separately when writing an article about a family if the last name pertains. It is becoming increasingly common, for example, for professional women to keep the last name they used before marriage. Thus the father and mother in many modern families have different last names. Children may have the father's last name, the mother's last name, a hyphenated name or some other combination of names.

In families where there are stepparents involved, last names may also be different within a single household. The same may be true in homes where the children live with their grandparents or other relatives. A writer should never assume that all the names are the same within a given household.

Jewish Names

Jewish name is not the Jewish equivalent of *Christian name.* It does not mean *first name,* but rather a name used during religious services and on religious documents.

In Israel, Jewish children are generally named in Hebrew. These are the names by which they are known by their friends, families and everyone else they meet. These are also the names used in religious services. As a result, most Israelis do not have separate Jewish names.

In Diaspora countries—countries outside of Israel—some Jews prefer to give their children more assimilated names. Those with non-Hebrew and non-Yiddish names are sometimes then given a separate set of Jewish names, names by which they are known mostly in religious services and on religious documents.

Maiden Name

Maiden name is becoming a dated term, in that it implies that before a woman is married she is a maiden and after she is married she has a new name. Many women find the term *maiden* objectionable.

Maiden name implies that all married women change their names upon marriage. Many married women do not change their last name upon marriage. Some keep their previous last name. Some combine names with their husbands to create a new name or a hyphenated name.

Reporters should not assume that all married women have maiden names as such. Editors should watch for this usage in copy.

Surnames

Surname means family name or last name, and is considered unbiased. Contrary to its sound, it is not a derivation of the masculine word, *sir.*

■ Old Wives' Tales

Do not use the expression *old wives' tale* as a substitute for the term *superstition.* Inaccuracies and misinformation should not be blamed gratuitously on old married women. The usage is gender biased, family biased and age biased. Instead, describe the so-called tale as a *superstition, rumor, irrational outcome* or *a superstitious story,* depending upon the reference, meaning and context.

11

Bias and Education

■ Education Bias Examples

The following are examples of different forms of education bias that commonly appear in publications or on broadcasts. Examine the sentences, and then determine how they should best be rewritten to eliminate bias.

The student was described as a computer whiz, a nerd and a geek, whose head was in the clouds.

For such an egghead, she was amazingly good at sports.

Up in his ivy tower, the professor probably had no sense of what it was like to survive in the Real World.

She dressed Ivy League, with preppy shoes and a blazer.

It doesn't take a brain surgeon or a rocket scientist to know that exercise is important.

■ Overview

Journalists are often guilty of two kinds of education bias: educated snobbery and anti-intellectualism. Educated snobbery is a matter of looking condescendingly upon people who are less educated than the writer. While less-educated people may seem like easy targets, writers tend to hesitate when it comes to revealing any bias in this direction. Anti-intellectualism is a matter of looking condescendingly upon people who are more educated than the writer. Highly educated people are apparently perceived as "fair game" by writers, judging from the frequency of disparaging remarks about higher education. Both constitute forms of bias.

■ Anti-Intellectual Terms

Contrary to what many journalists might imagine, anti-intellectualism seems to be more common within journalism than educated snobbery. An obvious example of massive anti-intellectualism was the Unabomer (spelled *Unabomber* in some publications) case, when the first articles on the suspect's arrest appeared. They were fast to list his education credentials and academic affiliations, and some columns implied that this supposed overeducation is what eventually led to his demise. Many journalists seemed to take delight in the resume partly because the suspect was affiliated with such elite educational institutions.

Doctor's Handwriting

All medical doctors do not write the same. According to popular American stereotypes, doctors inevitably have sloppy or indecipherable handwriting, and unreadable handwriting makes one a better physician. Obviously, these notions are false, as is the notion that as people get smarter, they become more difficult to comprehend. There is no "doctor's handwriting." These are anti-intellectual biases.

Egghead

Egghead is generally considered an acceptable synonym for *intellectual*. The word sometimes has a negative connotation, however. The image of an egghead is obviously an egg-shaped head. To some, this implies that very intelligent people necessarily have odd, awkward, egg-shaped or elongated heads. Although *egghead* is not usually meant as an insult, it is not necessarily considered a flattering label either. Some publications would argue that *egghead* implies that there is something wrong with being intellectual or smart, and implies a certain aloofness.

Head in the Clouds

People who pursue intellectual or theoretical discussions should not be presumed to have their *heads in the clouds*. The expression refers to those who are unable to act practically or reasonably. The expression is best attached to an action, rather than a person (a very fine distinction): One can behave as if one's head is in the clouds temporarily or even frequently. As a general rule, presuming that very smart people are unable to be practical indicates an anti-intellectual bias.

Intellectual

Although *intellectual* would appear to be a flattering adjective in all cases, in some social circles, *intellectual* is used as an insult. *Intellectual* may be defined as *rational,* or *using the intellect.* There is nothing biased about the word *intellectual,* unless it is used in a biased context. (Example: *Are you some kind of intellectual?*) Although the word is acceptable in most contexts, editors should be alert to negative usage and stereotyping by the writer to make sure there is no anti-intellectual bias intended.

INTELLECTUAL VERSUS ATHLETIC.   A high school student was excluded from a ball game because he was told that he was too intellectual to have any physical ability. Obviously the reasoning was faulty, but that is a common stereotype. Intellectuals are sometimes presumed to be clumsy, poorly coordinated and certainly not athletic. Editors should watch for these stereotypes, or statements that reveal a gee-whiz attitude when an intellectual's athletic performance is discussed, particularly if the individual is athletic. Having intellectual talent and athletic ability are not mutually exclusive, and both gifts should not be presented as opposites or ironies.

INTELLECTUAL VERSUS PRACTICAL.   At an interview, an applicant was asked if she was intellectual or practical.

"Both," she responded.

"You can't be both," the interviewer insisted adamantly. "You are either an intellectual or a practical person."

Aside from ignorance, what the interviewer displayed was intellectual bias. The interviewer seemed to believe that one could not be both a person of the mind and a doer at the same time, as if each was mutually exclusive.

Editors should be wary of such polarization of people in articles. Modern living requires that people think on a combination of levels: abstract and theoretical as well as tangible and practical. Because people think, it should not be assumed that they are incapable of doing. Because people do, it should not be assumed that they are incapable of thinking.

Ivy Leaguer

The Ivy League schools include: Harvard University, Yale University, Princeton University, Dartmouth College, Columbia University, University of Pennsylvania, Cornell University and Brown University. Students who attend any of these universities may correctly be called *Ivy Leaguers* or *Ivy League* students.

Some people use *Ivy League* or *Ivy Leaguer* to describe the way a person looks or dresses. They are referring to an image, not necessarily tied to what students on Ivy League campuses really look like or how they dress. The term is most commonly used by people who have not attended Ivy League universities and is meant as a compliment. The term is generally applied to white men who are clean-shaven, with short hair and who wear neat, conservative clothing. A writer who quotes someone describing a person as *Ivy League,* may be subtly promoting a stereotype of how top students look: male, beardless, conservative and Caucasian. Editors should be cautious with quotations that describe people this way. If the quotation is vital to the story, keep the expression in quotation marks. Attribute it, and explain its meaning in context.

Ivory Tower

The expression is *ivory tower* not *ivy tow*er, and it bears no relation to the Ivy League. According to the *Merriam Webster's Dictionary,* the usage refers to "an impractical often escapist attitude marked by aloof lack of concern with or interest in practical matters or urgent problems." It also means "a secluded place that affords the means of treating practical issues with an impractical often escapist attitude; especially a place of learning."

The second definition implies that thinkers and scholars are too removed to answer practical questions, an obvious intellectual bias. Editors should beware of such references, partly because the usage is a cliché, but also because it reveals a strong educational bias. If it appears within a quotation, the entire sentence should be kept in quotation marks, and the term should be attributed with the context explained clearly.

Overeducated Fool

Can a person be overly educated? Labeling a person *an overeducated fool* shows a bias against education and learning. Writers should be careful when quoting someone using the expression. Always use quotation marks. Attribute the expression, and explain the meaning of the quotation in context.

The Real World

Eliminate cliché references to *the real world* in stories about education and academic institutions.

According to common usage, one enters *the real world* after finishing one's education. For those who opt to continue working within the academic community as educators, *the real world* is postponed or avoided. The implication is that *the real world* exists everywhere except academic institutions. Such usage is obviously heavily biased, and implies that scholars and academics exist in a fake or fantasy world, removed from reality. It is a put-down of education and promotes the notion that students and educators are not accountable, burdened or responsible.

People who are employed by school districts, private schools, universities and colleges are as much a part of *the real world* as people employed by other companies and institutions. If the usage appears within a quotation that is vital to the story, the statement may be quoted directly, within quotation marks. It should also be attributed and explained in context.

Rocket Scientists

Many rocket scientists must be flattered or perhaps tickled when writers and speakers, thinking they are pointing out something obvious, start their sentence with, "It doesn't take a *rocket scientist* to figure out ..." The implication is obviously that the rocket scientist is the most intelligent kind of person. But the reference is also an anti-intellectual jab, implying that rocket scientists are somehow too educated for the issue at hand, as well as that the audience is simple-minded.

When a speaker resorts to this cliché, a writer or editor should not quote it directly. Instead, remove the quotation marks and paraphrase the gist of the sentence, the point the speaker is intending to make. Or just take out the first part of the sentence and directly quote the part of the sentence that follows "It doesn't take a rocket scientist to figure out that ..."

Brain Surgeons

See the previous entry under Rocket Scientists. Speakers, trying to make a point, often say, "It doesn't take a *brain surgeon* to understand ..." This expression is used as a variation of "It doesn't take a rocket scientist," and serves the same insulting function. In this case, it implies that brain surgeons are somehow overly educated, or more educated than everyone else, while it implies that the audience is filled with simpletons who are incapable of understanding anything conceptual.

When a speaker resorts to this cliché, a writer or editor should not quote it directly. Instead, remove the quotation marks and paraphrase the gist of the sentence, the point the speaker is intending to make. Or just take out the first part of the sentence and directly quote the part of the sentence that follows "It doesn't take a brain surgeon to understand that ..."

It Doesn't Take a Degree from Harvard or MIT

Refer to the entries under Rocket Scientists and Brain Surgeons. Speakers, trying to make a point, often say, "It doesn't take *a degree from Harvard or MIT* to know ..." The implication is that graduates of Harvard and MIT are more educated than everyone else, while it implies that the audience—though it may include college-educated people—is filled with simpletons who are incapable of understanding anything conceptual.

Again, this is a cliché. A writer or editor should not quote it directly. Instead, remove the quotation marks and paraphrase the gist of the remarks. Or just eliminate the first part of the sentence and directly quote the part that follows "It doesn't take a degree from Harvard or MIT ..."

Smart Aleck, Smarty-Pants, Wise Guy

Smart aleck, smarty-pants and *wise guy* are taunts that are understood to mean cleverness to the point of obnoxious behavior. The implication is that becoming too clever, wise or smart is bad, and that there is a limit on tasteful, comfortable intelligence.

In media quotations, these taunts are most commonly attributed to adults, speaking about poorly behaved children. They are often used in reference to children who constantly question or comment freely. The usage also appears frequently in crime stories, in discussions of suspects or criminals. In both cases, the implication is that it is obnoxious to be too clever, wise or smart, an anti-intellectual bias. In a crime story, it may not seem offensive to quote a law enforcement official referring to a suspect as a *smart aleck, smarty-pants* or *wise guy*. It is less tasteful, however, to quote an adult referring to a child this way, and generally reveals the adult's anti-intellectual bias.

Too Smart for One's Own Good

Can a person ever be too smart? Is there a maximum level of smartness that is optimal, after which intelligence becomes a drawback or burden? If the answer to either of these questions is yes, then it is possible to be *too smart for one's own good*. If not, the phrase is used as a putdown of a smart person who makes a mistake.

All people make mistakes. When people who are not considered intelligent make errors, writers tend to be more forgiving. When smart people make mistakes, however, others—particularly jealous others—are sometimes fast to blame the person's intelligence, as if to say, it is better not to be smart. The obvious implication is that the speaker (or the writer who quotes the speaker) is not as smart. The phrase reveals a bias against or subtle envy of intelligence.

Trendy Words That Reveal Bias

Students occasionally reveal an anti-intellectual bias in describing their contemporaries, often peers who study more or work harder than they do. Among the terms commonly used are *nerd, twit, geek, dork, dweeb, computer jock* and *computer nerd*. Writers should avoid using all of these terms. Although incorporation of such terms may sound youthful and trendy, they promote an anti-intellectual bias, and sometimes hint at jealousy on the part of the speaker who is not achieving as much.

When a person uses one of these terms in an interview, the reporter should inquire what is meant by the term. How does it apply to the person or people described? As a rule, it is better to specify the meaning behind the negative buzzwords in an article than to slavishly repeat the anti-intellectual slur in a quotation, thereby helping to promote bias.

Whiz Kids and Computer Whizzes

A young person who is comfortable using a computer should not be immediately labeled a *whiz kid* or *computer whiz*. Such labels merely suggest that the writer or editor is inept or uncomfortable with current technology. Most American schools are starting to require computer proficiency among high school students, and many require it to a lesser degree for primary school students.

Whiz kid references also appears commonly in articles about science, math, engineering and business achievements. Although the terms would seem flattering, implicit in the usage is an age bias. An adult in his or her 20s or 30s should not be referred to as a *kid*, even if the writer is significantly older and is impressed with the youth and ability of the person being described. The usage suggests the question, *How could somebody so young know or achieve so much?* This is obviously an age-biased question.

■ Educated Snobbery

Educated snobbery is sometimes used as a means of "acceptable" putdown when a writer wants to disguise a prejudice against someone's economic situation, race or ethnicity. Terms to examine include *underachiever, overachiever, dog, drone, automaton* and *gopher*. Editors need to learn how to recognize disguised references.

Automaton

Automatons are machines. Hard-working students and employees should not be described as *automatons*. Because a student or worker finds his or her work stimulating and becomes dedicated or even obsessive about excellence does not make the person an automaton. The usage suggests that the writer does not value hard work and is unable to understand dedication. The usage also suggests that the writer is showing a bias against the particular task, making a judgment that the study or labor is not meaningful.

Occasionally, hard-working people of other cultures are labeled *automatons,* either by writers or by observers quoted in articles, particularly in pieces about work and social conditions abroad or within a given community. In covering social climate and work conditions, a writer should look beyond the stereotype to find out why people are so devoted to their work. It should not be presumed that such people are machines.

Underachievers and Overachievers

An *underachiever* means a bright person who does not work to his or her potential. The term is insulting in two ways: It suggests that the person described is lazy or apathetic, and it suggests that the end result is never acceptable.

Overachiever is an even more insulting label than *underachiever*. An overachiever is one who works hard and achieves more than his or her supposed natural capability. The implication is that an overachiever is a relatively simpleminded person, with limited capacity. The implication is also that this person's success is undeserved and is only the result of working too hard, as if hard work is somehow wrong.

Both terms appear commonly in education pieces and business profiles. Writers should avoid using either label, since both require the writer to evaluate the potential of the person described, an evaluation that writers are not qualified to make. Editors should be wary about quoted material that incorporates either term. It is probably better to rephrase the quotation outside of quotation marks, omitting either term. If either term is to be used, the writer should attribute the usage carefully, and explain the usage in context.

In an interview with a teacher, for example, if the teacher says, "We need more funding, because most of the kids in this district are *underachievers*," the writer should explain why the teacher describes the students this way. Do the students have high IQ test scores but perform poorly in the classroom? Is there some other indication that the teacher has that the students have higher potential than they are showing? Are the students really performing badly, or does the teacher have unrealistic expectations? How are realistic expectations defined? Without a proper explanation by the writer, usage of *overachiever* and *underachiever* become examples of name-calling or quoted name-calling in an article.

■ Judging a School

Responsible education reporters attempt to cover their beat objectively by compiling statistics and examining a full range of schools and educational environments. Editors should be wary of reporting that stereotypes certain schools or school districts, thus revealing bias.

Editors who handle education stories regularly might ask some of the following questions to help assure even and unbiased coverage of education:

1. Does the education writer tend to repeatedly use the same school as an example of what the writer perceives to be excess? Does the writer impose his or her own ideas of excess, when writing about a school?

2. Does the writer always refer to the same school as an example of what the writer perceives to be poverty or underprivilege? Does the writer impose his or her own ideas of inadequacy when writing about a school?

3. Does the writer always characterize innovative programs as better than established programs? Or established programs as better than innovative programs?

4. Does the writer stereotype the students of a school based on the reputation of its surrounding ethnic or economic population?

5. Does the writer resent a community where a greater proportion of money is spent on education? Or a community where less money is spent on education?

6. Does the writer assume that certain populations are more difficult to teach than others?

7. How does the writer use statistics within an article? Are the statistics truly indicative of the quality of education? Or are the statistics mentioned as a way of manipulating information?

■ Touchy-Feely

Touchy-feely has become a buzzword to disparage educational methods that attempt to educate the child as a whole, incorporating feelings and psychology into the curriculum. People who use the term disparagingly generally favor approaches that are less nurture-oriented and more focused on mastery of skills. When an education writer labels a program *touchy-feely,* the writer is revealing a bias against certain teaching philosophies.

12

Bias and Values

■ Bias and Values Examples

The following are examples of different forms of values-bias that commonly appear in publications or on broadcasts. Examine the sentences, and then determine how they should best be rewritten to eliminate bias.

The student was scolded by the teacher, for being a kiss-up and a tattler.

The radioactive leak continued until a squealing whistle-blower notified the media.

The political candidate was considered a do-gooder by many of the voters.

The aide denied that he was the White House leak.

For her charitable work, she became known as the local Pollyanna.

■ Overview

Choice of words often gives away the writer's personal values. If a writer labels a project to be "worthy" of funding, for example, the designation is clearly a value judgment, based on the writer's understanding of worth. Some word usage is subtler, however.

■ Values-Related Terms

It is not uncommon in modern society to find references that belittle people who try to do good, as if doing good is inherently bad. Politicians are sometimes labeled *do-gooders* in the press. Well-behaved children are disparagingly referred to as *goody-goodies, Pollyannas, kiss-*

ups or *goody two-shoes*. Whistle-blowers are sometimes labeled *tattlers*, *leaks* or *squealers*.

Journalists should avoid using values-biased terms in news and feature stories. If such terms appear within a quotation and the statement is vital to the story, editors should make sure that the statement appears in quotation marks and that it is properly attributed and explained in context.

Do-Gooders

While a *do-gooder* sounds like a pleasant person, the connotation is meant to be negative. A *do-gooder* is someone who attempts to do good at the expense of what is practical or good in the long run. It has also been used to mean a *Monday-morning quarterback,* a *Johnny-come-lately,* someone who, after a misdeed or mistake, offers unwanted advice on how the task should have been done.

To use the term in writing implies that doing "good" is in some way bad or naïve, a value that the writer may not intend to reinforce. If a writer uses the term in quoting a speaker, the editor should make sure that an explanation and reason for the usage accompanies the reference.

Leaks and Squealers

Both leaks and squealers sound more annoying than flattering. From the journalism perspective, *leaks* are generally good. After all, to whom is the information leaked? To the journalism media, and then to the public.

Obviously, there is danger when top-secret government security information is leaked. In some cases, people who leak this kind of information are aiming to undermine the government or the safety of people, a cause in which journalists should not participate. (Obviously, journalists do not have the obligation to blindly print every threat or piece of propaganda that is hurled their way.) At other times, however, leaks are meant to improve conditions within a government office, by letting the public know about a silent behind-the-scenes threat that is otherwise hidden. Similarly, business leaks may be aimed at toppling business for competing companies, or leaks can be an "insider's" means of attempting to improve an industry. As a rule, journalists should be careful about accepting and spreading information, particularly when it comes to secretive and leaked information.

The journalists' aim is not to help topple any business. Attribution and reliability of sources obviously become very important when dealing with leaks.

At the same time, journalists should not write about *leaks* as if they're necessarily evil. Many good leaks have provided helpful journalistic information and tips, which were ultimately used to improve society. Leaking is often the only means an "insider" has of correcting an injustice (by making it public), sometimes a major injustice that would otherwise continue unnoticed by the general population.

Tattlers

A second-grade boy saw a child beat up another child on the playground. The second-grader ran to his teacher and told her. The boy was surprised when the teacher turned around and scolded him for being a *tattletale* or *tattler.* She said that tattling is a worse offense than fighting on the playground. Obviously, she was not a journalist.

Tattling is one of the important roles of journalism. The concept that the public has the right to know, and that public knowledge is one of the best defenses against corruption and wrongdoing in society, are major motivations for honest journalism.

Journalists that berate people in their writing for *tattling* are confused about their own role in the democratic system. Journalists who are faced with a quotation in which people are called *tattlers* should probably rephrase the quotation outside of quotation marks to eliminate parroting the jargon.

Whistle-Blowers

A *whistle-blower* is an informer, or one who draws attention to a wrongdoing by, figuratively, blowing a whistle. Often, the whistle-blower draws this attention to the misdeed by informing the news media and the public. The news media then blows the whistle, and becomes a vehicle of whistle-blowing.

Is this bad? Not according to the principles of American journalism. Whistle-blowing is one of the goals of journalism. In theory, investigative reporters are all whistle-blowers; and many traditional journalists say that all responsible reporters are investigative reporters. If the major goal of journalism is to inform the public, it seems ironic that some journalists then use the term *whistle-blower* as a derogatory term. Editors should be careful about negative usage, since any negative connotation indicates confusion about the role of journalism, and bias toward secretive corporate executives or political leaders.

■ Values in Quotations

Be wary of values-based terms that appear in quotations. Journalists are under no obligation to parrot quotations that are irresponsible or heavily biased, particularly if no explanation of the derogatory quotation or the reasoning behind it is available. Within quotations, taunts about values should be treated as seriously as epithets or any other heavily biased language.

If a speaker calls a political opponent a "Pollyanna," the writer covering the speech may see a reason to quote the term in an article, to give a sense of the speaker's values and the "flavor" of the speech. Instead of merely parroting the term, however, a good writer would then try to find out how and why the term *Pollyanna* was being applied. If this information is not spelled out within a speech, the writer should attempt to clarify the reference in a follow-up interview. If no interview or question-answer session is available, the writer should think twice about quoting flippant name-calling. When the term used sounds like a more potent insult, the need for following up becomes more obvious. For example, if a speaker calls an opponent a "racist," few writers would print the charge without an explanation of the speaker's choice of words.

Some writers view terms like *Pollyanna* and *do-gooder* as too innocuous to require following up. A good editor needs to recognize that when it comes to values reporting, what may seem harmless to one writer may be perceived as a fatal buzzword to a campaign or subject of an article. To a responsible editor, all labels should be suspect.

As a rule, editors should keep in mind that the journalist's job is not to slavishly quote whatever a speaker says, thereby helping to circulate unfounded political propaganda and name-calling. At the same time, the journalist's job is not to censor or "clean up" offensive usage. Responsible editors need to examine offensive terms and make sure they are adequately attributed and explained to the readers in context, if the terms are to be used at all within a given piece. If a speaker (or writer covering the speech) is unable to explain how the terms apply, the editor should not slavishly use the quotation, or should use it but explain that the reader was unable to defend the usage.

13

Appeals to "Positive Bias"

■ "Positive Bias" Examples

The following are examples of different forms of supposedly positive bias that commonly appear in publications or on broadcasts. Because positive bias is so difficult for many editors to detect and eliminate, 13 examples are provided. Examine the sentences, and then determine how they should best be rewritten to eliminate bias.

Asian Americans are always the most gifted in mathematics.

If you want a top lawyer, hire a Jewish attorney.

French men are the most romantic lovers.

Irish people know how to have fun at parties.

Scandinavian women are always the most attractive, with their beautiful blond hair and blue eyes.

Africans and African Americans have natural rhythm.

If you need precision work done, hire a German. They are the most exacting and efficient.

Californians are the most laid-back Americans, and they usually speak without any regional accent.

Southerners are friendlier because their slower pace allows them to enjoy life.

Hungarian mothers know how to feed you. They're great cooks and get offended if you don't clean your plate.

Women always have a much better sense of decorating. It's all part of the nesting instinct.

Methodists always cater conservatively, and they're careful to avoid lavish food displays.

The girls behaved like proper ladies when they were not on stage performing.

Positive bias does not necessarily mean flattery. If not all of these supposedly positive statements seem flattering to everyone, editors should note that what appears to one reader to be positive, seems more like negative stereotyping to the next reader. The objective editor should remove all bias.

■ Overview

Bias is not to be tolerated in objective journalism, even when the slant seems to be positive. Permitting positive bias implies that negative bias is acceptable as well. Positive bias opens the door to all biases, and what seems harmless and positive to one writer may seem offensive to the interview subject.

Positive bias is often harder to detect than negative bias. It is used commonly in marketing, where it is an acceptable means of promoting a product. A commercial example of popular "positive bias" is the appeal of Häagen-Dazs, an American creation that borrows heavily on a Danish image. The shops are decorated in red and white and light-toned wood, the colors of Denmark. The product appeals to many American customers' positive image of Denmark: clean, bright, modern and wholesome.

Likewise, Ben & Jerry's ice cream appeals to many Americans' positive feelings about the state of Vermont: clean mountain air, black-and-white cows, green pastures, blue skies and a bucolic setting, as well as the 1970s idealist lifestyle.

Both ice-cream companies provide visual examples of how positive bias is used effectively in marketing. Other ice-cream companies want consumers to identify their product with a wholesome southern image, an old-fashioned Pennsylvania Dutch image, a modern Swedish image, and a California fun-loving image. Within marketing, appeal to such positive biases is not only acceptable, but exemplary practice as long as the bias does not offend.

In journalism and objective editing, however, the equivalent bias needs to be eliminated. (Journalists are not promoters or publicists, and maintaining objectivity is essential.) For a journalist to advocate that Denmark and Vermont are somehow superior implies that the same journalist views other countries and states as inferior. Thus the editor is forced to reveal some degree of negative bias by promoting a positive bias.

Careless writers occasionally reveal their positive biases (while reinforcing other people's biases) when writing about *German efficiency, laid-back Californians, the work ethic of a New Englander, country hospitality, country cooking, French chic, Swiss punctuality, natural rhythm, fun-loving Irish*, etc.

◼ Descriptions without Bias

Including the positive traits or characteristics of a person, place or group within journalistic writing does not necessarily constitute positive bias. Contrary to the popular public image of journalism, journalists can write positive statements and still remain objective. Journalists need to watch diligently for stereotyping, both positive and negative, about characteristics of groups of people, however. A profile piece can describe an individual's characteristics or habits without trying to fit that individual into categories, whether ethnic, national, sexual or generational. In a feature piece, it is acceptable to write, "Mulvaney's family said he was a dedicated police officer, who knew every shop owner in the neighborhood and made them feel secure." It is unacceptable to write, "Mulvaney's family said that *like most Irish-American police officers,* Mulvaney was dedicated, and knew every shop owner in the neighborhood and made them feel secure."

◼ Positive Bias in a Quotation

When positive bias appears within a quotation, editors should still remove the positive bias from the copy. It is important to stress, however, that in order to eliminate positive bias from a quotation, an editor may trim a phrase from the quotation, but should not alter consecutive wording, rephrase within quotation marks or fabricate a quotation. Instead, remove the offensive portion of the quotation and insert an ellipsis.

This quotation is not acceptable: *"Like all Italian women,* Stella likes to feed her guests until they are full, and then she brings out the main course," her husband said.

In order to salvage the acceptable part of the quotation, the editor should remove the first phrase. This can be done by inserting an ellipsis: "... Stella likes to feed her guests until they are full, and then she brings out the main course," her husband said.

Because the bias appears at the beginning of the sentence and because the remainder of the sentence makes a complete sentence in itself, the offensive phrase can be edited out without an ellipsis as well and still be technically correct: "Stella likes to feed her guests until they are full, and then she brings out the main course," her husband said.

If the positive bias appears in the middle of a quotation, however, it may be more difficult to remove the bias without altering the quotation or the meaning of the quotation. If ellipses can be used in place of the biased portion of the statement without altering the context, the editor can insert ellipses and keep the rest of the quotation intact.

If the husband had said, for example, "Stella, *like all Italian women,* likes to feed her guests until they are full, and then she brings out the main course," an ellipsis can be inserted easily in place of the biased phrase. The altered sentence would be "Stella ... likes to feed her guests until they are full, and then she brings out the main course."

If omitting information and substituting an ellipsis result in alteration of the meaning of the quotation, however, the quotation should not be kept. Instead, it should be rephrased, and the quotation marks should be removed. Never keep the quotation marks if the quotation has been rephrased.

■ Trend Pieces

Trend pieces often try to characterize groups, and therefore tread on dangerous ground. Editors of trend pieces need to constantly question whether or not these pieces are contributing to previous stereotypes or creating new ones by grouping people together in an attempt to decipher a trend.

Trend pieces sometimes focus on a specific generation or interest group. Editors should watch for and eliminate all-inclusive words including *all, most, everyone,* and *as a whole.* Do not let the writer get away with a sentence like "All girls like diamonds," unless you know that the writer has interviewed "all girls." Likewise, do not permit a sentence like, "Everyone likes a parade," unless you know that the writer has interviewed "everyone." Similarly, "Most people enjoy the thrill of a roller coaster," is unacceptable, unless the writer has interviewed "most people."

Editors reading a trend piece written by a person who claims to be part of the particular trend should watch out for claims by the writer that "everyone" is following the specified trend. From the writer's vantage point, everyone with whom the writer h as contact may indeed be following that trend. But many of the readers are probably hearing about this trend for the first time and are not part of it and might even be offended at the suggestion that they are part of it.

Following are some types of sentences to avoid:

On college campuses this spring, *all the female students* are wearing multicolored nail polish.

What are retired people doing nowadays? Contrary to what you might think, *most* are surfing the Net.

The fashion doll has a new shape, featuring a flatter chest and wider hips, making her look more like *real women.*

Elementary-school-age boys prefer violent cartoons to educational television.

Generation X-ers eat their dinners out or order in, but *never* cook for themselves.

Although teenagers kicked the habit for years, *they are all* back to smoking again.

All urban and most suburban teenagers are into clubbing nowadays.

Most of the top executives have rediscovered the pleasures of a good cigar.

Parents, *as a whole,* tend to agree that it's much easier to raise boys than girls.

Recently, *the whole generation of people in their twenties* began lining up for tattoos and body piercing.

14

Editing Art for Bias

■ Biased Art Examples

The following are examples of different forms of biased art that commonly appear in publications or on broadcasts. Make a determination as to how each illustration should be handled to eliminate bias.

A photo taken at an anti-abortion rally shows two women burning their bras.

An art spread celebrating baseball is bordered by team logos, one of which depicts an American Indian, with an exaggerated toothy grin and wide eyes, another of which depicts a black child eating watermelon, and a third logo that reveals a Chasidic Jew with a pointy nose.

At a local arena, a TV camera focuses first on a fan's sign that says, "Go to Hell Gypsies." Then the camera pans across the stands to show fans singing a song that makes fun of Gypsies.

A political cartoon about the Middle East depicts an Arab man with an elongated pointy chin, pointy nose, and wicked-looking, pointed eyebrows, as he holds a curved knife in one hand and a money bag in the other.

A photo accompanying a story on a new peep show theater that has opened in a residential community shows publicity billboards outside featuring topless women.

■ Overview

If a picture is worth a thousand words, a biased illustration is the equivalent of many an insult. It may seem at first that art, particularly photos, cannot be biased, since unedited photos depict what is, as it is.

Yet novice photographers, photo editors, artists, art editors, and cartoonists should be aware that, contrary to common perception, subtle bias is often hidden in art. Publications handle visual bias differently. Biased art may range from "acceptable" but "offensive" illustrations to blatantly discriminatory depictions.

■ Typifying Groups

When writing captions for photos, the copy editor needs to be vigilant about not characterizing an entire population based on one photo of a group of people that might seem to represent that population. The first step might be to examine the photos that are offered as illustrations of the article. Are the photos fair to the article, or did the photographer focus on one small nonrepresentative group that behaved badly at the event? At a publication in California, one of the staff photographers had the tendency to only photograph young women whom he considered attractive—no matter what the event. If the editor feels that the photos were taken with a bias, the editor should question the photographer and inquire about the availability of additional photos that better illustrate the piece.

When there are no more suitable photos available, the copy editor should handle the captions with care. If a photo depicts a group of students drinking beer at an environmental demonstration, for example, the editor needs to write a caption that clearly explains that drinking was not the primary activity at the demonstration. The editor needs to let the reader know that the majority of people at the protest did not participate in the private drinking party. Selecting such a photo implies that the incident *typified* the event. This obviously degrades the intentions of the majority of the demonstrators.

One problem with the common journalism practice of having a copy editor (who was not present at the particular event) select photos and write captions is that the copy editor is at a loss to determine which photos in a selection typify an event. The photographer should limit the selection to photos that typify the event. If an editor sees a photo that would seem to degrade an event, the editor should ask the photographer if this was a widespread occurrence at the demonstration, or the exception to the rule. The caption should explain the context.

The photographer, at the same time, should not be focusing primarily on aberrant behavior when "covering" such a demonstration, but rather "slice-of-life" behavior. A camera can be a very powerful tool with which to misrepresent people or an event. A photographer should not be pursuing private people's shortcomings, unless those shortcomings play a pivotal part in the larger story.

This is not to suggest that photographers be censored in taking pictures. On the contrary, they should be free to photograph what they feel is important. In the later process of selecting photos to submit to the copy desk or art department for publication, however, photographers need to select photos that they feel are truly representational as well as interesting.

■ Demeaning Illustrations

As a rule, editors should note that newspapers have no obligation to print offensive illustrations. Such art does not enhance a newspaper's objectivity. Nor does it give the reader a greater understanding of the issues involved in a sports story. The exception is when the topic of the article is the offensive symbol itself.

Artists and art editors should be cautious about incorporating team symbols as illustrations in sports stories, although such art may be convenient or inexpensive. If a team symbol promotes bias, is belittling or contains an offensive caricature, objective publications should avoid printing symbols of that team in any article about the team. Printing such images only contributes to the promotion of offensive stereotypes. .

Some art editors contend that refusing to automatically publish certain emblems and symbols is a form of censorship. Yet most publications consider certain symbols, such as a swastika or an inappropriate sexual drawing, offensive enough to eliminate when it is only being used as part of an artist's illustration. (A different policy may apply for photos, when used and explained in context, and political cartoons.) In some cases, an art editor is left with the uncomfortable choice of whether to print the offensive caricature, helping to promote bias and stereotype along with the team, or to exclude such art, giving the offending team less visibility than other teams.

Style policies differ at different publications. Some publications may opt to avoid printing all team symbols as illustrations, rather than make a value decision on which symbols offend or have the potential to offend. Others may choose to print all but the ones deemed blatantly offensive.

Types of caricature features that are typically considered offensive are those that draw upon stereotypes. Some teams, for example, use logos that are offensive to Native Americans while attempting to be humorous or intimidating: bright red or yellow skin colors, obnoxious toothy smiles, facial expressions that are either overly naïve or uncomfortably stern.

■ Demeaning Photographs

The appearance of an offensive symbol on a uniform or in the background of a photo does not obligate a publication to print and endorse (or lend credence to) this symbol.

Print photographers and photo editors should pay attention to symbols. If the symbol appears on a team hat or uniform, the journalist could opt to eliminate a photo entirely or edit the photo to exclude the portion of the photo that contains the offensive art.

Some publications have strict editorial policies against editing art beyond cropping. At such publications, art could be tightly cropped to eliminate any offensive symbols. In other words, show the face of the player, but not the hat, if the offensive symbol appears on the hat. If the hat is worn snugly, and it is impossible to crop out the hat without chopping off too much of the head, eliminate the photo entirely. Choose another in its place.

At other publications, photos could be "touched up" or airbrushed to eliminate offensive slogans or symbols.

Fans who hold up ethnically offensive signs or pantomime offensive hand signals should not be photographed while promoting these biases. Such photos provide inappropriate illustrations, and the publicity encourages this insulting behavior by more fans seeking attention and by readers. The exception is when this biased behavior is the focus of the sports story.

■ TV Camera Angles

TV cameras should not focus on fans who hold up ethnically offensive signs, chant offensive slogans or songs, or pantomime offensive hand signals or portrayals of Indian lore, unless this insulting behavior is the focus of the news story. The same rule applies to focusing cameras on celebrities, politicians and team owners within the audience, who may imitate or feel pressured to conform to (thus endorsing) the mass behavior.

If the focus of the particular report is on a sport or game itself, insulting fans should not be granted gratuitous publicity. To broadcast insulting behavior is to publicize and endorse degrading biased images of people. In addition, such attention promotes similar biased copycat behavior and models this behavior for children and other spectators who may be watching from home.

■ Radio and Television Sound

Microphones should not offer publicity and endorsement to the chanters of ethnically offensive slogans or songs, unless the focus of the news report is the fans' insulting behavior.

Sound editors should eliminate offensive background chants from the audio, rather than letting some of the sound "leak" into the background noise. Such sounds do not provide informative "flavor" for a game. During idle moments of a game, between innings perhaps, microphones still should not pick up the sounds of rude or insulting fans. Lack of interesting sound is no excuse to record offensive chants.

■ Arrest Photos

Photographing an arrest scene may seem like a perfectly natural task for a photojournalist. And seeing that photo appear in print or on television may seem like a reasonable expectation. But photographers and photo editors need to consider the images that newspapers, magazines and television put before readers.

Photos in visible locations (publications, milk cartons and at the post office, for example) can be extremely useful in finding suspects and missing people. When a suspect is found, however, photos have less utility. This is not to suggest that the publication or television station should censor these photos and not let the public see the arrest. There may be good reason to show the arrest. What the public often sees, however, during an arrest, is a young man (men are seen more often than women) with his face covered by a hood or other garment, and only a hand sticking out holding onto that garment to shield his face from cameras. To the reader or viewer the hand appears to be either black or white. That is all that the reader or viewer sees of the suspect at the time of arrest, if no other photo is provided. The viewer then may subconsciously take a "tally" of how many white hands or black hands they see getting arrested on the TV news or in the newspaper. The end result may be heavily laden with prejudice based on skin color, since no other visual information is supplied.

Despite the tendency by the suspect to hide his or her face, arrests are very visual events for television cameras, which seek out visual material, and they create interesting action photos for print journalism. Therefore, arrests remain attractive subjects for photographers.

It would be journalistic heresy to suggest curtailing some of these photos, because that would be considered censorship. Besides, photographers could argue that there are many more elements to the arrest scene that may be of value to the readers. For example, they might argue that the arresting officers should be seen. And the location and environment may also be of news interest. The response is that editors need to be careful about publication of photos of arrests. If a photo is cropped so tightly that it only depicts the cloaked suspect with only one or both hands visible to the lens and no other people in the picture, its publication may not be justifiable from a bias perspective. If the photo is wider and shows a bit of the surroundings, its use may be justified. If other people are also shown in the photo, justification to use it increases.

■ Political Cartoons

Political cartoonists, like columnists, are supposed to have views, and therefore are permitted to harbor and divulge biases. Nevertheless, there are limits and lines that even political cartoonists should not cross when it comes to bias. Cartoonists should not, for example, characterize any one race, ethnicity, nationality or religion by stereotyping the group's appearance and depicting the entire group with the same elongated or exaggerated bodily features.

Cartoons drawn by Nazi artists before and during World War II targeted Jews, Gypsies and blacks in particular, presenting them with ugly, exaggerated features. The result of such cheap-shot cartooning is that the reader scoffs at and remembers the ugly appearance and stereotype, rather than attempting to understand the political message, if there is one. The aim of a political cartoon should be to express an opinion on an issue using visual symbols and images. The aim is not to belittle people or create ugly images of innocent people and enhance visual stereotypes of groups of people.

■ Publicity Brochures

Years ago, a young couple wanted to take a honeymoon in a Caribbean country, their first trip ever to this part of the world. They leafed through brochures that showed beautiful modern hotels, clean sandy beaches, turquoise waters and elegant gourmet restaurants. The people depicted in the brochures included a white couple riding horses on the beach, a different white couple dining in an elegant restaurant, and a white family playing together on an otherwise empty beach. The couple did not notice anything unusual since most Caribbean brochures featured similar pictures.

When the young couple arrived at their island retreat, they were surprised to find that most of the islanders were black. They had seen black people in the brochures for Jamaica, but in many of the other catalogs, all the people were white. Most of the brochures never showed any black people on the islands. The honeymooners were puzzled in retrospect by the absence of local residents in the brochures and were surprised that all of the guests were portrayed as white. Was it a conscious marketing decision? Apparently. Vacation brochures have been changing gradually over the years. Yet it is still relatively easy to find white-only brochures misrepresenting the Caribbean in particular, but other destinations as well.

There are many biased messages subtly conveyed by this misrepresentation. Depending upon the destination and the vacation being promoted, the subtle message can be interpreted to mean that business from black people is either insignificant, or worse, that they are not welcome. The lack of black representation in a welcoming brochure also appears to say that white people will somehow view the destination as undesirable if there are black people vacationing at the same resort—or even if they see black workers at the resort or living near the resort.

Does a publicist or a marketer have the obligation to show diversity if it is thought that such a depiction will hurt business? Perhaps that question is the wrong approach to the issue. National hotel chains have been finding that they are not losing business by using photos that show diverse hotel guests in their brochures. In fact, they are finding that such illustrations open them up to a wider spectrum of potential customers, since more people feel welcome. The same is true with major American universities that have been consciously increasing their portrayal of diverse representation in college catalogs.

As a general rule, publicists should show diversity, if there is diversity in a particular setting or if diversity is welcome. Hiding diversity only makes the publicist or marketer less credible with the consumer, as it insults many potential consumers.

■ Exclusion from Journalism Photos

Photojournalists, photo editors and television camera engineers should be aware that excluding whole groups of people from photos is a common visual form of bias, depending upon the context. Some well-meaning photo editors and art editors will discriminate unknowingly. In selecting photos to illustrate a piece on a Caribbean destination, for example, an editor may choose the photo of the white couple on horseback, because the composition of the picture itself is good or because the people look attractive to the editor. The editor might select the redheaded family for variety, to show that families also enjoy this destination. If the layout only allows enough space for two photos, the reader will only see white people depicted.

Is this necessarily bias? If the vast majority of the population is black, then failing to show any black people in the layout seems negligent, although many readers may not notice the difference, since they are accustomed to seeing lack of black representation in photos of the Caribbean. If the same scenario were transported to a different country, the negligence becomes more obvious. Imagine seeing a travel article on Japan in which all of the people depicted in photos appear to be Caucasian. The reader would immediately be puzzled and might wonder if there had been some mistake. Or imagine seeing a travel article on Japan in which all of the people shown are black.

If a photographer is biased and only photographs one "favored" group of people to illustrate a story, the photo editor should tell the photographer to go back and reshoot the story. If this is impossible (due to deadlines, budget or distance), the editor should seek out additional photos elsewhere to make the layout more representational.

Sometimes photo editors are not entirely to blame. If they are unable to send their own photographers to cover a story, they find themselves left to rely on publicity photos supplied by the destination or resort. If the destination only provides photos that exclude certain people, the editor is stuck with a dilemma. Most publications contain photo files, however. A conscientious editor should seek out photos that illustrate diversity, and use a previous photo that celebrates diversity, rather than a current photo that promotes exclusion, assuming the previous photo is not outdated. If no appropriate photo is available and the publication has an artist or staff of artists, perhaps a drawing would provide a more accurate representation than a photo. The editor should consider ordering such an illustration.

■ Exclusion from Illustrations

Artists have an obligation to portray diversity in their illustrations. Yet many journalism artists are still failing to do so.

Parents of students at a public elementary school that was referred to as a "miniature United Nations" wanted to design a welcome mat that would celebrate their students' diversity and make everyone feel welcome. When an artist submitted the final drawing, the group of students depicted cartoon-style on the mat were diverse: an Asian-looking girl with pigtails, a tan-skinned boy with black hair, a white-skinned girl with blond hair, and other white-skinned children. There were no black children, however, in the drawing. Had the mat been approved at that stage, the message would have been clear to the school's black students that everyone was welcome except them. Or perhaps they would have interpreted the exclusion to mean that they were somehow invisible or insignificant to the school.

So-called "oversights" can be offensive in journalism art. Artists need to pay extra attention to whom they include and exclude from illustrations, whether these drawings accompany news sections, features, sports stories, restaurant and arts reviews, business stories, travel pieces, real estate sections or editorials.

■ Head Shot Selection

In publications that print wedding photos and photos of business people who are promoted, many biases can be inadvertently revealed. A good editor will know how to avoid creating a biased page.

People who edit the social announcements pages are generally deluged with photos of young women in wedding attire, as well as head shots of smiling brides-to-be. Selecting which photos should be used is as much a political task as an art. Most publications immediately eliminate the full bridal photos, preferring instead to use smaller head shots in order to have enough space on the page to include more women.

The instinct of most new editors seems to be to pick the *prettiest* brides, or those that appeal to the editor most. They rationalize this decision by explaining that *pretty* brides create a more eye-catching page. This selection obviously reveals a lot about the visual biases of the editor, particularly when all of the brides portrayed have similar characteristics, whether it is blond hair, or long hair, or lots of jewelry or minimal makeup, etc.

An editor at a newspaper in southern California suggested that the best way to select photos for the announcements page was to intentionally choose the *ugliest* people—*the real dogs.* "Pick the ones that would never otherwise have a chance to have their picture in the newspaper," he suggested. They will become the most loyal readers, "and nobody will ever accuse you of bias." He would favor the ones who wore thick glasses for their wedding photos, the women with severe skin problems, the ones who were visibly overweight and the oldest-looking brides.

The California editor recommended the same procedure for the business pages, where career announcements and promotions included photos. He would intentionally pick whomever he designated as "not fitting the stereotype," which to him meant women, minorities, bald-headed men, obese people, elderly people, visibly handicapped people and those with any facial deformities.

While his policy of *ugliest* and talk of *real dogs* revealed an ugly bias in itself, the California editor was correct to seek out diversity in illustrating the wedding and career announcements. If the tendency at newspapers is to show only people who look alike, the pages become boring and fail to catch the eyes of readers. Editors should remember that what is attractive to one person is not necessarily attractive to the next, so any attempt to use photos of only so-called attractive or *beautiful people* only reveals the bias of the supposedly objective editor and tends to lead to lack of variety and interest.

Ultimately, there is no one correct way to select the right photos, although, as discussed, there are incorrect ways. Few publications have guidelines or criteria on selecting photos. Some have "dress codes," however, preferring head shots where brides are wearing bridal attire or veils, and where business executives are wearing business suits. As a general practice, editors should aim for fairness and diversity.

If men submit groom photos, publications probably have no good reason to exclude their head shots from the selection. Using a groom shot could, in fact, add to the diversity and interest on the page. In fact, excluding grooms could be perceived as bias. Likewise, editors need to recognize that young white women are not the only ones who make beautiful brides, but that black women, Asian women, Native American women, Latinos, older women and handicapped women also make beautiful brides. In any case, the job of the editor is not to be the biased judge of a beauty contest, but to provide fair coverage.

■ Graffiti

Graffiti is generally considered an illegal act of vandalism committed by one or two people. Some photographers feel that photographing graffiti encourages more graffiti by drawing undeserved attention to the so-called graffiti "artists'" work.

Whether or not to use a photograph or television shot of graffiti depends a lot on the context and what the graffiti says. If the piece is about a demonstration, for example, and the graffiti pertains to that demonstration, the photographer has good reason to photograph the graffiti. If the graffiti bears an insulting message unrelated to any news item, "John hates Joan" for example, there is obviously no reason to include a photo of such information in a publication or on television. If the graffiti seems to indicate a political or social stance on an issue that the photographer views as possibly indicative of a trend or emerging culture, the photographer may have reason to photograph the graffiti.

As a rule, a photo of graffiti should not appear in a newspaper without an explanation accompanying it and without authorship, either by an individual or a group claiming responsibility. In cases where it is unknown who is responsible for the graffiti, it is often better to either not publish the photo of the graffiti or to let the reader know that nobody has claimed responsibility for the graffiti. Historically, racists and other prejudiced people have been known to paint angry slogans in public places, with the intent of alarming people. Editors should be aware that publishing such graffiti may help further the cause of hateful people, by helping them to alarm more readers who otherwise would not be exposed to messages of hatred. If the slogans are tied in with a news story, perhaps that police are investigating the graffiti, for example, publishing the graffiti may be justified, although editors should also stay with the story long enough to report when police catch up with the "graffiti artists."

Editors are not in the business of censoring news, but if there is no news story to go along with graffiti, it is probably best not to publish photos of graffiti. A good photojournalist will question the meaning of graffiti when photographing it, allowing a good photo editor to then decide whether or not that information contains information worthy of a potential story.

■ Depiction of Women

While some groups may be conspicuously absent or underrepresented in the media, women are seen often in newspapers, magazines, movies and on television. The roles that they portray, and the positions in which they are seen, however, often reveal strong gender bias.

With more women playing more active roles in society, the task of reflecting this diversity should be easier for photographers and artists. When editors are offered choices in photos, they should actively seek photos that accurately reflect diversity of women's roles, instead of limiting women's appearances in newspapers to fashion pages, bridal announcements, film and entertainment pages, and home sections.

Clothing

Artists should not depict every girl wearing a dress, promoting the concept that girls are only girls when they wear less "functional" clothing.

Conclusion

Bias slips into modern "objective" journalism on a daily basis, even in the most respected news publications and broadcasts. In order to keep journalism free of prejudice, it is necessary to become aware of these lapses and recognize them. Although many respected publications have different editing policies toward eliminating bias, editors and journalism students need to examine and compare these policies in the vigilant ongoing effort to keep American journalism fair.

Journalists may not always agree on what constitutes fairness and what terms are biased. Yet in striving for fairness, journalists must fully understand the issues that determine objectivity. They must maintain a dialogue on terminology, and they must continue to examine current usage for all signs of prejudice and manipulation. In order to maintain credibility as objective journalists, they must seek to establish clear policies on the elimination of bias.

Obviously recognition of bias is the first step. Subjectivity and prejudice slip into journalism in the form of political bias, racism, ethnic bias, national bias, sexism, religious bias, ageism, bias based on people's appearances and disabilities, economic bias, social bias, bias against certain lifestyles, intellectual bias and visual bias. Until journalists are able to recognize all forms of bias, however, they will continue to find themselves promoting bias instead of fairness and objectivity.

One way to guarantee increased sensitivity and improved editing quality within major publications is to make sure that the staff itself is diverse. An ideal copy desk should include people of different ages, sexes, races, religions, ethnic backgrounds, nationalities, and lifestyles, who come together to edit and share their insights.

Recognizing the value and importance of multicultural representation within journalistic publications, the American Society of

Newspaper Editors released a mission statement in 1998, recommending that American newsrooms increase diversity in hiring to "reflect the racial diversity" of the society. According to the organization, 26 percent of the national population is minority (defined in this context as African American, nonwhite Hispanic, Asian-Pacific islander or Native American), but only 11.5 percent of newsroom employees are members of minority groups. The organization believes that it is in the best interests of journalism to increase the diversity of representation in America's newsrooms.

ASNE, the nation's largest organization of top editors of daily newspapers, produces literature on increasing and managing diversity in the newsroom.

Some publications may find that increasing diversity in the newsroom is difficult for geographical reasons. In such cases, editors have an extra obligation to gain expertise in American diversity and elimination of bias.

Because the English language evolves quickly, this book is intended only as a starting point in the study of bias. Copy editors and writers are encouraged to use it as a reference book, as moral support and documentation when being challenged by editors for eliminating bias in copy. Journalism students are encouraged to use it to gain expertise in bias as they embark on careers in which fairness and objectivity are both challenged and cherished.

References

1990 Census of Population. *Ancestry of the Population in the United States.* 1993. Washington, DC: U.S. Department of Commerce, Economics and Statistics Administration, Bureau of the Census.

1990 Census of Population. *Persons of Hispanic Origin in the United States.* 1993. Washington, DC: U.S. Department of Commerce, Economics and Statistics Administration, Bureau of the Census.

1990 Census of Population. *Social and Economic Characteristics of the United States.* 1993. Washington, DC: U.S. Department of Commerce, Economics and Statistics Administration, Bureau of the Census.

American Society of Newspaper Editors. 1998. Mission Statement.

Archer, Jules. 1991. *Breaking Barriers: The Feminist Revolution, From Susan B. Anthony to Margaret Sanger to Betty Friedan.* New York: Viking.

Arnold, George T. 1996. *Media Writer's Handbook, A Guide to Common Writing and Editing Problems.* Dubuque, IA: McGraw-Hill.

Ashabranner, Brent K. 1991. *An Ancient Heritage: The Arab American Minority.* New York: Harper Collins.

Auerbach, Susan, ed. 1994. *Encyclopedia of Multiculturalism,* 5 vols. North Bellmore, NY: Marshall Cavendish.

Bannerman, Helen. 1923. *Story of Little Black Sambo.* New York: Harper Collins Juvenile Books.

Barzun, Jacques. 1965. *Race: A Study in Modern Superstition.* New York: Harper & Row.

Bates, Stephen. 1993. *Battleground: One Mother's Crusade, the Religious Right, and the Struggle for Control of Our Classrooms.* New York: Poseidon Press.

Bogle, Donald. 1973. *Toms, Coons, Mulattoes, Mammies and Bucks; an Interpretive History of Blacks in American Films.* New York: Viking Press.

B'nai B'rith Style Book. 1983. Washington DC: B'nai B'rith.

Claiborne, Robert. 1973. *The First Americans.* New York: Time Life Books.

Committee on the Role and Image of Women in the Council and the Profession, National Council of Teachers of English. 1985.*Guidelines for Nonsexist Use of Language in NCTE Publications.* Urbana, IL: National Council of Teachers of English.

Coon, Carleton Stevens. 1982. *The Origin of Races.* New York: Knopf.

Davidson, Lawrence. 1998. *Islamic Fundamentalism.* Westport, CT: Greenwood Press.

Early, Gerald, ed. 1993. *Lure and Loathing: Essays on Race, Identity, and the Ambivalence of Assimilation.* New York: Allen Lane, The Penguin Press.

Epstein, Eric Joseph. 1997. *Dictionary of the Holocaust: Biography, Geography and Terminology.* Westport, CT: Greenwood Press.

Farber, Daniel A. 1997. *Beyond All Reason: The Radical Assault on Truth in American Law.* New York: Oxford University Press.

Fraser, Angus M. 1992. *The Gypsies.* Cambridge, MA: Blackwell.

Friedan, Betty. 1993. *The Fountain of Age.* New York: Simon & Schuster.

Friedman, Ina R. 1995. *The Other Victims: First-Person Stories of Non-Jews Persecuted by the Nazis.* Boston, MA: Houghton Mifflin.

Gerber, Judy, ed. 1998. *News Watch Project Style Guide.* San Francisco: News Watch.

Goldstein, Norm, ed. 1998. *The Associated Press Stylebook and Libel Manual.* 7th ed. New York: The Associated Press and Addison-Wesley.

Grimsley, Kirstin Downey. 1997. Baby Boomers Face Age Bias at Work. *Seattle Times,* 16 February.

Gutman, Israel, ed. 1995. *Encyclopedia of the Holocaust.* New York: Macmillan.

Hahn, Elizabeth. 1990. *The Inuit.* Vero Beach, FL: Rourke Publications.

Hammer, Trudy J. 1990. *Taking a Stand Against Sexism and Sex Discrimination.* New York: Franklin Watts.

Hancock, Ian. 1987. *The Pariah Syndrome: An Account of Gypsy Slavery and Persecution.* Ann Arbor, MI: Karoma Publishers.

Hazan, Helen. 1983. *Endless Rapture: Rape, Romance, and the Female Imagination.* New York: Scribner.

Hicks, David. 1980. *Images of the World: An Introduction to Bias in Teaching Materials.* London: University of London, Institute of Education.

Hoberman, John Milton. 1997. *Darwin's Athletes: How Sport Has Damaged Black America and Preserved the Myth of Race.* Boston: Houghton Mifflin.

Jardine, Alice, and Paul Smith, eds. 1987. *Men in Feminism.* New York: Methuen.

King, James C. 1981. *The Biology of Race.* Berkeley: University of California Press.

Kuper, Adam, and Jessica Kuper, eds. 1985. *Social Science Encyclopedia.* Boston, MA: Routledge & Kegan Paul.

Leab, Daniel J. 1975. *From Sambo to Superspade: The Black Experience in Motion Pictures.* London: Secker & Warburg.

Lerner, Michael. 1995. *Jews and Blacks: Let the Healing Begin.* New York: G. P. Putnam's Sons.

Lewis, Jordan, ed. 1976. *The New York Times Manual of Style and Usage.* New York: The New York Times.

Lowery, Charles D., and John F. Marazalek, eds. 1992. *Encyclopedia of African American Civil Rights: From Emancipation to the Present.* New York: Greenwood Press.

Maggio, Rosalie. 1991. *The Dictionary of Bias-Free Usage: A Guide to Nondiscriminatory Language.* Phoenix: Oryx Press.

Martindale, Carolyn. 1986. *The White Press and Black America.* New York: Greenwood Press.

Mather, George A., and Larry A. Nichols. 1993. *Dictionary of Cults, Sects, Religions and the Occult.* Grand Rapids, MI: Zondervan Publishing House.

Merriam Webster's Collegiate Dictionary. 1993. 10th ed. Springfield, MA: Merriam-Webster, Inc.

Miller, Casey. 1978. *Words and Women.* Garden City, NY: Anchor Press.

Montagu, Ashley. 1974. *Man's Most Dangerous Myth: The Fallacy of Race.* 5th ed. New York: Oxford University Press.

Newsday Stylebook. 1993. Melville, NY: Newsday

New York Times. 1998. Bias-Free Communication: Dwarfs, Midgets, and Little People. 26 April.

Osborne, Richard Hazelet. 1971. *The Biological and Social Meaning of Race.* San Francisco: W.H. Freeman.

Osinski, Alice. 1985. *The Eskimo: The Inuit and Yupik People.* Chicago: Children's Press.

Papper, Robert A. 1995. *Broadcast News Writing Stylebook.* Needham Heights, MA: Allyn & Bacon.

Pickens, Judy E., ed. 1982. *Without Bias, A Guidebook for Nondiscriminatory Communication.* 2d ed. New York: John Wiley & Sons.

Random House College Dictionary. 1984. Rev. ed. New York: Random House, Inc.

Rosenstein, Jay, producer. 1997. *In Whose Honor?* Point of View series of independent films. Ho-ho-kus, NJ: New Day Films.

Roth, Hy. 1978. *The Little People.* New York: Everest House.

Russell, Kathy, Midge Wilson, and Ronald Hall. 1992. *The Color Complex: The Politics of Skin Color Among African Americans.* New York: Harcourt Brace Jovanovich.

Scott, Charles I., Richard Crandall, and Thomas Crosson. 1994. *Dwarfism: The Family and Professional Guide.* 1994. Irvine, CA: Short Stature Foundation and Information Center.

Sway, Marlene. 1988. *Familiar Strangers: Gypsy Life in America.* Urbana, IL: University of Illinois Press.

Thompson, Roger M. 1993. *The Mormon Church.* New York: Hippocrane Books.

Thompson, Sue Ellen, ed. 1998. *Holiday Symbols.* Omnigraphics, Inc. Frederick G. Ruffner Jr. Publisher.

United Press International Stylebook. 1992. 3d ed. Chicago, IL: National Textbook.

Index